THINKING
SPREADSHEET

An Opinionated Guide to Problem Solving and Data Analysis
Using Microsoft Excel (or Your Favorite Alternative)

JOEL GRUS

Brightwalton

Thinking Spreadsheet:
An Opinionated Guide to Problem Solving and Data Analysis
Using Microsoft Excel (or Your Favorite Alternative)

Published by Brightwalton LLC

Seattle, Washington

brightwalton.com

ISBN-10: 0-9824818-1-0

ISBN-13: 978-0-9824818-1-3

CONTENTS

Acknowledgements

Wayne Winston taught me most of what I know about Excel, which puts me forever in his debt. Mike Morrow taught me a good chunk of the rest, but I'm pretty sure I've paid off all my debts to him by now.

John Perich, Mitch Hollberg, Jay Fundling, Brian Ma, and Chris Wiswell all read early drafts of this book and provided valuable feedback and corrections. Brian Dickens provided characteristically thoughtful suggestions on the book's structure and design. As is always the case, any errors or demonstrations of poor judgment that survived this feedback process are my sole responsibility.

I'm also thankful to all the people who over the years asked me a huge variety of how-to questions about Excel. Their problems were inspiration for many of the topics and examples in this book.

Above all, I am grateful to Ganga Subramanian, whose reaction to "I'm going to quit my job and write a book about spreadsheets!" was surely more positive than I deserved.

INTRODUCTION

There are many books about spreadsheets out there. Most of these books will tell you things like "How to save a file" and "How to make a graph" and "How to compute the present value of a stream of cashflows" and "How to use conjoint analysis to figure out which features you should add to the next version of your company's widgets in order to impress senior management and get a promotion and receive a pay raise so you can purchase a bigger boat than your neighbor has."

This book isn't about any of those. Instead, it's about how to Think Spreadsheet. What does that mean? Well, spreadsheets lend themselves well to solving specific types of problems in specific types of ways. They lend themselves poorly to solving other specific types of problems in other specific types of ways.

Thinking Spreadsheet entails the following:

- Understanding how spreadsheets work, what they do well, and what they don't do well.
- Using the spreadsheet's structure to intelligently organize your data.
- Solving problems using techniques that take advantage of the spreadsheet's strengths.
- Building spreadsheets that are easy to understand and difficult to break.

To help you learn how to Think Spreadsheet, I've collected a variety of curious and often whimsical examples. Some represent problems you are likely to encounter out in the wild, others problems you'll never encounter outside of this book. Many of them we'll solve multiple times. That's because in each case, the *means* are more interesting than the *ends*. You'll never (I hope) use a spreadsheet to compute all the prime numbers less than 100. But you'll often (I hope) find useful the techniques we'll use to compute those prime numbers, and if you're clever you'll go away and apply them to all sorts of real-world problems. As with most books of this sort, you'll really learn the most if you recreate the examples yourself and play around with them, and I strongly encourage you to do so.

Along the way you'll learn the basic ideas behind spreadsheets. You'll learn all sorts of useful shortcuts and time-saving tricks. You'll construct formulas until doing so becomes instinct. You'll amass a huge arsenal of functions, knowing when and when not to use each. By the end of the book you'll have mastered a wide variety of really advanced features.

As the title points out, this book is *opinionated*. It covers in detail topics that I consider important to Thinking Spreadsheet, and it goes out of its way to denigrate topics which I consider antithetical to Thinking Spreadsheet.

Accordingly, this is certainly not a "complete guide" to any program. There are plenty of features that I won't even mention, either because I don't care for them, because I don't understand them, because I'm afraid of them, or because I don't trust you to use them responsibly. Nonetheless, as "spreadsheet program" is an awkward-sounding phrase, and as most of you use Excel, the book will often refer to "Excel" even when speaking about spreadsheets in general. (This is what we in the writing business call "metonymy.")

Moreover, all of the examples and menu descriptions and illustrations are based on Excel 2007, as that's the version I happen to have. If you're using Excel 2010, you should barely notice the difference. If you're using Excel 2003 or older, the menu steps will be different, but everything else should be largely the same. If you're using some other spreadsheet program then I really can't guarantee that any specific example or function will work for you, although the basic concepts behind everything we do should somehow apply. Feel free to send me an email or ask the Internet if you can't figure how the instructions apply to your specific spreadsheet program.

There are a few sections of the book that are applicable only to Microsoft Excel. I'll try to call special attention to them, so that you don't waste too much time trying (for example) to build a Pivot Table in (for example) KrogerOffice. Occasionally it will be convenient to differentiate between "Old Excel" (2003 and earlier) and "New Excel" (2007 and later), which behave just differently enough to make you want to tear your hair out.

I expect that some readers of this book will have never used spreadsheets before, while others will have been using them for years. If you're in the second group, you might find some of the early chapters kind of basic. Based on the experiences of reviewers, the skew ought to be approximately 75% "I know that already!" and 25% "hey, I never knew that!" Accordingly, I recommend you at least skim the chapters on already familiar topics. You never know what you might learn.

Another reason for including the basics is so that throughout the rest of the book I can confidently assume you're familiar with them. I don't assume that you know the gory details of all the mathematics and statistics and science in the examples, and so I've tried to provide Wikipedia references in places where I think they'll be helpful.

I hope you find Thinking Spreadsheet valuable and useful.

Joel Grus
joelgrus@gmail.com

CHAPTER 1

WHAT SPREADSHEETS ARE AND ARE NOT

A **spreadsheet** is a **grid** of **cells** neatly arranged in rows and columns. Each cell can contain numbers, text, true-or-false values, or formulas that perform some sort of computation. Before we dive into the details, it's worth briefly discussing what spreadsheets are and what they're not.

Spreadsheets are Structured Data

The simplest use for a spreadsheet is to store data. For something really simple, like a grocery list, a spreadsheet is overkill. You'd do just as well writing it down on a notepad or on the back of an envelope.

But as soon as your data has *structure*, you can take advantage of the grid. For example, you could use a spreadsheet to organize your wedding:

	A	B	C	D
1	name	rsvp	gift	thankyou note
2	Jenny	Yes	cake platter	sent
3	Wendy	Yes	hand mixer	sent
4	Kevin	No	towel	sent
5	Karen	Yes		

Each row represents one guest, while each column represents a specific data point about each guest. Similarly, you could use a spreadsheet to manage your library of Star Wars novels:

	A	B	C	D	E	F
1	Title	Author	Published	Read	Rating	Fett Count
2	Darth Bane: Rule of Two	Drew Karpyshyn	12/26/2007	1/15/2010	8	0
3	The Death of Hope	Jude Watson	10/1/2001	1/20/2010	6	0
4	Outbound Flight	Timothy Zahn	1/31/2006	3/16/2010	4	0
5	Boba Fett: Crossfire	Terry Bisson	4/1/2003	4/3/2010	10	184

Here each row represents one book, while each column represents a specific data point about each book.

Spreadsheets are Relationships

These examples so far don't use the real power of spreadsheets, which involves specifying the *relationships* between your data and the things you'd like to know.

If you want to know how many books mention Boba Fett, that's necessarily the number of values in the "Fett Count" column that are greater than zero. If you want to know how many books were published in 2007, that's necessarily the number of dates in the "Published" column that are between 1/1/2007 and 12/31/2007. If you want to know the most recently read book by an author whose name starts with T, that's necessarily the book whose value in the "Author" column starts with T and whose value in the "Read" column is largest among all books whose author starts with T.

Each of these describes a relationship between some value you want to know and your data. To answer each of these questions is simply to translate each relationship into a formula that Excel understands.

Spreadsheets are not Databases

A **database** is a program whose primary purpose is **storing and retrieving data**. For example, the Department of Motor Vehicles maintains a database that keeps track of license plate numbers and the people to whom they're assigned.

On a small scale, you can use spreadsheets as databases. Many people do, and several of our examples will. This is especially convenient when your data fits neatly into a small table and when you intend to interact with your data only through the spreadsheet itself. If your state has issued only 100 license plates, then a spreadsheet might be a good way to store that information.

Databases are often designed to interact with other programs. When you want your data used as part of a website or in an application, you should probably store it in an actual database. Data that lives in a spreadsheet can be easily interacted with only as a spreadsheet.

What's more, spreadsheets have strict limits on the number of rows and columns they can contain. If amount of the data you want to store exceeds these limits, your data won't even fit in a spreadsheet.

On the other hand, databases really only store and retrieve data. They don't analyze data, they don't perform computations, and they're not good for capturing formulaic relationships. To get a database to do these things, you typically have to write computer programs that interact with the database. If you need to do analysis, a spreadsheet can easily capture summaries of your data and calculations based on your data that automatically update whenever your data does. Most of this book will be devoted to exploring such summaries and calculations.

Spreadsheets are not Computer Programs

A **computer program** is typically a sequence of instructions. The computer follows the instructions in order until told to stop.

Many problems can be solved either with spreadsheets or with computer programs. For instance, later we'll build a spreadsheet to calculate income tax. We'll do this by storing the tax brackets in our spreadsheet grid, specifying the income elsewhere in the grid, and finally creating formulas that specify how the tax liability depends on these data. Our primary concern will be the *relationships* between the data and the output we want computed. As we change the data, those correctly-specified relationships will ensure that our output changes properly.

You could instead write a computer program to compute income tax. In that case you'd have to specify the *procedure* to get from the data to the desired result. Then you'd instruct the computer to follow that procedure and output the tax liability. If the brackets changed, or if your income changed, you'd have to modify the instructions accordingly and run the program again.

These are two different ways of thinking about the same problem. The spreadsheet way involves relationships among structured data in a grid. The programming way involves an algorithm to follow. If you approach your problems in terms of algorithms, you'll have a hard time getting spreadsheets to do what you want. Accordingly, a significant part of this book will be devoted to helping you think about your data problems in terms of relationships.

It turns out that there are actually ways to cram programming functionality into spreadsheets. But by doing so you forfeit the power of the "grid of relationships" approach, in which case you largely forfeit the advantage of using spreadsheets. Accordingly, Thinking Spreadsheet frowns on these techniques.

CHAPTER 2

THE FUNDAMENTALS

A typical spreadsheet file (**workbook**) consists of multiple grids (**worksheets**). The worksheets are shown as tabs at the bottom of the page, and you can switch among them by clicking on the different tabs.

In recent versions of Excel there are also command-containing **ribbons** above the grid, which you can explore by clicking on their names.

At different times, we might use "spreadsheet" to refer to either a workbook or a worksheet. Which one should be clear from the context.

Cells

Each worksheet is a grid of **cells** arranged in rows and columns. When referring to cells the standard convention is to refer to columns with letters and rows with numbers. The column goes first.

So, for instance, A1 is the top left cell of the worksheet. A2 is the cell directly below A1, and B1 is the cell immediately to the right of A1.

	A	B	C
1	This is cell A1.	This is cell B1.	...
2	This is cell A2.	This is cell B2.	...
3	...	...	...

After 26 columns there's no letters left, so we start naming columns with 2-letter combinations. The cell to the right of Z3 is AA3, then AB3, and so on. There's no reason you should ever get past column ZZ (and, in fact, many spreadsheet programs won't let you get that far), but if you did then you'd use three-letter combinations: AAA, AAB, AAC. Recent versions of Excel will let you go all the way to column XFD (which is the 16,384th column, if you're counting).

	ZY	ZZ	AAA	AAB
1		Some		
2		programs		
3		even		
4		don't		
5		go		
6		this		
7		far!		

Spreadsheets also have limits on how many rows a worksheet can contain – older versions of Excel will only let you have 65,536 rows, and newer versions will let you have slightly more than a million. If you have more than a million rows of data, then a spreadsheet is maybe not the right tool for your problem.

	A	B
1048571		
1048572	Looks	
1048573	like	
1048574	we've	
1048575	hit	
1048576	rock-bottom!	

As most people have little interest in keeping track of rows and columns in their head, the letters and numbers will typically be labeled (unless some cruel person has turned these labels off, in which case you have my permission to find this person and punch him). The current row and column are highlighted in a different color, just to make your life easier. In addition, above the sheet to the left is a **Name Box** which will also tell you the active cell, unless you've explicitly given it some other name.

B2	▼	f_x	The dark border sho

	A	B	C
1			
2		The dark border shows this is the active cell, and the highlights above and to the left show we're in column B and row 2.	
3			

Now, when you're discussing spreadsheets with your friends, you know how to refer to things. "That number in D10 makes no sense!" "I think you made a mistake right there in F3." "If DQ14536 is correct, I'll eat my hat!"

If you want to refer to a cell in a different worksheet, you need to start with the worksheet name and an exclamation mark. The top left cell on Sheet3 is Sheet3!A1. If the sheet name has spaces in it, put it in single quotes: 'Other Sheet'!A1. You can include the single quotes even if there are no spaces in the sheet name, but you don't have to.

Ranges and Arrays

You can also refer to **ranges** consisting of multiple cells. Usually the cells will form a rectangle, which you specify by giving the top left cell, then a colon, then the bottom right cell. For instance, A1:C1 is a range that's 3 cells wide and 1 cell high,

while A1:A3 is 3 cells high and 1 cell wide,

and B2:C4 is 2 cells wide and 3 cells high.

If you leave off the row or column specifiers, you'll get entire columns or rows. For instance, B:C is a range two cells wide and the entire spreadsheet high, and 2:5 is a range four cells high and the entire spreadsheet wide.

Selecting Cells and Ranges

To select a single cell, you can either click on it or navigate to it using the arrow keys. To select a rectangular range of cells, you can click one corner cell and – without releasing the mouse button – drag to the opposite corner. Alternatively, you can select one corner, then hold down Shift while selecting the opposite corner.

You can select an entire column by clicking on the column header and an entire row by clicking on the row header.

If you want to select an unusually-shaped collection of cells, Ctrl-Click will *add* whatever you click on to your selection. So if you click on A1, then Ctrl-Click on B2 and Ctrl-Click on C3, just those three cells will be selected.

What can you do with selected cells? Many things, as we'll see in a bit.

Arrays

An **array** is a collection of data organized into rows and columns. Although A1:B3 is a *range*, the data in A1:B3 is an *array*. In an Excel context people tend to use the terms interchangeably, since anywhere Excel wants an array it will also accept a (rectangular) range and understand that you really mean "the array of values in this range." However, the reverse doesn't work – there are some places where Excel really requires *ranges* rather than arrays. This isn't a huge deal, because most of the time when we need an array we'll specify it using its range anyway.

Arrays are incredibly useful, as they allow you to treat chunks of data as single units. Using arrays you can think about "the sum of the values in A1:B100" instead of "A1 plus B1 plus A2 plus B2 ... plus B100." It's much easier to conceptualize "find the value 12 in A1:A100" than "look for 12 in A1, then in A2, then ...." Structuring and dealing with our data as arrays (instead of as individual cells) will allow us to do many wonderful things.

Constant Arrays

One way of getting arrays that aren't ranges is by specifying them on the fly. We call these **constant arrays**. You specify a constant array by using curly braces to mark the start and end of the array, commas to separate items in rows, and semicolons to divide one row from the next.

For instance, {1,2,3;4,5,6} represents an array with 2 rows and 3 columns. Its first row is {1,2,3} and its second row is {4,5,6}. Likewise, {1;2;3;4;5;6} represents an array with 6 rows and 1 column. Each row contains just one number. Don't try to create a constant array with differently-sized rows. That won't work.

Using constant arrays is not common, and we won't do it very often.

Values

The simplest thing you can do with a cell is to put a **value** in it. (If you want to get nitpicky, the real simplest thing you can do is leave it blank, but I'm pretty sure you're capable of doing that without my assistance.) Broadly speaking, there are three kinds of values: numbers, text, and Booleans.

A number can be an integer, like 0, or 25, or -12. It can be a decimal, like 3.14159. It can be a percentage, like 5% (which is really the same as 0.05). It can be a date, like 9/11/2001 (which is really the same as 37,145, for reasons we'll explain later), or a time, like 7:12 PM (which is really the same as 0.8, for reasons we'll explain later), or even a date-time combination like 9/11/2001 7:12 PM (which is really the same as 37.145.8, for reasons we'll explain later).

To put a number in a cell, you just select the cell, type the number, and hit either the Enter key, the Tab key, or one of the arrow keys. Try it. Go ahead, this book's not going anywhere. If you type a number (or anything else) into a cell that already contains something, you'll overwrite it. If you start typing into a cell and then think better of it, you can hit the ESC key, which will abandon your typing and restore the cell to however it was before you started typing.

Text is, well, text. It could be a name, like Joel, or an address, like 1600 Pennsylvania Avenue, or a paragraph, like the one you're reading. (I tried to insert this paragraph into itself as an example, but my word processor didn't like that.)

You can also include numbers as text by prefacing them with an apostrophe. So if you type '1600 into a cell, you're storing the four-character text 1600. (This works with non-numbers too: if you put 'Joel in a cell, you're storing the four-character word Joel. Of course, you could also just type Joel without the apostrophe.)

Finally, a Boolean is the logical value TRUE or FALSE. If you type TRUE (or true) into a cell, Excel will know that you mean the Boolean TRUE and will even capitalize it for you. It might not be obvious why you'd ever want to do this, but it will become clear in a few chapters. As you might guess at this point, you could store "true" as text by prefacing it with an apostrophe.

One thing to notice is the default way that Excel justifies the cell's value.

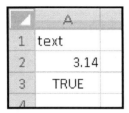

If it's text, it gets justified to the left. If it's a number, it gets justified to the right. And if it's a Boolean, it gets centered. Sometimes numbers accidentally get stored as text versions of numbers, and this can be a quick way to spot the mistake.

Formulas

We specify relationships among our data by creating **formulas**. A cell with a formula *computes* its value.

There are some non-relationship reasons to do this. For instance, Excel makes a nice calculator. If you want to know the value of 2 + 3, you can use a formula to compute it. You can also endow cells with "self-awareness." Using formulas, a cell can figure out what row or column it's in.

But by far the most important use of formulas is to capture relationships by having a cell's value depend on the contents of other cells.

The Simplest Formula

To learn about formulas, it makes sense to start off with the simplest formula. We'll use a formula to specify that cell B1 should have the same value as whatever is in cell A1.

A formula always starts with an equals sign. In fact, anything that starts with an equals sign, Excel will think it's a formula. So if you type

= means equals

into a cell, you'll see instead #NAME?, which is Excel's way of telling you that something bad has happened. In this case, it thinks that your formula refers to the intersection of two ranges called 'means' and 'equals', which Excel doesn't recognize. If you wanted the cell to actually show '= means equals' then (as you might guess at this point) you need to preface it with an apostrophe.

Go to cell B1 (either by moving there using the arrow keys or by clicking on it) and type

=A1

and press Enter. You've just defined a relationship: B1 should contain a value equal to whatever is in A1.

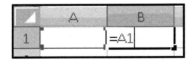

Even though there's nothing in A1, cell B1 shows a 0. This is because in formulas that "seem like" arithmetic, Excel treats a blank cell as having the value 0. That might seem a little odd to you, but it ends up being kind of handy. For instance, if you want to add together the values of a bunch of cells, and one of them is blank, you'd probably rather add the values of the rest of the cells (which is what happens when a blank cell gets treated like a zero) than get some sort of error (which is what might happen if a blank cell were treated in some other way).

Here's where the magic happens. Go to cell A1 (either with the arrow keys or by clicking there) and type 1 (and hit Enter). You should see cell B1 automatically change its value to 1. (If it doesn't, then something is terribly wrong with your computer and you should throw it out with the trash and buy a new one. Or else try again.)

Try typing other things in A1. When you type text, cell B1 should show the same text. When you type numbers, cell B1 should show the same numbers. When you type TRUE, cell B1 should show TRUE. The formula maintains the relationship as the data changes.

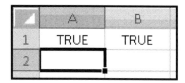

At this point we've got two cells that both show TRUE. But one of them will keep containing the value TRUE even if we change everything else in our spreadsheet. The other contains the formula =A1, which has the value TRUE only as long as cell A1 does. Obviously there's got to be some way for us to tell the difference.

In fact, there's several ways. The first is the **formula bar** right above the spreadsheet grid. If you click on a cell (or use arrows to select it), the formula bar will – true to its name – show the formula behind it.

Click on A1, and the formula bar will show TRUE. Click on B1, and the formula bar will show =A1.

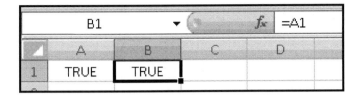

Alternatively (and possibly better), if you press the F2 key (or double-click on the cell), the formula will appear in the cell itself. What's more, if your formula refers to any other cells (like ours refers to A1), the references will appear in different colors, and the cells themselves will be outlined in those same colors. As long as you're not color-blind, you can quickly see what other cells your formula depends on. (Unless they're off the screen, of course.) You can even click and drag the outlines to change the formula's references.

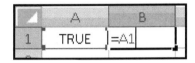

If you have a lot of cells whose formulas you'd like to see, you can go to the "Formulas" ribbon and click the "Show Formulas" option in the "Formula Auditing" section.

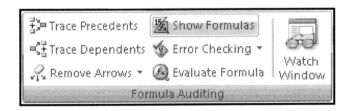

Suddenly every cell will display its formula rather than its value. This can help you quickly see what's going on, but you probably don't want to leave it like this. Click "Show Formulas" again to return things to normal.

Sorting

One thing that Excel excels at is sorting data. This is slightly unfortunate, as sorting data is not always a Thinking Spreadsheet thing to do.

A key principle of Thinking Spreadsheet is that spreadsheets should automatically adapt to changes in their data. But when you make changes to sorted data, the result is usually *unsorted* data. This means that if you have a spreadsheet that *relies* on data being sorted, you also have to rely that anyone who changes the data immediately re-sorts it.

This doesn't mean that sorting data is always a bad thing to do. It will often be the case that you want to sort data to get a better understanding of it or to initially clean it up. As long as your spreadsheet doesn't *rely* on the data being sorted, this shouldn't be a problem.

For sorting purposes, numbers come first, then text, then Booleans. Smaller numbers come before larger numbers. Words earlier in the dictionary come before words later in the dictionary. And FALSE comes before TRUE.

How to sort

Excel sorts *rows*. If you have a bunch of numbers in column A and a bunch of names in column B and you tell Excel to sort by column A, you will also end up changing the data in column B. If the smallest value in column A is 1, then sorting will move that value to the top and bring along the corresponding value in column B. It's possible to get Excel to sort only column A while leaving column B untouched, but this isn't the default behavior.

To make your life simple, the data you want sorted should be in a rectangular range, with no other data immediately adjacent.

It's most common to start by selecting just one cell in data you want sorted.

In that case, Excel will sort the rows of the biggest rectangular range that contains the selected cell and that doesn't contain any blank rows or columns. If you set up your data in a reasonable way, this should be exactly what you want.

If that's not the range you want sorted, you'll have to explicitly select the range you want before sorting. If there's other data immediately adjacent, Excel will stop and ask whether you want to include it. So if you want to sort A1:A100 while leaving B1:B100 unchanged, you'll have to explicitly select A1:A100 and then refuse Excel's attempt to expand the range.

In the below table you can see some of the Academy Award winners over the past few years:

	A	B	C	D	E
1	Year	Award	First	Last	Movie
2	2008	Best Actress	Kate	Winslet	The Reader
3	2007	Best Actress	Marion	Cotillard	La Vie en Rose
4	2009	Best Cinematography	Mauro	Fiore	Avatar

Notice that the years are not in the right order. This is easy enough to fix. At the top of the page on the Data ribbon is a section called "Sort and Filter." If your ribbon doesn't look like this, click on where it says "Data" at the top of the workbook.

You have two options. The simpler involves the A-Z down-arrow button. If you click anywhere in the Year column and then click the A-Z down-arrow button, Excel will sort the rows by year in ascending order.

	A	B	C	D	E
1	Year	Award	First	Last	Movie
2	2007	Best Actress	Marion	Cotillard	La Vie en Rose
3	2008	Best Actress	Kate	Winslet	The Reader
4	2009	Best Cinematography	Mauro	Fiore	Avatar

Sometimes Excel won't realize you have column headers and will try to sort those as well. If this happens, swear at the computer, click undo, and try the second method below.

If you'd clicked the Z-A down-arrow button, it would have sorted the list in descending order instead.

That's great when you only want to sort based on the data in one column, but often you want to specify additional columns for Excel to use to "break ties." Here there are two "Best Actress" awards, and so (if you wanted to sort by Award) you might want to specify another field to look at next.

For example, let's say we want our list sorted first by Award (from Z to A) and then by Movie (from A to Z). In that case we'll need to use the "Sort" feature. Click somewhere in the movie list and then click the Sort button.

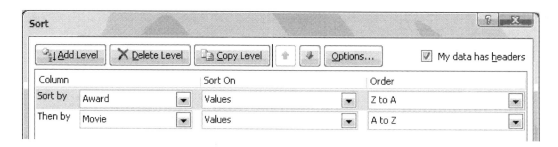

A window will pop up. Make sure "My data has headers" is checked, then choose "Award" under "Sort by" and choose "Z to A" under "Order." Next click "Add Level" and specify "Movie." Finish and click OK.

	A	B	C	D	E
1	Year	Award	First	Last	Movie
2	2009	Best Cinematography	Mauro	Fiore	Avatar
3	2007	Best Actress	Marion	Cotillard	La Vie en Rose
4	2008	Best Actress	Kate	Winslet	The Reader

At last it's sorted in the order we want.

Formats

Consider the number 4.1. You might want it to show up just like that, as 4.1. Or maybe you want to hide the decimal and show it as 4. Maybe it's a dollar amount, and you want to show it as $4.10. Or maybe it's exact to ten decimal places and you want to show it as 4.1000000000. Maybe it represents a percentage and you want to show it as 410%. It's even possible (although not likely) that you want to show it as a fraction: 4 1/10.

None of these choices changes the value in the cell. It's always 4.1. But Excel lets you choose the format in which it's displayed. Type 4.1 in cell A1, and with that cell selected, go to the Number section on the Home ribbon.

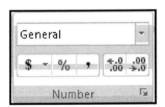

Clicking the $ button will format it as currency: $4.10. Clicking the % sign will format it as a percentage: 410%. Clicking the , button will format it as a number with 2 decimal places: 4.10. The other two buttons increase and decrease the number of decimal places shown.

If you click on the down arrow next to "General," you'll see a whole list of formats you can choose from.

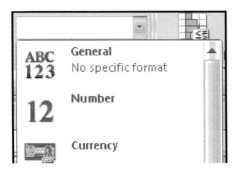

If you're really picky and none of these meets your fancy, you could choose "More Number Formats." You could also type Ctrl-1, or right-click and choose "Format cells." Any of these will bring up a window with lots of choices.

There's a huge number of options here, some of which duplicate functionality available on the Home ribbon, some of which do not. Feel free to spend your leisure time exploring the "Format Cells" options, but we won't spend a lot of time discussing them in this book.

Decoration

You can also change the look and feel of cells. Most of these options are in the Font section of the Home ribbon.

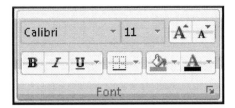

The dropdown with the name of the font (here, Calibri) lets you change the font of selected cells, and the dropdown next to it lets you specify the size of the font. The "A up arrow" and "A down arrow" increase and decrease the size of the fonts.

The "B" makes the contents of a cell appear bold, the "I" italic (slanted), and the "U" underlined. The grid of lines next to these lets you choose various styles of borders for your cells. The paint can changes the background color of a cell, while the "letter over color" next to it changes the color of the cell's contents.

If you know how to make cells **bold**, and if you know the General, Number, Comma, Short Date, and Percentage formats, you know enough for Thinking Spreadsheet.

Resizing Rows and Columns

Sometimes a column isn't wide enough to see its entire contents, and sometimes a column is wider than it needs to be.

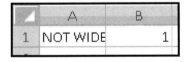

There are several ways to fix this. If you right-click on the column header, you'll see a Column Width option, which gives you the option to specify the width in "number of standard characters." Since no one thinks in terms of "number of standard characters," this isn't always useful.

More helpfully, you can click on the right border of the column header (which will create a popup showing the current column width)

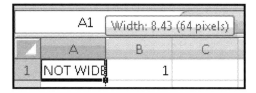

and drag to whatever width you want

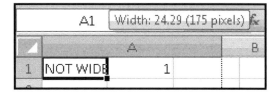

and release.

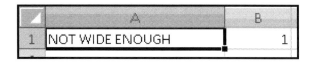

If you select multiple columns, click-and-drag will resize them all (to the same size).

Finally, if you select one or more columns and double-click on the right border of one of their column headers, the columns will resize so that each is just wide enough for its data.

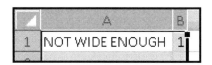

If you have a cell with a lot of data in it, this can make its width expand wider than your screen, in which case you can't even see its right border, and you'll need to use Right-Click - Column Width (or Undo) to fix things.

Row Heights

All these same procedures work to adjust row heights, but you'll rarely need to adjust the row heights.

Conditional Formatting

Sometimes you might want a cell's format to automatically vary depending on its contents. For example, you might want cells containing the value TRUE to be colored green and cells containing the value FALSE to be colored red. Or you might want the color of a cell to get darker the larger its value and lighter the smaller its value.

Conditional formatting will let you do these things, although it arguably violates the "transparency" plank of Thinking Spreadsheet. There's no easy way to spot cells that are conditionally-formatted unless you know to look for the conditional formatting.

Nonetheless, there are times when it's useful, so we'll briefly go through the options. If you're using Excel 2007 or later, you can find Conditional Formatting in the Styles section of the Home ribbon.

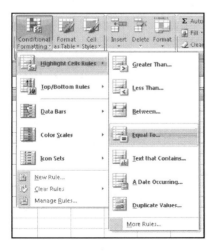

Highlight Cells Rules

Highlight cells that are greater than a specified value or equal to a specified value. Perhaps you need to highlight customers with negative balances or library patrons with overdue books equal to TRUE.

Top / Bottom Rules

Highlight the top (say) ten values in your selection, or the bottom (say) 10% of values.

Data Bars

Draw colored bars *inside the cells*, with longer bars corresponding to larger values.

Color Scales

Highlight the cells according to some color scheme. One popular scheme is to highlight large values in green, average values in yellow, and small values in red, with the largest values being the darkest green and the smallest values being the darkest red.

Icon Sets

Similar to color scales, except with little pictures of traffic lights or arrows in the cell instead of highlighting.

Use a formula

If you select "New rule" you can specify an arbitrary formula (which we'll learn about soon) and highlight cells for which the formula equals TRUE.

Feel free to play around with these, but we won't use them again.

CHAPTER 3

EXTENSIBILITY

One key feature of spreadsheets is the ability to quickly extend your work from one part of the grid to another. If you have a formula involving the data in column A, it's easy to instantly create analogous formulas involving the data in column B, in column C, and so on. We'll examine a variety of ways to do this and think about when it might be useful.

Cut Copy Paste

Unless you are new to a computer, you are probably familiar with Copy, Cut, and Paste. You probably copy news articles and paste them to your Facebook page. You probably edit your emails by cutting paragraphs near the top and pasting them down near the bottom.

In a spreadsheet these behaviors are full of subtleties. A spreadsheet cell has a value. It has a formula. (If you typed the value in directly, then its "formula" is the same as its value.) It has a format. The default Paste will paste all three of these. (Cells can also have other things attached to them, like comments and validation, but neither is particularly important to Thinking Spreadsheet.)

By far the most interesting part of Copy-Pasting in a spreadsheet is that when you Copy-Paste a formula, its references will change. If the new location is two cells to the right, the new formula will have its references moved two cells to the right. A reference to A1 will become a reference to C1. A reference to B3:D5 will become a reference to D3:F5. A reference to Z:Z will become a reference to AB:AB.

Similarly, if the new location is three cells down, its references will also be shifted down by 3 cells. A reference to B2 will become a reference to B5. If you copy a formula from C3 to B2 (up 1 and left 1), its references will all be shifted up 1 and left 1.

To illustrate this, put the values 1, 2, and 3 in cells A1:A3. And in cell B1 enter the formula =A1.

We're going to copy it and paste it into B3. Click on the cell B1, then right-click and choose Copy. (Or, as in most other programs, press Ctrl-C.)

The dotted line around cell B1 shows it's what we currently have copied.

Now click on cell B3, right-click, and choose Paste. (Or use Ctrl-V.)

Since we pasted two cells down, the reference is now to A3:

Why does Excel move references? It's a feature. Imagine that our data is in A1:J100 and that cell A101 contains a formula that refers to A1:A100. Then when we Copy-Paste that formula into B101, its reference will change to B1:B100. This is a quick way of specifying that the relationship between B101 and B1:B100 should be the same as the relationship between A101 and A1:A100, and it's much easier than crafting a new formula.

Of course, the rows work similarly. If a formula in K1 refers to cells A1:J1, then when we Copy-Paste the formula down to K2:K100, each pasted copy will refer to its current row.

If the references didn't move, you'd have to type in a new formula 100 times!

This reference-moving isn't always desired behavior. Sometimes you don't want your references to move, and very soon we'll see how to make sure they don't.

When you *Cut* and Paste, references in the Cut cell don't move. This is because Cut-Paste usually means you're *relocating* your work rather than trying to extend it. (References *to* the cell you cut *will* move, which is probably also the behavior you want.)

Paste Special

Sometimes you need to paste only some of the information from a cell. Perhaps you want to paste just the formatting but not the formulas, or vice versa. Or maybe you've copied a bunch of complicated formulas, but you'd rather paste their values.

Excel provides a Paste Special command that does all this and more. On the right-click menu, right below the Paste option, there's a Paste Special option.

You can also get to it if you click the down arrow beneath Paste at the top left of the Home ribbon:

If you have Excel data copied and you choose Paste Special, you'll see a menu like the following:

You can choose options either by typing the underlined letter or by clicking on them. There are a lot of options here, and we'll only discuss some of them. (As always, you're encouraged to experiment with the others.)

Formulas pastes only the formulas, omitting formatting and other things (like comments, which we won't be using). You might use this if your target cells already have formatting that you want to keep.

Values pastes only the values, and (in particular) replaces the formulas. There are a few reasons why you might want to do this. First, you may want to save the outcome of some complicated analysis before you change its inputs and formulas. Obviously, when you change the inputs and formulas the values will change, so you have to make a by-value copy of them if you want to keep them around.

It may also be the case that you want to copy a small amount of the output of one spreadsheet into another. You can, it turns out, keep the formulas and have one spreadsheet refer to a completely different one. But this is generally a bad solution – you'll have to keep the spreadsheet files together and not change their locations and worry about inter-workbook references breaking. It's usually simpler just to move the values over.

A third possibility is that you have a bunch of very slow formulas that you want to bypass. For instance, perhaps you have 100,000 rows of data, each of which needs to do a time-consuming VLOOKUP() into another sheet with 100,000 rows of data. If you're confident that none of the data will change, you might copy all the cells and then paste them by value onto themselves so that the time-consuming calculation only needs to happen once. If you're only sort of confident the data won't change, you might leave the formulas in the top row and value out the rest. If you decide you need the formulas again, you can just copy or fill them down.

Forma_ts (notice that the key for this is 't') pastes only the formats, not the values or formulas. If you've gotten the format in some cell just the way you want it, you can use this to apply the same format to other cells.

_M_ultiply will multiply whatever is in the target cells by whatever you've copied. If you copy only one cell, all of your target cells will get multiplied by the value of what you've copied. If you copy an array of cells, an equally-sized array of cells will be multiplied. If the cells you're pasting into only contain values, their values will be replaced with new values; if the cells you're pasting into contain formulas, the formulas will be modified to include the multiplication.

A_dd, **_S_ubtract**, and **Di_vide** all behave similarly.

The only other option we'll worry about is **Transpos_e**, which will flip your rows and columns. A range with 3 rows and 2 columns will be transposed into a range with 2 rows and 3 columns:

	A	B	C	D	E	F
1	Original			Transposed		
2	1	4		1	2	3
3	2	5		4	5	6
4	3	6				

Transpose can be combined with other Paste Special options, or can act alone (in which case it pastes everything).

Non-Excel Paste-Specials

If you copy data from outside of Excel, you'll get different Paste Special options. For instance, if you copy data from a webpage, you'll have options to paste it as HTML, Unicode Text, or Text. (Generally you'll want to choose Text.) If you copy data from Microsoft Word, you'll get several options, and again you'll generally want to choose Text. Sometimes the book will tell you to Paste-Special-Text, and this is what we mean. If you ever get an unexpected menu when you try to Paste Special, it's probably because your copied data is from a different program.

Having Your Fill

Another way of extending your work is Fill, which takes some feature of a cell or range and uses it to "fill in" a larger range. Fill does many complicated things, and often won't behave the way you expect it to. We'll go over the most useful basics.

The first way to fill is by selecting a rectangular range and using the Fill command in the "Editing" section of the "Home" ribbon. When you choose it you'll see several options, the most useful of which are Fill Down and Fill Right.

Fill Down is equivalent to Copy-Pasting the top row of your selection into the remainder of your selection. If the top row of any column contains a value, that same value will be filled in the entire column. If the top row of any column contains a formula, that formula will be filled in the entire column, with its references changing just as if you'd Copy-Pasted it.

Similarly, Fill Right accomplishes the same thing as copying the leftmost column of the selection and pasting it into the remainder of the selection.

Fill Left and Fill Up are similar, although in practice they're much less useful. There are a few other options that we won't discuss.

Drag Fill

There's a second way to fill that behaves slightly differently. You may have noticed that when you select a cell or a range there's a little square at the bottom right of the bold border:

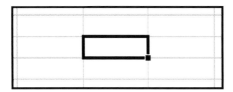

By clicking and dragging this square, you get a slightly different (and slightly unpredictable) fill behavior.

> If you click anywhere else on the border and drag, Excel will Cut the selected cells and Paste them wherever you drag them to.

The simplest case is if you select a single column with either formulas or values (but not both) and drag the square to the right. In this case it behaves the same as our previous Fill Right. For instance, put 1, 2, and 3 into A1:A3, then click and drag the square over to row C:

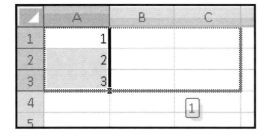

As you drag, you can see a tiny pop-up window indicating what value is being filled in the first (here, topmost) cell. This isn't interesting in this case, but it will be useful in a minute. In the "after picture" you can see a little "drag plus" box below and to the right of our dragged range. If you click it you'll get some options to change how your drag fill behaves. We don't want to change how it behaves, so we'll ignore the box, and eventually it will go away.

If instead you select a single row and drag the square *down*, it mostly behaves just like our previous Fill Down.

There are some exceptions. If you Drag-Fill a date, you'll get a sequence of subsequent dates.

Notice how here the tiny "latest fill" pop-up is slightly more useful, as it saves us the trouble of having to count rows to end at a specific date.

Similarly, if you Drag-Fill a time (e.g. 9:15) you'll get a sequence of hour-later times. If you Drag-Fill a month you'll get a sequence of months. If you Drag-Fill text that ends in a number (e.g. Level1) you'll get a sequence of texts with increasing numbers (Level2, Level3, ...).

Because of this, if you Drag-Fill the text-version of a number (like '1) you'll get an increasing sequence of text-versions of numbers ('2, '3,) but if you Drag-Fill an actual number (like 1) you'll just get a lot more 1's.

You can get an actual sequence of numbers with Drag-Fill, but normally you have to start with at least two numbers. If you put 1 in A1 and 2 in A2 and then Drag-Fill starting with both cells, you'll get your sequence.

You could have also done this by dragging a single 1 down (creating a column of 1s) and clicking the "drag plus" box to force Excel to fill a *series*. However, then you would have had to work without the pop-up progress counter.

If instead you'd started with 1 in A1 and 3 in A2, drag fill would have generated the sequence 1,3,5,7,....

This pretty much only works for arithmetic sequences, that is, sequences that involve adding the same increment each time. If you start with (for example) 1,2,4, Excel will get confused and produce something ugly. So don't do that.

There's one other curiosity. If you put the value 1 in cell A1 and Drag-Fill down, you'll get a column of 1's. However, if you put 1 in cell A1 and the formula =A1 in cell B1, and if you then Drag-Fill both cells down, you'll get an increasing sequence in column A.

In short, Drag-Fill can produce unexpected behaviors in all but the simplest cases. Don't be surprised when it does.

Double-Click Fill

There's also a third way to fill. Let's say you have a column of data and you need to add a new column next to it. In this example, put the numbers

1 through 5 in A1:A5 (using a drag-fill if you want). Our goal is to have formulas in B1:B5 that equal the value in column A.

First, type

=A1

into cell B1:

	A	B
1	1	=A1
2	2	
3	3	
4	4	
5	5	

Now if you double-click on the Drag-Fill square, Excel will (in essence) Drag-Fill down as far as there's data in the column to the left. Here, column A has data down to row 5, so double-clicking is the equivalent of Drag-Filling down to B5:

	A	B
1	1	1
2	2	
3	3	
4	4	
5	5	

	A	B
1	1	1
2	2	2
3	3	3
4	4	4
5	5	5
6		

This can be a speedy alternative to Drag-Fill-ing thousands of rows. However, it's always a good idea to check that your fill made it all the way down. If there are errant blanks in the previous column or non-empty cells in the column you're filling, your fill will stop as soon as it reaches them.

The Almighty $

As we've seen repeatedly, when you paste or fill a formula that uses references, they change. If cell B1 refers to A1 and you copy its formula down to B2, the new formula will refer to A2. If you copy its formula over to C1, the new formula will refer to B1. Sometimes this is desired behavior, but sometimes it isn't. Sometimes you want copied versions of the formula to keep referring to A1.

To let Excel know that it shouldn't move your references, you can use $ signs. A $ in front of a row or column specification tells Excel not to change it when you copy or fill. So a formula that refers to $A$1 ("never change column from A, never change row from 1") will keep referring to $A$1 no matter where you copy it. A formula that refers to $A:$A ("never change start column from A, never change end column from A") will keep referring to the first column no matter where you copy it. A formula that refers to the range $C$3:$D$5 ("never change start column from C, never change start row from 3, never change end column from D, never change end row from 5") will keep referring to that exact same range no matter where you copy it.

You don't have to $ both the row and the column. You can $ only one or the other. A reference to $G10 will keep referring to column G if you copy it to the left or right, but it will refer to $G9 if you copy it to the row above and $G11 if you copy it to the row below. Similarly, a reference to G$10 will keep referring to row 10 if you copy it up or down, but it will refer to F$10 if you copy it to the left one column and H$10 if you copy it to the right.

A classic example of this functionality is a multiplication table. If you write one set of factors across the top row and another down the first column, then your multiplication formula needs to keep referencing the top row and the first column as you fill out the table. This means the reference to the first column needs to $ the column letter, and the reference to the top row needs to $ the row number:

◢	A	B	C	D	E	F
1		1	2	3	4	5
2	1	=$A2*B$1				
3	2					
4	3					
5	4					
6	5					

If you gloss over the fact that we haven't yet discussed how to multiply in Excel, you can see that the formula will keep looking to column A for its first argument and row 1 for its second argument as we copy it across and down. This is much easier than typing a different formula into every cell!

When you're specifying a range, you have even more options. For instance, in B1 you might have a formula that references $A$1:$A1 ("never change start column from A, never change start row from 1, never change end column from A, but do allow the end row to change"). If you were to copy the same formula to B10, the new copy would reference $A$1:$A10. This is a common "include everything that's happened to this point" pattern, and it's likely you'll find it useful.

If you don't like typing $ signs, the F4 key will cycle through the options. Type =A1 in cell B2. Don't hit Enter, but instead press the F4 key. You'll see your formula change to =$A$1. If you hit F4 again, the formula will change to =A$1. Press F4 once more, and the formula will change to =$A1. One last time, and it will return to =A1. For something more subtle, like $A1:B$3, you'll probably have to $ it manually.

One thing to note: Paste-Special-Transpose will change your $ signs. Type 1 into cell A1 and =$A1 ("never change the column from A, but let the row change") in cell B1, then Copy and Paste-Special-Transpose both cells into D1:D2.

The formula pasted into D2 will be =D$1 ("never change the row from 1, but let the column change")! If you think about it, this is probably the behavior you want, but just be aware of it.

Insert and Delete

If you don't leave enough space for whatever you need to do, you can always insert more. (Unless you've already used up the allowable number of rows or columns, in which case you can't.)

Inserting a row or column

Most commonly you'll insert an entire row or an entire column.

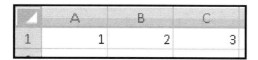

Let's say you need a new column where you'll add the value 1.5. First select the column *after* where the new one should go by clicking its header.

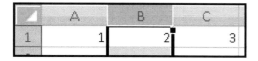

Now right-click and choose Insert.

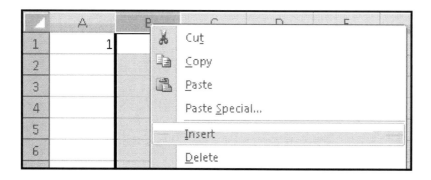

Everything starting at the column you selected has been moved one column to the right.

Since inserting the new column is roughly the same as Cut-and-Pasting everything to its right, references will adjust in the same way they would if you Cut-and-Pasted.

Any formulas that referred to cells in column C will be updated to refer to those cells' new location in column D. Formulas that referred to cells in column D will likewise be updated to refer instead to column E, and so on. Similarly, formulas that referred to ranges that span the inserted column will automatically expand; a formula that previously referred to A1:C1 will (after the insert) be updated to refer to A1:D1. This is good, as it means that (in most cases) inserting rows or columns won't break your pre-existing formulas.

One tricky issue is that inserting rows or columns *next to* a range won't expand it. If you have a formula that refers to B1:C2, then inserting a new column between columns B and C would expand the range to B1:D2. But inserting a column to the left of column B or to the right of column C won't expand the reference at all. (Inserting a column to the left of column B will of course *move* your reference to the right.) This means if you want the range to expand, you need to either add the column in the middle of the range or manually update the formula.

Inserting a smaller range

When you insert a column, Excel knows to move all subsequent columns to the right. When you insert a row, Excel knows to move all subsequent rows down. But if you select (for example) A1:B2

	A	B	C	D
1	1	2	3	4
2	5	6	7	8
3	9	10	11	12
4	13	14	15	16

and try to insert, Excel will ask you what you want:

If you choose "Shift cells right," Excel will shift your selection to the right but leave the other rows unchanged.

	A	B	C	D	E	F
1			1	2	3	4
2			5	6	7	8
3	9	10	11	12		
4	13	14	15	16		

"Shift cells down" behaves analogously.

The behavior of formulas that refer to the shifted cells is slightly more complicated. References to ranges move only when the insert shifts the entire range. In our above example, a formula that refers to A1:A2 will – after the insert – refer to C1:C2. However, a formula that refers to A1:A3 will not change at all, since A3 was not affected by the insert. This will trip you up at some point, so be careful.

Delete

The "opposite" of insert is delete. If you delete a column, all of the columns after it will get shifted left. If you delete a row, all of the rows after it will get shifted up. If you delete a rectangular range, Excel doesn't know whether to replace it with the cells below it or to its right, and so it will pop up a menu and ask whether you want to replace it by shifting cells left or up.

If you have formulas that refer to deleted cells or to ranges consisting entirely of deleted cells, they'll turn into #REF! errors. If they refer to ranges and you delete some (but not all) of the rows or columns in the range, the formulas will shrink accordingly. If they refer to ranges and you delete some (but not all) of the cells in the range, then the formulas won't change at all. Again, be careful with this behavior!

Insert Copied Cells

In our previous examples, we always inserted blank cells. However, if you Cut or Copy data before you Insert, Excel will insert cells containing that data. As with Pasting, Cut-and-Insert is primarily for relocating cells and their contents, while Copy-and-Insert is for duplicating them.

If you Copy and then Insert, the behavior is no different than if you were to first Insert a same-sized (blank) range and then Copy-Paste the data into it. Cells that you Copy-Insert will change their references just as if you'd pasted them.

If you Cut and then Insert, then Excel actually Deletes the original cells once you're done. If you Cut a column and Insert it somewhere else, Excel will completely get rid of the old column. (Whereas with Cut and Paste Excel would have left it blank.)

All Clear

When you Delete cells, other cells move in to fill their place. You can also just *Clear* the cells to empty them out.

On the Home ribbon in the Editing section, there's a Clear dropdown that gives four options. Clear All totally blanks out the cells. Clear Contents empties the cells' contents while leaving their formats unchanged. Clear Format does the opposite.

The Delete key also Clears Contents. If you need one of the other Clears, you'll have to use the Ribbon.

Find and Replace

In the Editing section of the Home ribbon, there's a Find and Select drop-down that's mostly useful for Find (also Ctrl-F) and Replace (also Ctrl-H).

Find will search the cells of your spreadsheet for whatever you tell it to. You can find one match at a time or all cells that match. By default Find looks at formulas. If you enter the value 2 in cell A1 and the formula =A1 in cell A2, then Excel will find the number 1 only in cell A2 (since it's in the formula) and the number 2 only in cell A1 (since the value you typed in counts as a formula). You could instead search based on values, in which case 2 would be found in both cells and 1 in neither.

Replace not only finds what you tell it to, but replaces it with something else. If you have a bunch of formulas using the SIN() function and you need to replace them with the COS() function, you could Replace "SIN(" with "COS(". Be careful, though. If your formulas also used the ASIN() function, Excel would find and replace those instances of "SIN(" too.

If you select part of your spreadsheet before using Find or Replace, Excel will only Find or Replace within your selection.

CHAPTER 4

SHORTCUTS THAT WILL AMAZE YOUR FRIENDS AND CONFOUND YOUR ENEMIES

Right-clicking through menus and using the scroll bars and searching through ribbons gets really old, really fast. Luckily, there's lots of short-cuts you can use. And once you get good at using them, you'll be able to spreadsheet so effectively that people will think you're some sort of wizard. Eventually they might even encourage you to write a book, which I hope you do, just as long as it doesn't compete with this one.

Tab and Enter

When you input something into a cell, you'll usually use either Tab or Enter to let Excel know that you're done. Typically Tab moves the active cell one to the right while Enter moves it one cell down.

However, if you have a lot of data to input, you can combine Tab and Enter in clever ways.

In cell A1, input 1 and Tab. The active cell will move to B1. Input 2 and Tab again. The active cell will move to C1. Now input 3 and this time Enter. The active cell will go down to row 2 but will return to column A, which is where you started using Tab.

When you need to type in many rows and columns of data, using Tab to move across and then Enter to go back to the start of the next row can save you a lot of cursoring (or mousing) around.

Cut and Copy and Paste

Instead of using right-click or the Home ribbon, you can copy the current selection with Ctrl-C, you can cut it with Ctrl-X, and you can paste from the clipboard with Ctrl-V.

There are several ways to Paste-Special. If you hold down both Ctrl and Alt and press V, you'll get the Paste Special menu. On some keyboards this is an unwieldy combination of keys, so there's a couple of other ways.

For historical reasons, if you hold down Alt and then press 'e' and then 's', you'll get the Paste Special menu, at which point you can type 'v' for values, 't' for formats, 'f' for formulas, and so on. (That's if you've got Excel data on your clipboard. If you have an image or some webpage data, you'd get the appropriate "paste special" options for those instead.)

If your keyboard has a "right-click" button on it, you can also "right-click" and then press 's' for the "Paste Special" option. Probably because I use this shortcut all the time, they changed it in Excel 2010 so that now you have to press 's' twice.

Going To

If you type a cell (e.g. B3) in the Name Box, you'll be magically transported to that cell, and if you type a range (e.g. B3:D5) it will be magically selected.

You can do the same with Ctrl-G, which brings up the "Go To" box. Typing in a cell or range or name will go to and select it just as if you'd typed it into the Name Box.

Zipping around with Ctrl-Arrow

Sometimes you'll have spreadsheets with thousands of rows and hundreds of columns of data. You'll need to look at the top, then the bottom, then the top, then the right.

A slow way to get to the bottom of your data would be to press the down arrow repeatedly. Another way would be to use your mouse to move the slider bar on the right side of the spreadsheet or click on the down arrow just below it.

But a much faster way is to use Ctrl-Arrow. If you hold down the Ctrl key on your keyboard and press one of the directional arrows, you'll move really, really far in the arrow's direction. How far?

If the next cell in that direction is empty, you'll go all the way until you reach a non-empty cell. If there are no non-empty cells in that direction, you'll go all the way to the edge of the sheet.

If the next cell in that direction is non-empty, you'll go as far as you can without reaching an empty cell.

So if you're at the top of a column with lots of numbers (and no blanks), Ctrl-down will take you all the way to its bottom. At that point, Ctrl-up will take you back to the top. If there are blank cells in the column, Ctrl-down will take you to just above the first one.

Selecting with Shift-Arrow

Often you'll want to select multiple cells at once. That way you can copy them all at the same time. Or, if you've already copied something, you can paste it into all the cells at the same time. Or you can fill down from the top row or fill right from the left column.

One way to select cells, of course, is to click and drag with the mouse, releasing the mouse button after you've chosen the cells you want.

But that requires you to take your hands off the keyboard, wasting valuable seconds.

Fortunately, you can do the same thing with Shift-Arrow. Move the active cell to A1 again (either with the arrows or the mouse). Now hold down Shift and press the right arrow twice:

Notice that the name bar shows that you've selected 1 row and 3 columns. Press Shift again (if you let go of it) and press the down arrow twice:

And now you've selected the same 3x3 range.

Filling Multiple Cells With Ctrl-Enter

Now that you've got the 3x3 range selected, type 1, hold down Ctrl, and press Enter:

Ctrl-Enter tells Excel to fill every cell that's selected with whatever you typed. You can input a formula as well. Excel will put your exact formula in the top left cell and then extend it using its usual rules.

For instance, select B2:C3, type =A2+B1 and then Ctrl-Enter:

Since that formula is going in B2 (and has no $ in it), it means "this cell's value is the sum of what's in the cell to my left and what's in the cell right above me." You can see that indeed that's what happened.

Combining Shift-Arrow and Ctrl-Arrow

If Ctrl-Arrow zips and Shift-Arrow selects, what happens when you combine them? Let's try it. Make A1 the active cell, hold down Shift and Ctrl and press the down arrow once.

You've just selected the first column A1:A3. Now while still holding down Shift and Ctrl press the right-arrow, and you've selected the whole 3x3 range A1:C3.

This is a very common pattern for cutting (or copying) and pasting large amounts of data:

- Ctrl-Arrow to get to the data
- Ctrl-Shift-Arrow to select all the data
- Ctrl-X to cut the data (or Ctrl-C to copy the data)
- Ctrl-Arrow to get to the new location for the data
- Ctrl-V to paste the data

None of this is difficult, but if you do it quickly while people are watching it looks like magic. Use this to bolster your Thinking Spreadsheet reputation!

Keyboard Fills

You can also use keyboard shortcuts to fill. If you select a range, Ctrl-D will fill down (based in whatever is in the top row), and Ctrl-R will fill right (based on whatever is in the leftmost column).

Combining all these shortcuts allows you to quickly manipulate huge chunks of data. Let's say you need to change the formula in B2:C3 so that it adds 1 to the value in the cell above and the value in the cell to the left.

Method 1: Ctrl-Enter Again

Select the range B2:C3 by selecting cell B2 and then using Ctrl-Shift-Right and Ctrl-Shift-Down. Now type

=A2+B1+1

and finish with Ctrl-Enter. All four cells will get their formulas updated.

Method 2: Copy and Paste

Select only cell B2, and change its formula to =A2+B1+1. Now copy the new formula (using Ctrl-C), select B2:C3 (using Ctrl-Shift-Right and Ctrl-Shift-Down), and paste it (using Ctrl-V).

Method 3: Select then Modify then Fill

Select B2:C3 again. Type in =A2+B1+1, but only hit Enter. This only changes the formula in B2. But the range B2:C3 is still selected. Now fill down using Ctrl-D. This fills the formulas from row 2 down into row 3. Nothing in column C will change, but cell B3 will get the new formula from B2. Finally, fill right using Ctrl-R. The new formulas in B2 and B3 will be copied into column C, as desired. (We could have filled right first, then down, and it also would have worked.)

Method 4: Modify then Select then Fill

Select and change only cell B2. Now select the range B2:C3, fill down, and fill right.

Pete and Repeat

We saw that when you're entering a formula, the F4 key cycles through the different ways of $-ing your references. When you're not entering a formula, F4 means "repeat what I just did."

If you just inserted a column, F4 inserts another column. If you just deleted a row, F4 deletes another row. If you just applied the Percentage format to some cells, F4 will apply the Percentage format again (and hopefully you've selected a different set of cells). The possibilities are endless, although "insert again" and "delete again" are the ones you'll probably find most useful.

Do and Undo

As in many other programs, Ctrl-Z will undo the last action. Want to un-Paste? Ctrl-Z. Un-Fill? Ctrl-Z. Un-Format? Ctrl-Z. Un-Delete? Ctrl-Z. Un-Insert? Ctrl-Z.

If you're one of those people who can't make up his mind and you decide to *re*-do what you just un-did, use Ctrl-Y.

The Quick Access Toolbar

In newer versions of Excel (2007 and later), you can place commands you use often into a Quick Access Toolbar.

You might see the Quick Access Toolbar above the ribbon

(It's the part with the picture of the floppy disk and the undo arrow.)

Or you might see it below the ribbon

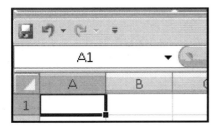

Or you might not see it at all. If you don't (or if you see it above the ribbon), right-click anywhere in the ribbon and choose "Show Quick Access Toolbar" below the ribbon.

As its name implies, you use it to *access* Excel features *quickly*. There are a few ways to add things to the quick-access toolbar. The easiest way, if your desired accessee is an option in one of the ribbons, is to simply right-click on it and choose "Add to Quick Access Toolbar."

For instance, you might find that you need to Sort-A-to-Z all the time. Go to the Data ribbon and right-click on the Sort-A-to-Z icon:

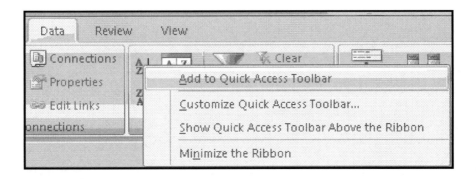

If you click on "Add to Quick Access Toolbar", it will suddenly appear!

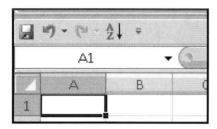

You might also want to add options that don't appear on any of the ribbons (or that you have trouble finding). In that case you'd instead choose "Customize Quick Access Toolbar" and wade through the dizzying selection of addable toolbar buttons. You might enjoy playing around with these choices, and you might even learn some new Excel features you never knew about.

Mostly, though, you can just right-click and add things from the ribbons.

Chapter 5

Functions

A critical part of Thinking Spreadsheet is using formulas to capture relationships, and to create clever formulas you'll need to use functions.

Using a Function

When you took Algebra in tenth grade, they probably taught you to think of functions as "black boxes," but a series of high-profile airline crashes has given that term somewhat negative connotations, so we won't use it.

Instead, we'll say that a **function** is a rule that takes zero or more **inputs** and produces an **output** that depends on them in some way. The output is typically a number, some text, or a Boolean. The input can be any mixture of the three, an Excel range, or even nothing at all.

For instance, "always output 1" is a function with no inputs.

"Input a number and output the square root of that number" is a function with one input. (Don't feel bad if you don't know what a square root is, I won't tell anyone.)

"Input a string and a number and output the numberth character of the string" is a function with two inputs.

To tell Excel to use a function, you have to give it the name of the function, followed by its inputs (if any) in parentheses. Functions with 0, 1, or 2 inputs would look like the following:

    FUNCTION()
    FUNCTION(INPUT1)
    FUNCTION(INPUT1,INPUT2)

Of course, you don't actually type "FUNCTION" or "INPUT1," you type the actual name of the function and the actual values or locations of the inputs. We will always write our functions in ALL CAPS, but it's not required. (Excel will automatically UPPERCASE them for you if you don't.)

Excel knows lots and lots and lots of functions. Some are easy to understand; some are devilishly complicated. Some were invented just last week; some are included only so that spreadsheets created by the Watergate burglars can still be opened. Some of them are used primarily by the virtuous; some are the province only of the wicked. Properly using these functions is at the core of Thinking Spreadsheet and will occupy a significant chunk of this book.

A function can only appear in a formula, which (I'm sure you remember) always needs to start with an equals sign. Do not think this means that a function itself must always be preceded by an equals sign, only the formula must.

So if we wanted a cell to contain the value of a function with no inputs, we would have to type

    =FUNCTION()

If we wanted it to contain twice the value of the function, we could type

    =2 * FUNCTION()

or

    =FUNCTION() * 2

Notice how the equals sign is only at the start. Notice also that I included spaces in the formula to make it easier to read. This is pretty much always acceptable and pretty much never required. You could have typed

=2*FUNCTION()

and it would not have made any difference to Excel. Do what you like.

Function Inputs

When a function needs inputs, you can specify the input values explicitly:

FUNCTION(3.14)

You can also tell Excel to look in a specific location for the values by providing an appropriate reference:

FUNCTION(A1)

or

FUNCTION(B2:C8)

And, perhaps most magically, you can use the output of one function as the input to another:

FUNCTION(2,OTHERFUNCTION(B3,1))

That last one is a mouthful, so let's look at it. We're telling Excel to compute an output using the rule FUNCTION. And we've given it two inputs. The first input is the number 2, which I expect you understand. And the second input is the output from when you take the function OTHERFUNCTION and apply it to the two inputs "value of what's in B3" and 1.

By composing functions like this, we'll be able to do all sorts of crazy and wonderful things.

You should always be careful not to mix up the inputs. For instance, the POWER() function takes two inputs, the first called "Number" and the second called "Power." You won't need to know these names to use the function. You'll use it as POWER(2,3) or POWER(A1,C4). But you will need to know that the exponent is the second input, not the first. Using POWER(3,2) will give you the wrong answer if you want 2 to be the Number and 3 to be the Exponent.

Using $ to Tweak Functions

We saw earlier how careful use of $ signs in our references allowed us to write formulas only once and then extend them throughout a spreadsheet. They can also make it easier to repeat and tweak functions.

For instance, imagine that you have some data in A1:E1, and that in columns F and G you want compute FUNCTION1() and FUNCTION2() using that data. If you give F1 the formula

    =FUNCTION1($A1:$E1)

then you can quickly Copy-Paste it into G1 (without changing its references) and then manually change FUNCTION1 to FUNCTION2. Without the $ signs, Copy-Paste would have shifted the reference to B1:F1, and you'd have to do additional work to fix it. Of course, in this example, it's not too much more work just to enter the FUNCTION2() formula from scratch, but with more complicated formulas you can save a great deal of work using $-Copy-Paste-tweak.

A related case is when you want to change another input to the function. Let's say in F1 you need to compute FUNCTION(A1:E1,1), while in G1 you need to compute FUNCTION(A1:E1,2). If your formula in F1 is

    =FUNCTION($A1:$E1,1)

then you can just Copy-Paste it into G1 and change the 1 to a 2. Without the $, Copy-Paste would change the reference to B1:F1.

Special f_x

At the start of the formula bar, you should see f_x. This is the wondrous "insert function" button, and it has two related uses.

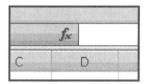

First, if you have no idea what function you'd like to use (or if you're interested in browsing through the functions available to you), clicking the f_x will pop up a menu that allows you to search for and browse through all the functions Excel knows about.

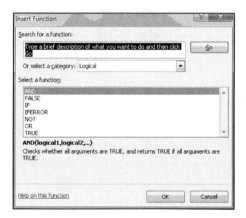

You can use the search box to look for a function (or do a "vanity" search to see if there are any functions named after you), or you can choose a category from the dropdown box and browse to see what functions are available.

Alternatively, on the "Formulas" ribbon there are several dropdown boxes that can help you find relevant functions:

Once you choose a function, you'll see a description of its use and inputs:

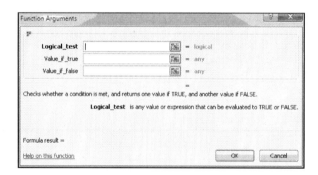

You can either type the value or reference you want right into the box, or (when you want the input to be a reference) you can click the funny-looking square just to the right of the input box and then use the mouse or keyboard to select the cells you want to reference.

Even if you know what function you want, you can still use f_x to see detailed explanations of the inputs it expects. If you type

=IF(

into a cell and then click on the f_x button, you'll get the same pop-up box that you would have gotten if you'd chosen the function from a menu.

If you want to know even more than the brief descriptions that are shown automatically, click the "Help on this function" link in the bottom left corner and you can read help pages until you're blue in the face.

Function Pop-ups

If you only need the *names* of the function inputs, you can just rely on the pop-ups that Excel automatically provides. When you start typing a function name, Excel will show you all the functions that start with whatever you typed:

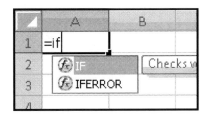

Once you choose one, Excel will show you the names of the inputs it expects, with optional inputs enclosed in [square brackets]:

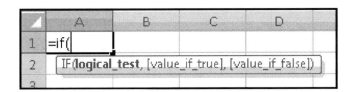

As you specify the inputs, Excel will **bold** the input you're currently supplying, which can be helpful when creating complicated formulas:

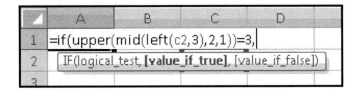

Investigating Function Parts

As we've mentioned, one way to create complex formulas is by *nesting* functions one inside another. When these formulas go awry, it can be tough to figure where they went wrong. In a new worksheet, in cell B1 input the formula

=EXP(LN(A1))

which will give you a #NUM! error. (Don't worry that we haven't yet learned the EXP() or LN() functions, we'll get to them much later, and their details aren't important right now.) We'd like to figure out where the error is coming from.

If you click f_x, you'll get a popup describing the outermost function:

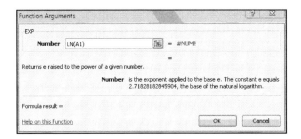

You can see that the function's input LN(A1) is producing the #NUM! error, and that the EXP() is just passing it through. To investigate further, go the formula bar, click on the LN() part of the formula, and click f_x. You'll get a popup just for the LN() function, which you can explore and try to fix things. (It turns out that LN() requires a positive number as its input.)

When you have elaborate formulas with multiple functions, exploring their details is often the only way to understand them.

Eliminating Function Parts

Still with the formula

=EXP(LN(A1))

in B1, put the value 1 in A1. Click cell B1, and in the formula bar select just the LN(A1) part of the formula. If you press F9, Excel will evaluate whatever you've got selected and replace it with its value. In this case, LN(A1) equals 0, and so after you press F9 the formula will become

=EXP(0)

If you press Enter or Tab, it will be permanently changed. If you were just checking, you can hit ESC to abandon the changes.

Showing Your Work

As we've seen, Excel lets you create pretty complicated formulas. For instance, in cell B1 you might have

=FUNCTION2(FUNCTION1(A1, 6), 7)

In most cases we'll read from the inside out: "Compute FUNCTION1 with the value of what's in A1 as the first input and 6 as the second input. Then compute FUNCTION2 with the preceding result as the first input and 7 as the second input."

An alternative way of doing the same thing is to put each step in its own cell. In B1 you could have

=FUNCTION1(A1,6)

Then in C1 you'd have

    =FUNCTION2(B1,7)

Of course you'd get the same result. Each way has its pros and cons. The
first method doesn't clutter up your spreadsheet with intermediate outputs
that you don't need. If you're confident that what you're doing is right, and
you want to keep your spreadsheet clean-looking, it might be preferable.

The second form makes it easier to understand what your formulas are doing.
If you end up with a weird-looking result, you can quickly see which step
went awry.

There's one situation where the second approach is unambiguously better,
and that's when you have to use an intermediate result multiple times.
Consider the following:

    =FUNCTION4(FUNCTION3(A1,8),FUNCTION3(A1,8))

In this example, FUNCTION3(A1,8) will be computed twice. If it's a function
that takes a long time to compute, then your spreadsheet will be twice as
slow as it needs to be. If instead you put =FUNCTION3(A1,8) in B1 and
=FUNCTION4(B1,B1) in C1, you'd only be computing FUNCTION3 once.
In complicated spreadsheets with complicated functions, this can make your
computations a lot zippier.

Now, for pedagogical reasons, this book will lean heavily toward the second
"show your work" method. That's primarily in order to illustrate exactly
what we're doing, not because it's necessarily better.

CHAPTER 6

I AM ERROR

If you do something Excel doesn't like, it's not shy about letting you know. (Not unlike your downstairs neighbor.) If your formula produces an odd-looking result starting with a pound sign (#), then probably you've got some kind of error.

Error Messages

To see what we're up against, we'll go through each of the error messages you might see.

#######

Technically, this isn't an error. It just means that Excel can't display whatever is in the cell showing the #######. Typically this happens for one of two reasons.

First, maybe the cell isn't wide enough. Put the value 1 into a cell, and click the "Add Decimal Points" button until the cell has to expand. Now drag the right border of the column to shrink the column width, and you'll see it.

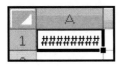

Alternatively, maybe you're trying to format a number in a way that doesn't make sense to Excel. For instance, if you try to format a negative number as a Date, you'll get this. Type -1 into A1, and then on the Home ribbon under the Number dropdown box, select "Short Date." Since Excel doesn't know how to display -1 as a date, you'll see the ####### again.

Nonetheless, in both circumstances, the values exist just fine. Formulas that rely on a ###### value will work without a problem, and so this isn't really an error. It's just a problem with the formatting.

#NULL!

You'll probably never encounter this error. I've never encountered this error. No one I know has ever encountered this error. If someone I knew ever did encounter this error, I'd probably stop speaking to him. Nonetheless, I've included it for the sake of completeness.

When you list multiple ranges separated by spaces (like A1:C1 A1:B4), Excel interprets that as their intersection (in this case A1:B1). But what if the ranges don't intersect at all? For instance, there are no cells that lie in both ranges A1:C1 and A2:B4. And if you try to use their intersection A1:C1 A2:B4, you'll get the #NULL! error.

Of course, you're never going to intersect two ranges, and therefore you're never going to see the #NULL! error. So forget I mentioned it.

#DIV/0!

Remember in third grade when you were learning arithmetic, and your teacher told you that you couldn't divide by zero, and then you asked why not, and she told you that in a commutative ring it was impossible for the zero-element to have a multiplicative inverse, and then you asked why not, and then she showed you that if it did then you could prove that 1=0, and then you asked why one couldn't equal zero, and then she made you draw a circle on the chalkboard and stand with your nose in it for the rest of the day?

Well, Excel has similar opinions about dividing by zero. And so when you try to divide by zero, or by a cell that contains zero, or even by a cell that's empty (which Excel will treat as a zero for arithmetic purposes), you'll get the #DIV/0! error (which itself seems to be dividing by zero). This one's easy enough to avoid: don't divide by zero!

As we'll see when we learn the AVERAGE() fuction, you'll also get a #DIV/0! error if you try to compute the average of a range that doesn't contain any numbers.

#REF!

This error means you're trying to refer to a cell or range that doesn't exist.

For instance, in cell B1, insert the formula =A1. Now highlight column A, right-click, and choose Delete. In the cell with your formula (which is now A1, since Excel shifted everything one column to the left when you deleted what used to be column A), you'll see #REF!, and if you look at its formula, it will show as =#REF!. That's because the cell it wants to refer to (what was A1, before we deleted it) is gone.

Another way to get a #REF! error is to refer to cells that are "off the sheet." Starting with a fresh worksheet, again put the formula =A1 in B1, and then copy-and-paste it into A1. Excel will try to move the reference so that it looks at the cell *to the left of* A1, which is off the worksheet, which gives you a #REF! error.

The #REF! error is pretty easy to avoid: don't delete parts of the spreadsheet that other parts of the spreadsheet rely on, and don't refer to parts of the spreadsheet that don't exist. Usually when you get a #REF! error you want to Undo (Ctrl-Z) whatever you just did.

#NAME?

This error means Excel has no idea what you're talking about. Most commonly this occurs because you've made some sort of typo. For example, if you're trying to use the DATE() function, but you accidentally type HATE() instead, Excel won't be able to find the HATE() function and will give you this error.

Additionally, when you give a formula an explicit string as one of its arguments, you have to put the string in double quotes. The (boring) formula

    ="Spreadsheet"

gives its cell the same value as if you'd just typed Spreadsheet as its value. The (incorrect) formula

    =Spreadsheet

gives its cell a #NAME? error.

#VALUE!

This error usually means that you gave a formula a type of data it didn't know how to deal with. Arithmetic involving text, for instance, will give you this error. Also, text searches that don't match will give this error. For instance, if you wanted to check whether there's an I in TEAM (there isn't), you'd use the formula

    =FIND("I","TEAM")

which would give you a #VALUE! error. (Don't worry that you don't yet know the FIND() function, we'll get it to it later. For now just trust me that it works the way I say.)

#NUM!

You'll see this error if you give a math formula a value that it's not designed to handle. For instance, Excel won't let you compute the square root of a negative number. This one usually means a *math* error more than a spreadsheet error.

#N/A

This one is sure to be your favorite. The #N/A stands for Not Available. It means, unsurprisingly, that a value that Excel needs is for some reason not available. An unexpected #N/A might mean that you're trying to LOOKUP an item in a list that doesn't contain it, or it might mean one of dozens of other things that don't have much to do with each other.

Invisible Errors

Unfortunately, Excel can't always tell when you make a mistake, because sometimes your mistakes aren't obviously mistakes. If your finger gets heavy and you type B11 when you mean B1, it's possible your formulas will still work but just give the wrong answer. Sometimes you'll give functions the wrong arguments – for instance, POWER(2,3) and POWER(3,2) are not equal to each other, and if you use the wrong one you'll get the wrong answer.

Fixing invisible errors is hard. First you have to notice that something is wrong. Then you have to figure out what it is. As irritating as #NUM! and #VALUE! can be, at least they let you know there's a problem. Invisible errors always cause the worst headaches!

Intentional Errors

Incredibly, sometimes you want a cell to contain an error. And if you type one of the error messages into a cell, Excel will act as though the cell had actually produced the error. Usually the error you want is the value #N/A, to indicate that a value is Not Available. (If you just wanted to mess with people you could manually enter some #DIV/0! errors into your spreadsheet, but in my experience no one finds this particularly clever.) Some types of graphs will plot blank cells as zero values, so if you want to show actual missing data points you have to fill in the blanks with #N/A. You can also use the function NA() which takes no arguments and returns a #N/A error.

Or perhaps you want to make sure that all your data points have meaningful values before you use them in a computation. If they're blank, often the calculation will produce a result anyway; for example, if you're taking a SUM(), blank cells will just get treated as if they contained 0. However, if you fill them initially with #N/A, then your SUM() calculation will also show up as #N/A until every single value has been filled in properly.

Now, as we'll see throughout the book, there are many other (usually better) ways of making sure that a computation has all the data it's looking for. But there's a slight possibility this intentional error trick might come in handy someday.

Handling Errors

Errors convey information, and sometimes you'll be more interested in the information than the error itself.

For instance, if you want to know whether a list contains an item, one way to find out is to try to MATCH() the item in the list and then check whether the result is a #N/A error or not. If you want to know whether a string contains a substring, you could try to FIND the substring in the string and then check whether the result is a #VALUE! error or not. Excel provides a few functions to do this.

ISERROR() takes one input and returns TRUE or FALSE, depending on whether the input is one of the above errors or not. The formula

=ISERROR(A1)

will return TRUE if there's currently an error in cell A1, and FALSE if there's not. Similarly, the formula

=ISERROR(FIND("I","TEAM"))

will return TRUE, as indicated earlier. The one error ISERROR() won't catch is the aforementioned ########, which we pointed out isn't really an error.

Occasionally (typically for reasons related to the previous section) you might want to distinguish between #N/A errors and other errors. Whenever that's the case, ISERR() will return TRUE for any error that's not a #N/A error, and FALSE otherwise. Complementarily, ISNA() will return TRUE for a #N/A error, and FALSE otherwise. Probably you'll never care about this distinction, and probably you should just use ISERROR(). That's what we'll do for the rest of the book.

If you want to *handle* errors, you can use the function IFERROR(), which takes two inputs. If the first input is not an error, the function will just pass it through as the output. If the first input is an error, the output will equal the second input.

So, for instance,

=IFERROR(A1,"error in A1!")

will return the value of what's in cell A1, unless that's an error, in which case it will return the string "error in A1!"). Similarly,

=IFERROR(FIND("I","TEAM"),"There's no I in TEAM!")

will do what you expect it to.

It's easy to mix up ISERROR (which only takes one input) and IFERROR (which takes two). Try not to.

Circular References

When you enter a formula, Excel undergoes a complicated rigmarole of steps to make sure that whatever cells your formula depends on are updated, whatever cells those cells depend on are updated, and so on.

If you're not careful, you can end up with a never-ending cascade of references. A simple example occurs if you type =A1+1 in cell A1. This means that the value in cell A1 should be one greater than the value that's in cell A1. It's easy to see that this isn't possible. (If you're mathematically inclined, you might object that it would be possible if we allowed infinite values in cells, but we don't, and it's not.)

The preceding example would probably never happen unless you made a typo (or were messing around). However, a more realistic scenario would be one in which, for example, A1 references B1, B1 references C1, C1 references D1, and then D1 references the SUM of everything in column A. This too is a circular reference, and Excel will give you a warning message if you try it.

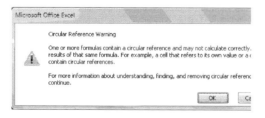

It turns out that there are a number of really advanced, somewhat oddball things you can do with Excel that actually require you to use circular references. But we're not going to discuss any of those in this book, and so – as far as we're concerned – circular references are to be avoided like the plague.

Data Validation

One way to prevent errors is to disallow certain inputs. For instance, if you have a cell in which a user of your spreadsheet is supposed to input his age, you might want to force him to enter a number greater than 0. If someone is supposed to input his phone number, you might want to force him to enter something that looks like a phone number.

If you're interested in this, there's a Data Validation feature on the Data ribbon in the Data Tools section. If you click on it you'll get a popup to specify the sort of validation you want.

You can choose to force a Whole number, a Decimal, a Date, a Time, or a Text length, each of which gives you the option of specifying a max and a min. If the input is age, for instance, you might want a whole number between 0 and 150, or (if you're some sort of life extension fanatic) maybe just greater than 0.

If you put this sort of validation in a cell, you might want to customize the Input Message tab, which gives the spreadsheet user an indication that their inputs have to meet the validation criteria, and you definitely want to customize the Error Alert tab, or else users who input invalid data will get an unhelpful "The value you entered is not valid" message.

List Validation

By far the most useful application of validation is when you have a (small) list of acceptable values, as you can specify that they appear in a dropdown box.

You can enter the values separated by commas

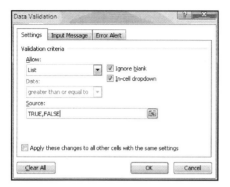

or you can enter a reference to a range containing the allowable values. As long as you keep "In-cell dropdown" selected, the cell will get a dropdown menu with its allowable values.

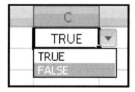

If done wisely, this can make your spreadsheets much simpler for people to use.

Custom Validation

If you choose the "Custom" option you can specify an arbitrary formula that needs to be TRUE for the input to be valid, which allows you to create arbitrarily complex validations. However, we can't fruitfully discuss these until later, when we learn more about formulas involving Booleans.

CHAPTER 7

FINDING AND IMPORTING DATA

Once you get started doing data analysis, you'll quickly discover the need to get data *into* Excel. These data could come from some other program, a text file that someone emailed you, a web page, or a flyer you stole off a telephone pole.

One obvious way to get any data into Excel is to type it in. If the data is from a printed flyer, that's probably what you'll have to do. But if the data is already on the computer, there are (in most cases) easier ways. It will be important not just to get the data into Excel, but to do so in a way that takes advantage of the grid.

Excel-Readable Formats

If you're extremely fortunate, you may find a source of data that allows you to download an Excel-ready file, either .xls (which is the older Excel format), .xlsx (which is the newer Excel format), or .csv (which is just a comma-separated text file). When this is the case, you can download the file and open it in Excel directly.

For example, the Google Finance page for Microsoft's historical stock price

http://www.google.com/finance/historical?q=NASDAQ:MSFT

has a "Download to Spreadsheet" button on it (or did at the time this book went to press). If you click it, a spreadsheet will open with the prices in it.

Pasting from the Web

If there were no such button, you could instead copy the data and Paste-Special-Text it directly into Excel. (Why Paste-Special-Text? Because we're interested in the data itself, not the HTML formatting. If you just Paste what you copied, which is the same as Paste-Special-HTML, the results will depend in an unpredictable way on whatever extra HTML junk the web designer included. Paste-Special-Text ensures that we only get the data we want.)

Show. **Daily** | Weekly			Jul 27, 2009	- Jul 26, 2010	Update
Date	Open	High	Low	Close	Volume
Jul 26, 2010	25.86	26.20	25.80	26.10	67,157,294
Jul 23, 2010	25.84	26.02	25.25	25.81	108,520,012
Jul 22, 2010	25.51	25.99	25.47	25.84	73,016,369
Jul 21, 2010	25.60	25.65	24.98	25.12	73,297,593
Jul 20, 2010	24.86	25.48	24.70	25.48	45,530,162
Jul 19, 2010	24.96	25.30	24.91	25.23	38,181,760

To get these into Excel, first select the entire table by highlighting it with the mouse, then right-click and copy it, and finally Paste-Special-Text it into Excel:

	A	B	C	D	E	F
1	Date	Open	High	Low	Close	Volume
2	26-Jul-10	25.86	26.2	25.8	26.1	########
3	23-Jul-10	25.84	26.02	25.25	25.81	########
4	22-Jul-10	25.51	25.99	25.47	25.84	########
5	21-Jul-10	25.6	25.65	24.98	25.12	########

Notice that Excel was clever enough to realize that the first column contained dates. (You can tell by the way it slightly reformatted them.) After resizing the columns, we can see all the data:

	A	B	C	D	E	F
1	Date	Open	High	Low	Close	Volume
2	26-Jul-10	25.86	26.2	25.8	26.1	67,157,294
3	23-Jul-10	25.84	26.02	25.25	25.81	108,520,012
4	22-Jul-10	25.51	25.99	25.47	25.84	73,016,369
5	21 Jul 10	25.6	25.65	24.98	25.12	73,297,593

And now you're ready to do all sorts of analysis.

Text to Column

Sometimes you'll get data simply as text, separated by commas or tabs or some other character. For instance, our stock prices might have shown up like this:

```
Date,Open,High,Low,Close,Volume
26-Jul-10,25.86,26.2,25.8,26.1,67157294
23-Jul-10,25.84,26.02,25.25,25.81,108520012
22-Jul-10,25.51,25.99,25.47,25.84,73016369
21-Jul-10,25.6,25.65,24.98,25.12,73297593
20-Jul-10,24.86,25.48,24.7,25.48,45530162
```

If you copy the data and Paste-Special-Text it into Excel, it will get jammed into a single column.

	A	B	C	D	E
1	Date,Open,High,Low,Close,Volume				
2	26-Jul-10,25.86,26.2,25.8,26.1,67157294				
3	23-Jul-10,25.84,26.02,25.25,25.81,108520012				
4	22-Jul-10,25.51,25.99,25.47,25.84,73016369				
5	21 Jul 10,25.6,25.65,24.98,25.12,73297593				

Excel put the entire first line in A1, the entire second line in A2, and so on. Text-to-Column will split the data into columns for us.

How will Excel know where to end a column and start the next? Sometimes data is delimited. In this example we have commas that separate one column from the next, but you might instead have tabs, spaces, semicolons or something else. Less commonly, you might have fixed-width columns, so that the first 5 characters are one column, the next 8 another, and so on.

With all the data in A1:A101 selected, go to the Data ribbon and choose the Text to Columns option:

You'll get a wizard that allows you to choose whether your data is delimited or fixed-width. Once you click Next, Excel will guess incorrectly that your data is delimited by tabs:

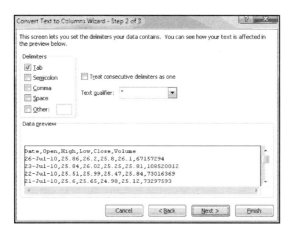

Uncheck "Tab" and check "Comma" instead. The wizard will then show what the split would look like:

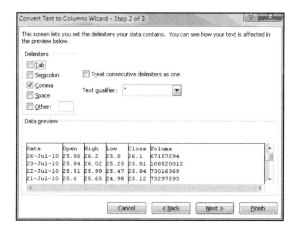

Click Finish, and you'll get your data in columns, as desired.

Once you use Text-to-Columns with (say) commas as your separator, Excel will keep thinking of commas as separators until you close the workbook or perform another Text-to-Column with a different separator. After you split your stock price data into columns, any further text you paste with commas in it (for instance, if you pasted "Gates, Bill") will also get split into columns, which is often not what you want.

If this happens to you, click on a non-empty cell and run Text-to-Column again with Tab as the delimiter.

Importing Text Files

If the data you need is already in a text file, a comma-separated file, or a tab-separated file, you can import it using the "From Text" option in the "Get External Data" section of the Data ribbon. After browsing to and choosing the file, you'll get a series of menus that are basically identical to the Text-to-Column wizard we went through in the previous section.

After describing the data to Excel, it will ask you where you want to put it. You can either choose a cell (which it will use as the top left corner of your data) or specify a new worksheet, in which case Excel will add one.

Importing from a Database

Excel can also import data from a database on your computer or on your network. The exact nuts and bolts of how to do this depend on the database type and how it's configured and what tables your data lives in, which means we're not going to discuss it here.

Cleaning and Normalizing

Data that you gather will often need **cleaning**. They might be full of stray spaces, missing values, typographical errors, extra separators, or countless other things that make them not immediately usable. Throughout the book we'll see different techniques for cleaning your data, although the core technique is always ingenuity.

Data will also often need **normalization** to enforce a sort of internal consistency. It's hard to do state-by-state analyses when the State in your dataset is sometimes written as "North Carolina," sometimes as "N. Carolina," and sometimes as "NC." We'll also see techniques for these situations, but again cleverness and attention to detail are what really matter.

If you aren't careful about cleaning and normalizing your data, you'll likely end up with all sorts of errors and mistakes. Be attentive.

CHAPTER 8

BASICS OF VISUALIZATION

I said I wasn't going to spend much time writing about workaday topics like "how to print" and "how to make charts." Nonetheless, at various points in the book I'll need to use charts to illustrate what I'm doing, and it hardly seems fair not to empower you to do the same.

The Charts We Care About

Although Excel contains many different chart types, in this book we will only use three: the Column/Bar Chart, the Line Chart, and the Scatter Chart. (What Excel calls a "Column Chart" most normal people would call a "Bar Chart." Excel uses "Column Chart" when the bars are vertical and "Bar Chart" when the bars are horizontal. We'll adopt this same terminology and talk about "Column Charts," but we won't be very happy about it.)

A chart is simply a way to visualize data. In most situations we'll have some data (the "dependent variable," typically numeric) that depends on some other data (the "independent variable," not always numeric). Following a convention that was established by algebra teachers, we'll usually refer to the independent variable as x and the dependent variable as y.

To demonstrate the different types of graphs, we'll use some very simple data that don't mean anything but that make nice pictures.

x	y
1	100
100	950
10	400

To start with, let's put the data into Excel. Our life will be easier if we remove the x header. By default Excel thinks that any column with a header contains dependent variables, since it's not uncommon to plot multiple series of dependent variables in the same chart. If we were to leave the data as above, Excel would think we had two dependent series, one called x and one called y and it would plot them both using its default independent variable, $\{1,2,\ldots\}$.

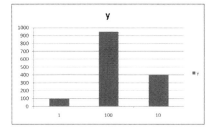

To create a column chart, click anywhere in the data, go to the "Insert" ribbon, click on "Column" under charts, and choose the top left option.

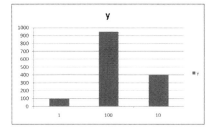

If you do the same with "Bar" you'll produce a bar chart, which you can see is just the column chart turned on its side (and with the data going from bottom to top).

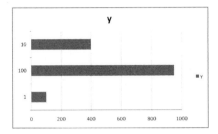

A line chart will plot your data in order and evenly spaced on the x-axis. So the point with x-coordinate 100 will be plotted halfway between the points with x-coordinates 1 and 10, even though 100 is larger than 10. A line chart treats these numbers as labels only.

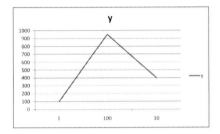

Finally, a scatter chart (sometimes called an "X-Y Chart") will place points on the chart based on *both* their x-coordinates and y-coordinates. The point with x-coordinate 1 will be plotted farthest to the left, the point with x-coordinate 10 will be plotted slightly to its right, and the point with x-coordinate 100 will be plotted far to the right. If you choose the version with segments connecting the points, the segments will be drawn according to the ordering of the original data; the points themselves are just points and don't depend on the ordering at all.

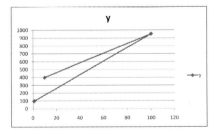

Just to be confusing, if you create a Line chart whose independent variable is a date, Excel will plot and connect the points in chronological order, which is not quite "line chart" behavior and not quite "scatter chart" behavior.

When should you use one chart over another? As a general rule, if you want to compare quantities, use a column chart. If you want to show trends in data, use a line chart. And if you want to show relationships between multiple variables, use a scatter chart. These are not absolute rules; they're only starting points. Nonetheless, they're good starting points.

Tweaking Charts

Excel won't always draw charts the way you want it to. Usually, if you right-click on some element of a chart, you can customize it. If you right-click on a line in a line chart, you can change its color and width. If you right-click on the x-axis, you can change its starting point and ending point and labels and tick marks. If you right-click on a column in a column chart, you can add labels to it.

Additionally, if you select a chart, Excel will add three "Chart Tools" ribbons. The "Design" ribbon lets you change the chart type (for example, from Line to Column), select different data for the chart, and apply a variety of built-in visual styles. The "Layout" ribbon has options to add or remove axes, axis titles, chart titles, gridlines, and other similar elements. The "Format" ribbon doesn't do much you'll find useful.

You should play around with these if you like the idea of customizing your charts, but we're not going to dwell on them.

Pie Charts

Beginning charters often like to use pie charts. This is unfortunate, as it's very hard to judge the relative sizes of pie slices.

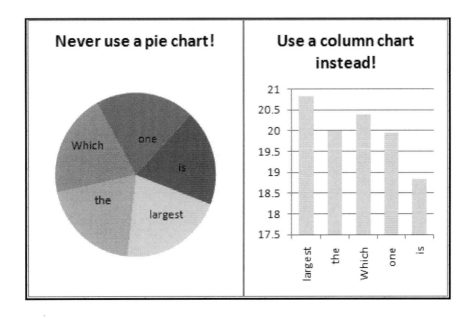

3-D Charts

Some people also like to add 3-D effects to their charts, which pretty much always makes them more difficult to read.

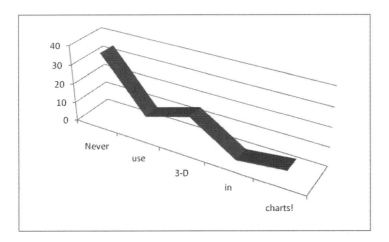

CHAPTER 9

PLUSES AND MINUSES

Excel makes a great calculator, except that it doesn't fit in your pocket and doesn't use a font in which 07734 is "hELLO" when you turn it upside down.

Rithmetic

If you learn nothing more than how to do arithmetic in Excel, you'll already be able to get a great deal of value out of spreadsheets. (On the other hand, if you learn nothing more than how to do arithmetic in Excel, I'll be very disappointed in you, as most of my writing will end up having been for nothing.)

To start with, you can add two numbers using +. The formula

    =2+3

will add 2 and 3 produce the value 5.

Similarly, the formula

    =-1+1

equals 0, and the formula

=1.5+0.1

equals 1.6. You can subtract numbers in the same fashion, using a - sign instead of a + sign. For instance, the formula

=2-3

will produce the value -1, and the formula

=1.5-0.1

will produce the value 1.4.

You can also multiply and divide using * and /. The formula

=2*3

equals 6, while

=1.5/0.1

equals 15. As mentioned earlier, you probably want to avoid dividing by 0.

If you divide two numbers which aren't multiples of each other, you'll get a decimal answer. This can be exact or an approximation. For instance, if you divide

=1/8

you'll see 0.125. This is exact, since 1/8 is exactly 0.125.

On the other hand, if you divide

=2/3

you'll see something like 0.666667. The exact answer would be 0.666666... continuing forever. But Excel can't keep track of that many decimal places, so it eventually rounds off.

You can use cell references instead of numbers. The formula

=A1*4.5

equals the value in cell A1 multiplied by 4.5, and the formula

=A2-3

returns 3 less than the value in cell A2. You don't have to use any numbers at all – the formula

=A1/A2

returns the value of what's in A1 divided by the value of what's in A2. (Of course, you'll get a #VALUE! error if your cells don't contain numbers, and a #DIV/0! error if you try to divide by a cell that contains 0 or is blank.)

There's nothing restricting you to only two numbers at a time either. The formula

=A1+B2+C3+D4

adds four cells that lie on a diagonal line, and the formula

=A1*B2*C3*D4

multiplies them. However, you need to be extra careful when you do this, or things might get confusing.

For instance, consider the formula

=2+3*4

Naively, this could mean "add 2 and 3, and then multiply the result by 4." Or it could mean "add 2 to the result of multiplying 3 and 4."

Similarly, consider the formula

   =10-5-1

This could mean "subtract 5 from 10 and then subtract 1 from the result." Or it could mean "subtract 1 from 5 and then subtract the result from 10."

Excel doesn't like ambiguity, so it follows a specific (and pretty standard) order of operations. Multiplication and division occur first, and they take place from left to right. After that, addition and subtraction occur, and they also occur left to right.

So in our first example, since multiplication comes before addition, we first multiply 3 * 4 and only then add 2. The answer is 14 (as you can check yourself).

In our second example, we only have subtractions, so we simply work left to right. First, we subtract 5 from 10 and then subtract 1 from the result. The answer is 4 (as you can check yourself).

If you want to force a different order, you need to use parenthesis. In fact, part of Thinking Spreadsheet is always using parenthesis to specify order of operations, even when the formula would work correctly without them.

That is, you really ought to use 2+(3*4), even though 2+3*4 would give the same answer. There are two reasons for this.

First, using parentheses greatly reduces your chances of accidentally messing up the formula. It makes your intentions absolutely clear, which helps you get it right and also helps anyone who has to modify your work.

In addition, the formula with parentheses is much easier to read. When you look at the second type of formula, you have to spend extra time thinking about how Excel will interpret it. With the parentheses, it's obvious. An extra second of typing now will save you minutes or hours of headaches later.

The only time this rule doesn't apply is when you're only multiplying or only adding. There's no possible ambiguity in 2+3+4, nor in 2*3*4. It's obvious what each formula means, and the order of operations in each is completely irrelevant.

Otherwise, use the parentheses.

Division Joy

What's 5 divided by 2? Well, if you're in third grade it's "2 remainder 1", and then when you're in fourth grade it's "2 and a half" and then when you're in fifth grade it's 2.5. We're going to put on our third-grade hats for a few minutes.

When we divide two (positive) numbers, the number we're dividing is called the *dividend*, and the number we're dividing by is called the *divisor*. And since we're in third grade, we find the *quotient*, which is the largest integer we can multiply the divisor by and get a number that's no bigger than the dividend. And we get a *remainder*, which is how much is left over. Necessarily the remainder will be at least 0 but less than the divisor.

For instance, if we were computing 14 / 3, we'd find that the quotient was 4 (since 4 * 3 is not bigger than 14 but 5 * 3 is) and that therefore the remainder must be 2, which is the amount left over when you subtract 4 * 3 from 14. If we were computing 25 / 8, we'd find the quotient equal to 3 (since 8 * 3 is not bigger than 25 but 8 * 4 is) and the remainder equal to 1. And if we were computing 20 / 5, we'd find the quotient equal to 4 and the remainder equal to 0.

Luckily (for people who need to do integer division), Excel provides functions to do the work. The function QUOTIENT() takes two inputs, the dividend and the divisor, and outputs the quotient. So

=QUOTIENT(25,8)

returns the value 3. Its counterpart MOD() takes the same inputs and outputs the remainder. Thus

=MOD(25,8)

returns the value 1.

The MOD() Squad

It turns out that MOD() is not only useful for integer division.

MOD() is also a way of setting up *equivalences* between numbers. If two numbers differ by a multiple of 12, then they'll have the same remainder when you divide them by 12. And so when you MOD() them by 12, you'll get the same answer.

This makes MOD() useful for doing what you might have learned as "clock arithmetic." What time is "17 hours after 11:00"? Well, it's

=MOD(11+17,12)

which is 4. If we want to worry about AM/PM, we can use military hours, which go from 0 to 23, and MOD() by 24.

If we start a 43-hour forced march at "1900" (which is military speak for the 19th hour, or 7pm), then we'll finish at

=MOD(19+43,24)

the 14th hour, or 2pm. It will be

=QUOTIENT(19+43,24)

or 2, days later.

Pseudo-randomness

MOD() also is useful for generating "pseudo-random numbers," numbers that look sort of random but aren't. (Computers are typically designed to follow specific instructions, and so most programs that use "random" numbers are actually producing them through some sort of deterministic process using MOD().)

Imagine that you have a list of employee ID numbers, and you want to divide your employees into three roughly equally-sized groups. (Perhaps you need to lay off 1/3 of the company but you don't care which 1/3.) Then you could assign groups with

=MOD(*ID*,3)

That's the remainder when you divide the ID by 3, so it's either 0, 1, or 2. Assuming that there aren't any odd patterns in how employee IDs are assigned, then the three groups should be about the same size. It's not random, since there's a specific rule for it, but it's likely that the results will appear random.

Divisibility

Sometimes you'd like to know whether one number is divisible by another number. That's the same thing as saying that there's no remainder when you do the division, which happens precisely when MOD() equals 0. We'll see examples of using MOD() to test for divisibility later in the book.

Give Me a SIGN()

So far we've mostly been working with positive numbers, but negative numbers are sometimes useful too. Excel has a pair of functions that come in handy when you're working with a mixture of positive and negative numbers. And they're both pretty simple.

The first is SIGN(), which takes a single numeric input and outputs its sign. If you give it a positive number, SIGN() outputs the value 1. If you give it a negative number, SIGN() outputs the value -1. And SIGN(0) is equal to 0.

Its counterpart is ABS(), which is short for absolute value. The absolute value of a number is the value you get if you *ignore* its sign. So ABS(3) is 3, and ABS(-3) is also 3. ABS(0), in case you were wondering, is 0.

There's two relations between these two that might come in handy. First, any number is equal to its SIGN() multiplied by its ABS(). If the number is positive, its SIGN() is 1 and its ABS() is itself. If the number is negative, its SIGN() is -1 and its ABS() is itself multiplied by -1. And if the number is 0, then its SIGN() and ABS() are both 0. In every case, multiplying the SIGN() and ABS() gets you back the original number.

A second relation (with an analogous proof) is that the ABS() of a number is equal to the number multiplied by its SIGN(). You can check this yourself.

Both of these functions will be useful additions to our toolbox, although neither is terribly interesting on its own.

Short ROUND()

Sometimes you need to transform a number into a simpler number. Maybe you don't care about the decimal part of it, or maybe you're only concerned with the closest multiple of 10. Excel has lots and lots and lots and lots of functions that do this, and we'll go over them, and still you'll end up confusing them and have to look back at this chapter. That's OK. We'll group them into three categories, depending on what sort of parameters they want.

No Parameters

The simplest of these functions is INT(), which takes one numeric input and returns the next integer less than or equal to it. You should think of it as "decrease until you hit an integer."

So, for instance, INT(2.5) equals 2. INT(2) equals 2. INT(0.5) equals 0. INT(-0.5) equals -1 (which is the next integer less than or equal to -0.5). INT(-1) equals -1.

Slightly less useful are EVEN() and ODD(), which you should think of as "move away from zero until you hit an even (or odd) integer." EVEN(1) equals 2, while EVEN(-1) equals -2. ODD(1) equals 1, since it's already an odd integer. ODD(2.5) equals 3, while ODD(-2.5) equals (-3).

What about ODD(0)? Does it move up (to 1) or down (to -1)? Try it and find out!

I'll be surprised if you ever use EVEN() or ODD().

Decimal Places

Sometimes you want to round a number to have only a certain number of decimal places. This is exactly what the function ROUND() does. It takes two inputs: first the number you want rounded, and second, the number of decimal places.

ROUND() works the way that you learned in grade school. It looks at the digit after the last one you want. If that digit is 5 or more, it increases the previous digit, otherwise it leaves it alone:

Function	Result	Why
ROUND(1.46,1)	1.5	Digit after 1 decimal place is 6
ROUND(1.44,1)	1.4	Digit after 1 decimal place is 4
ROUND(1.44,2)	1.44	Digit after 2 decimal places is (implicitly) 0
ROUND(1.46,0)	1	Digit after 0 decimal places is 4

ROUND() does the same with negative numbers, so ROUND(-1.46,1) would be -1.5 and ROUND(-1.44,1) would be -1.4.

You can also specify a negative number of decimal places, which rounds to the left of the decimal point.

Function	Result	Why
ROUND(1627,-1)	1630	Digit "after -1 decimal place" is 7
ROUND(1627,-2)	1600	Digit "after -2 decimal places" is 2
ROUND(1627,-3)	2000	Digit "after -3 decimal places" is 6
ROUND(1627,-4)	0	Digit "after -4 decimal places" is 1

The last example may be a little surprising. It might help to think about it as ROUND(01627,-4), which makes it easier to see why it rounds to zero.

Two related functions are ROUNDUP() and ROUNDDOWN(). ROUNDUP() always rounds away from zero, no matter what the next digit is. And ROUNDDOWN() always rounds toward zero, no matter what the next digit is.

Function	Result	Why
ROUNDUP(1627,-1)	1630	Always away from zero.
ROUNDDOWN(1627,-1)	1620	Always toward zero.
ROUNDUP(-1.44,1)	-1.5	Always away from zero.
ROUNDDOWN(-1.44,1)	-1.4	Always toward zero.

For reasons I can't figure out, there's also a function called TRUNC() (which is "truncate" truncated) that does exactly the same thing as ROUNDDOWN(). It's easier to type, I suppose.

Multiples

Rather than specifying a number of decimal places, you might want to specify a multiple instead. The function MROUND() rounds its first input to the nearest multiple of its second input.

Function	Result	Why
MROUND(4.1,0.25)	4	4 is the closest multiple of 0.25.
MROUND(4.2,0.25)	4.25	4.25 is the closest multiple of 0.25.
MROUND(4,3)	3	3 is the closest multiple of 3.
MROUND(5,3)	6	6 is the closest multiple of 3.
MROUND(4.5,3)	6	4.5 is exactly halfway between 3 and 6. In that case we MROUND away from 0.
MROUND(4,-3)	#NUM!	You can't round a positive number to a negative multiple, nor vice versa.

Notice that you get an error if the number to round and the multiple have opposite signs! Don't do that.

CEILING() will round a number to the nearest multiple away from zero, and FLOOR() will round a number to the nearest multiple toward zero. They basically do what you'd expect functions called MROUNDUP() and MROUNDDOWN() to do. (However, there are no functions MROUNDUP() and MROUNDDOWN(), so don't try to use them!)

Like MROUND(), CEILING() and FLOOR() will give you errors if your inputs have opposite signs, so make sure they don't.

CHAPTER *10*

SUMMARY JUDGMENT

Once you start dealing with larger datasets, you'll often need to *summarize* the data in various ways. For instance, if you have a list of test scores, you might want to know their average, or how many scores are in the list, or the largest score.

SUM() Like It Hot

SUM() is one of the most useful functions I know. It sounds simple: SUM() simply returns the sum of its inputs. However, like many things that sound simple, it isn't.

Summing Values

One way to use SUM() is by giving it an explicit list of values as inputs. If all these values are numbers, SUM() will just add them up. If some of these values are Booleans, SUM() will count each TRUE as 1 and each FALSE as 0. If some of these values are text representations of numbers (like "3" or "-1.5"), then Excel will pretend you just typed the number itself. But if even one of the values is text that doesn't represent a number, you'll get a #VALUE! error. (If one of the values is an error, then you'll get an error as well.)

Let's look at some examples:

Function	Value	Why
SUM(1,2,3)	6	1+2+3=6
SUM("1","2",3)	6	numbers stored as text are converted to text
SUM(TRUE,TRUE,FALSE)	2	TRUE treated as 1, FALSE treated as 0
SUM("one","two",3)	#VALUE!	"one" is not (to Excel) the representation of a number as text

Of course, anywhere you can use a value, you can also use a function that returns a value. For instance, the formula

=SUM(MOD(10,3),SIGN(-1),9)

would evaluate to SUM(1,-1,9), which would be 9.

Summing References

You can also give SUM() references to cells or ranges of cells, in which case it behaves slightly differently. When SUM() is given a reference, it looks at the contents and ignores everything except numbers. It ignores Booleans. It ignores all text, even numbers stored as text. It ignores blank cells.

For instance, type the text **one** in A1, TRUE in A2, and 3 in A3. Now in cell A4 enter the formula

=SUM(A1:A3)

Excel ignores the text and Boolean and gives you the answer 3. If you'd directly typed =SUM("one",TRUE,3), it would have returned a #VALUE! error.

You can also sum across multiple ranges at once, like SUM(A1:A3,B2:B4,D9). If you want to get really crazy, you can sum a mixture of ranges and values:

SUM(A1:A3,TRUE,"3",FALSE,ABS(-1.5),D4)

You'll probably never do something so convoluted; however, you might at some point want something like one more than the sum of a range: SUM(A1:J1,1).

Multiplication

If you'd rather *multiply*, you can use PRODUCT(), which is the multiplicative equivalent of SUM(). It treats values and references the the same way that SUM() does. If you give it references, it will multiply all the numbers in them and ignore everything else.

You can probably think of lots of situations where you might want to add up a whole bunch of numbers: accounting, football, science, gardening, alchemy, darts, or basically anything else where you're trying to keep track of money, points, or how much lead you've turned into gold.

It's harder to think of situations where you need to multiply a lot of numbers. It's possible you'll never use PRODUCT() at all.

Example: Keeping the Pennies

Your bank is instituting a new "Keeping the Pennies" forced-saving program. If you choose to enroll, every time you make a purchase with your check card they'll round the amount up to the nearest dollar and deposit the difference in a savings account. For example, if you buy a $2.75 latte, they'll take $3 out of your checking account but put 25 cents into your savings account. If you buy a $9.99 CD, they'll take $10 out of your checking account but put a penny into your savings account.

You're not sure whether to enroll in this program. To help you decide, your bank let you download all of your check card transactions from last year, so you can find out how much you would have been forced to save.

To start with, go to ThinkingSpreadsheet.com and find the transaction listing:

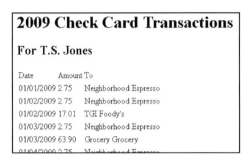

(I assumed your name was T.S. Jones. It is, right?)

Select all of the transactions, copy, and Paste-Special-Text into a new spreadsheet.

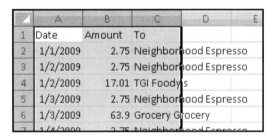

The columns are apparently not wide enough, so widen them.

Now we need to figure out how many pennies we'd keep from each transaction. For clarity we'll do this in two steps, although in practice you'd probably combine them.

First, in column D, we'll round the transaction amount up. We'll use ROUNDUP(), but we could just as easily use CEILING().

We want to round the transaction amount up to the next whole number. That is, we want to round it up to zero decimal places, which means in D2 we can use the formula

=ROUNDUP(B2,0)

and fill down using a Double-Click-Fill. The pennies kept are just the difference

=D2-B2

	A	B	C	D	E
1	Date	Amount	To	Round Up	Pennies
2	1/1/2009	2.75	Neighborhood Espresso	3	0.25
3	1/2/2009	2.75	Neighborhood Espresso	3	0.25
4	1/2/2009	17.01	TGI Foody's	18	0.99
5	1/3/2009	2.75	Neighborhood Espresso	3	0.25
6	1/3/2009	63.9	Grocery Grocery	64	0.1

In practice you might skip the "Round Up" column and combine the two preceding steps:

=ROUNDUP(B2,0)-B2

Finally, we just need to sum the pennies:

=SUM(E2:E463)

You would have ended up with $133.51 extra in your savings account. (Taken out of your checking account, of course.) That's probably not going to be enough to retire on.

"You got your SUM( ) in my PRODUCT( )!"

There's also a hybrid between SUM() and PRODUCT(), with the strikingly unoriginal name of SUMPRODUCT(). It takes as its inputs one or more arrays, all of which must have the same dimensions. If they don't, you'll get a #VALUE! error.

Since the arrays all have the same numbers of rows and columns, each possible location (e.g. row 2, column 3) identifies exactly one element in each array. For each location, SUMPRODUCT() multiplies the corresponding elements in all the arrays. And then it adds up the results.

For instance, consider the formula

=SUMPRODUCT(A1:B3,C5:D7)

Its inputs are two arrays with the same dimensions: three rows and two columns. The function will multiply corresponding elements: A1 (first array, first row, first column) with C5 (second array, first row, first column), B1 (first array, first row, second column) with D5 (second array, first row, second column), and similarly for the other 4 positions. Then it will return the sum of these products. The final result will be the same as if we'd entered

=(A1*C5)+(B1*D5)+(A2*C6)+(B2*D6)+(A3*C7)+(B3*C7)

but with a lot less typing.

The similar SUMSQ() will square (multiply by itself) every number you give it then return the sum of the results.

If you give SUMSQ() an array, the result is exactly the same as if you gave the array to SUMPRODUCT() twice.

Example: The Gradesheet

You're teaching a class in which the students have a term paper, two midterms, and a final. You want the term paper to count for 20% of their grade, each midterm to count for 25%, and the final exam to count for 30%.

Put these weights in B1:E1, the labels in B2:E2, and some grades in B3:E3.

	A	B	C	D	E
1		20%	25%	25%	30%
2		Term Paper	Midterm 1	Midterm 2	Final
3	Student 1	95	60	80	85

Then in F3 you can compute the overall grade (for the student in row 3) as

=SUMPRODUCT(B$1:E$1,B3:E3)

You should find an overall grade of 79.5.

Putting a $ on the 1 (and not on the 3) allows you to copy this formula down for additional students. The first reference will keep referring to the weights in row 1, while the second will move to refer to each student's grades.

Now imagine the Dean demands that the final count for 50%, each midterm 20%, and the term paper only 10%. All you have to do is change the weights in row 1, and your whole grade sheet will be updated!

	A	B	C	D	E	F
1		10%	20%	20%	50%	
2		Term Paper	Midterm 1	Midterm 2	Final	
3	Student 1	95	60	80	85	80

Imagine further that you need to give a third midterm. Highlight column E, right-click, and choose Insert.

	A	B	C	D	E	F	G
1		10%	20%	20%		50%	
2		Term Paper	Midterm 1	Midterm 2		Final	
3	Student 1	95	60	80		85	80

The final exam and grades will both shift one column to the right, leaving a blank spot for your third midterm. Even better, your SUMPRODUCT() arguments will have automatically expanded to B$1:F$1 and B3:F3. This means that as soon as you fix the weights and add in the third midterm grades, the overall grades will be correctly calculated.

This only works because you inserted a column in the middle. If you'd added the column to the left or to the right of the existing grades, the formulas wouldn't have expanded, and you'd have to fix them by hand.

Down for the COUNT()

Whereas SUM() adds numbers, COUNT() simply counts them. Otherwise, the two functions behave pretty similarly. If you give COUNT() values that are numbers, text representations of numbers, or Booleans, it will count them. If you give it any other text, it won't.

Function	Result	Why
COUNT(1,2,3)	3	all 3 are numbers
COUNT("1","2",3)	3	numbers stored as text are converted to text
COUNT(TRUE,TRUE,FALSE)	3	TRUE treated as 1, FALSE treated as 0
COUNT("one","two",3)	1	"one" and "two" are not (to Excel) the representation of a number as text

One clear difference is that COUNT() happily ignores values that can't be interpreted as numbers, whereas SUM() would produce an error.

Like SUM(), if you give COUNT() references as inputs it will ignore everything that's not a number. And this is most commonly how you'll use it.

If you have a list of numbers in column A, then

   =COUNT(A:A)

tells you how many are in your list. If you add more numbers, or if you delete some of the numbers, those changes will automatically be reflected. If your column has a header then (unless the header is a number itself) it won't be counted.

If for some reason you wanted to count more than numbers, the slight variation COUNTA() will count everything except for blank cells. You may have occasion to use this at some point, but COUNT() is much more common.

Along similar lines, AVERAGE() gives you the average of its inputs, behaving (as we've now come to expect) differently depending on whether you give it values or references.

AVERAGE() is essentially SUM()/COUNT(). In particular, if you give it references that don't contain any numbers, you'll get a #DIV/0! error.

Quick Sum and Count

If you select a range of cells, Excel will show you statistics at the bottom right of the window.

Average is the AVERAGE() and Sum is the SUM(), but Count is actually the COUNTA(), the number of non-blank cells in your selection. If you right click on the bar, you can also enable Max, Min, and "Numeric Count," which is the COUNT().

Example: A Pseudo-Random Number Generator

As mentioned earlier, computers can't actually generate random numbers. Instead they produce numbers that "seem" random. One common way of doing this involves what's called a "linear congruential generator," which we're going to build.

The procedure is not terribly complicated. We start with a number, called a "seed." We then multiply it by a constant factor, add a different constant factor, and MOD() the result by a third constant factor.

For instance, a really simple (and not very good) generator takes the seed, multiplies it by 29, adds 3, and MOD()s the result by 32. It then uses the result as the next seed and repeats.

Whenever we MOD() a number by 32, the result will be between 0 and 31. Also, for a fixed choice of constants, the result of the generator depends only on the seed. This means that whenever we see a number repeat, we'll consequently see the entire sequence of pseudo-random numbers repeat. And since there are only 32 possible outputs, if we generate more than 32 random numbers then necessarily we'll see the same number twice, which means our sequence will start repeating itself over and over again. So this not very good sequence will produce at best 32 pseudo-random numbers.

To see this, put these factors in a spreadsheet and use 10 as the seed:

◢	A	B
1		
2	multiply:	29
3	add:	3
4	mod() by:	32
5		
6	seed:	10

We'll start generating numbers in B7:

=MOD((B6*$B$2)+$B$3,$B$4)

If you're astute you'll notice that the above formula has more $ signs than it needs. Since we're going to fill this formula down, we certainly need to $ the row numbers on B2, B3, and B4. Since we're not going to copy the formula side-to-side, it doesn't really matter whether we $ the B. So why did I do it? Two reasons.

First, the first time you press F4 to $ a reference, it $'s both the rows and the columns. So when I hit F4 after typing B2, it became $B$2. Since the formula will work correctly with $B$2, I saved myself some work and left it like that.

Second, I find that it requires a surprising amount of mental energy to decide whether the appropriate reference is $B2 or B$2. When you truly need (say) the row to change and the column not to change, then you do have to think through it. But if (like here) you want the row not to change but don't care what the column does since you're never going to copy it side-to-side, then using $B$2 actually lessens your chance of getting the formula wrong.

Throughout the book you'll see me using $ on both rows and columns when it would suffice to only $ one or the other, and this is why.

Copy or fill this formula all the down to B50.

6	seed:	10
7		5
8		20
9		7
10		14
11		25

You can check that after 32 numbers, the entire sequence starts to repeat. And that was with a good choice of parameters. If instead we'd multiplied by 4, we would have quickly gotten stuck on 31 forever:

	A	B
1		
2	multiply:	4
3	add:	3
4	mod() by:	32
5		
6	seed:	10
7		11
8		15
9		31
10		31
11		31

In a real application, we'd use much larger numbers. I got the following parameters from the Wikipedia article "Linear congruential generator."

	A	B
1		
2	multiply:	1664525
3	add:	1013904223
4	mod() by:	4294967296

Change to these parameters, and copy the formula in B7 all the way down to B10006, to generate 10,000 pseudo-random numbers. They're all between 0 and 4294967295, which isn't terribly useful for applications. It would be more useful if they were between 0 and 1, which will be the case if we divide them by the modulus.

In C7, simply input the formula =B6/$B$4 and then copy it down.

6	**seed:**	10	
7		1030549473	0.239943497
8		797165516	0.18560456
9		2863095995	0.666616483
10		163339998	0.038030557
11		209336485	0.048739949
12		424041664	0.00001c150

We don't yet know enough statistics to investigate "how random" these numbers are, but we can check their average, which we'd expect to be approximately 0.5 if these numbers were really uniformly drawn from [0,1). If you check

=AVERAGE(C7:C10006)

you'll find that it's 0.497413778. Try changing the seed and see what happens to the average.

Probably you'd never need to create your own pseudo-random number generator. The ones included with Excel (which we'll explore in later chapters) work well enough. But if you ever needed a reproducible set of pseudo-random numbers (for instance, if you wanted someone to be able to duplicate your analyses), then you might have to generate your own.

MAX() and MIN()

Besides SUM() and COUNT() and AVERAGE(), there's two more common statistics that you'll often want to know about your data. MAX() returns the largest value from the values or ranges you give it as inputs; MIN() returns the smallest value. As you're used to by now, both will ignore non-numbers in references but will happily include TRUE and FALSE and numbers-as-text that are explicitly included as inputs. So MAX(TRUE,FALSE) would equal 1 (since it understands TRUE as 1 and FALSE as 0), but if you were to put TRUE in A1 and FALSE in A2, then MAX(A1:A2) would equal 0 (which is how Excel thinks of the MAX() or MIN() of an empty range).

If you understand how SUM() and COUNT() work, then you also understand how MAX() and MIN() work, so we won't dwell on them.

Example: Tax Brackets

Here in the United States we have a progressive income tax. As your income increases, you pay a higher tax rate.

For instance, here are the marginal tax rates for a single taxpayer in 2010:

Taxable Income	Marginal Tax Rate
$0-$8,375	10%
$8,375-$34,000	15%
$34,000-$82,400	25%
$82,400-$171,850	28%
$171,850-$373,650	33%
More than $373,650	35%

It's important to understand how marginal tax rates work. Each tax rate applies *only* to the range to its left. If your taxable income is $10,000, you pay 10% income tax on the first $8,375, and you pay 15% only on what's left in the 15% bracket. If your taxable income is $500,000, you pay 35% tax only on the amount above $373,650; the income below this is taxed at the different rates shown in the table.

We're going to build a spreadsheet to calculate tax liability. We'll start by putting the above data into Excel. We'll also include a cell to input our income, which we'll assume is $50,000 to start, and a cell to output our tax liability:

	A	B	C	D	E
1				Starting At	Marginal Rate
2	Income:	50,000		0	10%
3	Tax Owed:			8,375	15%
4				34,000	25%
5				82,400	28%
6				171,850	33%
7				373,650	35%

If we wanted to be fancy we'd do our computations all at once, but things will be clearer if we break them up into several steps:

1. Calculate how much income falls into each bracket.
2. Compute the taxes owed out of each bracket.
3. Add them up.

To start, in F1 let's add the label "Income in Bracket." Then in F2 we need to compute how much of our income lands in the first bracket. If the total income is less than $8375, all of the income falls in the bracket. If the total income is greater than $8375, only $8375 of it falls in the bracket. This means the formula for F2 needs to capture "whichever is less: our income or $8375." And since the brackets might change, rather than hardcoding $8375, we'll point our formula to D3, where it lives:

=MIN($B$2,D3)

The tax for this bracket is the marginal rate multiplied by the amount in the bracket, so (after adding the label "Tax" in G1) the formula for G2 should just be

    =E2*F2

In order to compute how much income falls in subsequent brackets, it will be helpful to use column H for "Income Left." After you put that label in H1, you'll need the formula

    =$B$2-F2

in H2.

fx	=$B$2-F2			

D	E	F	G	H
Starting At	Marginal Rate	Income in Bracket	Tax	Income Left
0	10%	8,375	837.5	41,625
8,375	15%			
34,000	25%			
82,400	28%			
171,850	33%			
373,650	35%			

The second bracket will require slightly different formulas. The income falling in this bracket is the smaller of the size of the bracket and the income left to be taxed. That is, the second bracket covers the next (34000-8375)=25625 of income. If there's less income than that remaining, we put all of what remains into this bracket. If there's more, we'll put only the 25625. That means the formula for F3 is

    =MIN(H2,D4-D3)

The formula for the tax you can just copy down (it's still the marginal rate

multiplied by the amount in the bracket). And the new "income left" will
have to be the previous "income left" less whatever we've taken out in this
bracket. So the formula for H3 will be

=H2-F3

f_x	=H2-F3			
D	E	F	G	H
Starting At	Marginal Rate	Income in Bracket	Tax	Income Left
0	10%	8,375	837.5	41,625
8,375	15%	25,625	3843.75	16,000
34,000	25%			

This same reasoning (and hence the same formulas) should work for all but
the last bracket. So we can copy or fill them down all the way to row 6.

D	E	F	G	H
Starting At	Marginal Rate	Income in Bracket	Tax	Income Left
0	10%	8,375	837.5	41,625
8,375	15%	25,625	3843.75	16,000
34,000	25%	16,000	4000	0
82,400	28%	0	0	0
171,850	33%	0	0	0
373,650	35%			

The last bracket, however, will need a different formula in column F, because
it has no stopping point. The income in the last bracket is simply whatever's
left, which means the formula for F7 is

=H6

The Tax and Income Left formulas are still the same, so they can be copied
down.

Finally, we can figure out the tax owed. It's just the sum of the taxes for each bracket. So the formula for B3 is simply

    =SUM(G2:G7)

You can give it a nice comma format if you like.

Try changing the income amount. Try 5,000. Try 100,000. Try 500,000. Does it work the way you expect?

In practice this isn't how you'd compute taxes. A simpler way would be to pre-compute the tax amounts at the bracket boundaries and then just add the last amount.

So you might build a spreadsheet that already "knew" the tax on an income of 34,000 would be 4,681.25. Then it would notice that our 50,000 income fell in the 34,000 to 82,400 (25%) bracket and just compute the tax as

    4.681.25 + 25% * (50,000 - 34,000).

Unfortunately, we don't yet have the Excel expertise to compute taxes this way. Luckily, the way we did it works just as well (and is just as depressing).

Technique: Running Totals

Sometimes when you go to stores they'll have a take-a-penny jar by the cash register. The idea is that if your total is something like $4.03, you can take 3 pennies from the jar instead of having to get lots of coins back from your $5 bill. Conversely, if your bill is $4.96, you can put your change in the jar instead of hanging on to 4 cents that will only get lost in your couch anyway.

Your friend works at one of these stores, and all day long he watches how many pennies each customer leaves or takes. One day he hands you the list of transactions and asks you to find out the most pennies that were in the tray at any one time:

3, 4, -1, -2, -3, 1, 1, 1, -2, 4, 2, -1, -1, -4, 1, -2

(It was kind of a slow day for business.)

We'll use a spreadsheet to model the take-a-penny jar. In column A, we'll keep track of the transactions. And in column B, we'll track how many pennies are in the jar.

	A	B
1	Transaction	In Jar
2	3	
3	4	
4	-1	
5	-2	
6	-3	

The first thing to observe is that the number of pennies in the jar at any given time is equal to the sum of the transactions up to that point. After the first customer puts in 3 pennies, there's 3 pennies in the jar. After the next customer puts in 4, there's 3+4=7. After the next one takes out a penny, there's 3+4-1=6 pennies. And so on.

There are two ways to capture this in Excel. The first is to use the SUM() function and $ signs. In B2, we want to sum just the value in A2. In B3 we want to sum A2 and A3. In B4 we want to sum A2, A3, and A4. And as we keep going, in every row we want to sum the cells in column A starting at row 2 and ending at the current row. This means the formula to put in B2 is

=SUM(A$2:A2)

The missing $ on the last 2 means that when we copy this formula down it will reference A$2:A3, A$2:A4, and so on, just as we want. Enter the formula in B2 and copy it down.

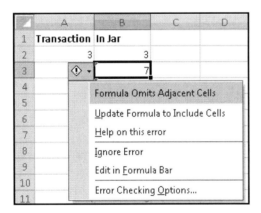

The little green triangles mean that Excel is trying to second-guess us. If you click on one of those cells and click on the hazard flag that appears, you'll see why:

This is Excel's way of telling us that there are nearby numbers that aren't included in our SUM(). Since this is by design, ignore it. (Or dig into the menus and disable this warning, if you feel like living dangerously.)

Since we're interested in the largest number of coins in the tray, we need the MAX() of what's in column B.

    MAX(B:B)

will work and tells us that at one point there were 8 pennies in the tray. You could also use

MAX(B3:B17)

but if you decide to add more transactions at the bottom this formula won't
see them. Later on we'll learn more subtle ways to build formulas that shrink
and grow as necessary, but for now just MAX() the whole column.

There's another way to do this. Delete the formulas in column B so we can
start over. After the first transaction, the running total is equal to the first
transaction, so enter the formula

=A2

in cell B2.

After each subsequent transaction, the new total is just the new transaction
added to the previous total. So in cell B3, use the formula

=A3+B2

and copy it down. It's easy to check that we get the same result as before.

Why would you choose one over the other? Well, the SUM() method is
simpler in that it uses only one self-explanatory formula. If you look in
cell B4 and see SUM(A$2:A4), you know precisely what its value means.
If you see A4+B3, you have to check the formula in B3 (and subsequently
in B2) to be sure of what the formula is doing. Some people consider it
more aesthetically pleasant to have a single formula that works for the entire
"running total" column than to have different formulas for the first cell and
the remainder.

On the other hand, the A3+B2 approach has its own benefits. It does a lot
less work. When you get to row 20, it's still only adding two values: A20 and
B19. The SUM() approach has to add the nineteen numbers in A2:A20, even
though A2:A19 have already been added up in the previous row. If you have
thousands of rows of data, the SUM() approach is doing a lot of unnecessary
computation and can really slow your spreadsheet down.

Additionally, there are other "running total"-type computations that have no analogue of the SUM() function. For instance, you might want to concatenate a column of words into a list. As we'll see later, there is a CONCATENATE() function, but it doesn't work on arrays. The only way to build such a list is to use the second approach: start with the first word and then build a "running list" by concatenating one additional word in each row.

In short, you should understand both of these methods, so that you can use whichever is most appropriate.

The LARGE() and SMALL() of it

Sometimes you don't just want to know the MAX() element, but also the second largest, third largest, and so on.

The LARGE() function takes two inputs. The first is an array, and the second a number specifying which largest element you want. LARGE(A1:A10,1) returns the largest number in A1:A10. LARGE(A1:A10,4) returns the fourth-largest number in A1:A10. LARGE(A1:A10,11) will give you a #NUM! error, since there is no eleventh-largest number in A1:A10.

LARGE() ignores cells that don't contain numbers. This means that LARGE(A1:A10,9) will give you a #NUM! error unless at least 9 of the 10 cells in A1:A10 contain numbers.

There's also a SMALL() function that you can use to find the smallest number in an array, the second-smallest, and so on. It behaves identically to LARGE(), except that it returns the smallest numbers instead of the largest numbers.

You can do the reverse with the RANK() function. It takes two inputs, a numeric value and an array, and returns the "rank" of the number in the array.

If the number is the largest number in the array, RANK() will return 1. If it's the second largest number in the array, RANK() will return 2. If the number isn't in the array at all, you'll get a #N/A error, and if the number isn't a number (for instance, if you try to find the rank of "A") you'll get a #VALUE! error.

If ever you want the rank from smallest to largest (so that the smallest number in the array is 1, the second-smallest is 2), you can give RANK() a third input of TRUE. If the third input is FALSE (or if you only use two inputs), you'll get largest-to-smallest.

Technique: Sorting Numbers Without Sorting

When we discussed sorting, we pointed out that it's not always a Thinking Spreadsheet thing to do, because sorted data has a tendency to become unsorted when it changes.

For instance, imagine that five of your friends are raising money for your favorite charity. As the resident expert in Thinking Spreadsheet, they've asked you to keep track of their fundraising.

You set up a simple spreadsheet based on their initial numbers:

	A	B
1	**Person**	**$ Raised**
2	Alex	60
3	Barbara	90
4	Chris	70
5	Doug	80
6	Ellen	40

You could sort it and find that Barbara had raised the most money. But then if Alex emailed you and said he'd now raised $100, your data would be unsorted again once you made the change. To keep the list in order, you'd have to remember to re-sort it every time you updated the numbers.

Instead, we'll create a copy of the table that re-sorts itself when you change the original data. To start with, over to the right, let's put labels 1 to 5 to represent the rankings:

	A	B	C	D
1	Person	$ Raised		Ranking
2	Alex	60		1
3	Barbara	90		2
4	Chris	70		3
5	Doug	80		4
6	Ellen	40		5

We'll want the #1 ranking to represent the most money raised, so we'll be using LARGE(). (If we wanted the #1 ranking to represent the least money raised, we'd use SMALL() instead.) In E2, enter the formula

=LARGE($B$2:$B$6,D2)

and copy down:

	A	B	C	D	E
1	Person	$ Raised		Ranking	$ Raised
2	Alex	60		1	90
3	Barbara	90		2	80
4	Chris	70		3	70
5	Doug	80		4	60
6	Ellen	40		5	40

Try changing the numbers and making sure that the rankings change accordingly.

You might object that this spreadsheet only "sorts" the amounts. It doesn't tell you *who* is the top fundraiser. This is a good objection. Unfortunately, we haven't yet learned enough to add that functionality. So save this spreadsheet somewhere. We'll come back and add more features soon enough!

CHAPTER *11*

DATE NIGHT

Start building spreadsheets, and pretty soon you're going to run across the need to use dates. If you're doing accounting or financial modeling, you'll need to know the dates of your cash flows. If you're building a model to beat the stock market, you'll want to know the dates of historical prices. If you're building a project schedule, you'll need dates. If you're making travel plans, you'll need dates. No matter what you do, you'll need to use dates!

How Excel Represents Dates

In Excel, a date is just a number with special formatting. The documentation calls it a "serial number," which makes me think of the army or prison, so we'll just call it a number. If you type 1/1/2010 into a cell, you should see 1/1/2010, but behind the scenes Excel is storing the number 40179. Each day corresponds to an increase of 1 in the number, so that 1/2/2010 is actually the number 40180, and 12/31/2009 is actually the number 40178.

The number corresponding to a date is almost "days starting at 1/1/1900." The number 1 is the date 1/1/1900, the number 2 is the date 1/2/1900, and so on. But Excel erroneously thinks 1900 is a leap year, and so the number 60 is the fake date 2/29/1900. Because of this, 61 means 3/1/1900, but if you counted correctly it would be day 60. Similarly, 1/1/2010 is the 40,178th day, but it gets the number 40179. None of this should really affect you unless you use dates from the year 1900, which you won't.

You can see the number underlying a date by changing the format of its cell to "General." Conversely, if you're seeing the number, you can show it as a date by changing the format to "Short Date."

This representation enables easy date arithmetic. If you add 14 to a date, you'll get the date that comes 14 days later. If you subtract one date from another, you'll find how many days apart they are. However, you can't do this arithmetic all in one line. If you have 1/1/2010 in cell A1, then A1+14 equals 1/15/2010, as you'd expect.

But the formula

=1/1/2010 + 14

equals 14.0005. (You may get more or fewer decimal places.) Because of the equals sign, Excel treats the slashes as division operators. It's as if you'd input

=((1/1)/2010) + 14

To explicitly use a date in a formula, you have to use the DATE() function, which requires a year, a month, and day. So to find the date 14 days after 1/1/2010, you could use

=DATE(2010,1,1)+14

which correctly outputs 1/15/2010.

If you're just typing dates into cells, then it's much easier to input them directly. But when you need to specify them directly in formulas, don't forget the DATE() function.

When typing in dates directly, you can sometimes take shortcuts by leaving off the year. For instance, if you type 1/1, Excel will guess that you mean the current year. In 2010 it will automatically use the value for 1/1/2010. In 2011 it will automatically use the value for 2011. And so on.

You can also abbreviate the year. If you type 1/1/10, Excel will understand that you mean 2010. (Unless you mean 1910 or 2110, in which case it's misunderstanding what you mean.) In my copy of Excel 2007, 1/1/29 gets converted to 1/1/2029, while 1/1/30 becomes 1/1/1930. This behavior will change maybe in Excel 2025, so if you're using that version be extra careful.

Example: Balancing Your Checkbook

Now that we know arithmetic and dates, we can use Excel to balance our checkbook. (This will be the first time I've balanced a checkbook in approximately 20 years.)

Our very simple checkbook register will have only 6 columns.

1. Date: the date of a transaction
2. Number: the check number.
3. Description: of the transaction.
4. Payment: the amount, if we're making a payment
5. Deposit: the amount, if we're making a deposit
6. Balance: remaining after the transaction.

We'll start our account with a zero balance:

	A	B	C	D	E	F
1	Date	Number	Description	Payment	Deposit	Balance
2			opening balance of 0			0

And we'll fund our account by depositing a paycheck for $500. Let's say we did this on 1/2/2010:

	A	B	C	D	E	F
1	Date	Number	Description	Payment	Deposit	Balance
2			opening balance of 0			0
3	1/2/2010		paycheck		500	

To benefit from using Excel, we should really use a formula to compute our balance. Which formula should we use? Well, after any transaction, we compute our balance by taking the previous balance, adding any deposits, and subtracting any payments.

Therefore, in F3, we'll add the formula

=F2+E3-D3

	F3		▼	f_x	=F2+E3-D3	
	A	B	C	D	E	F
1	Date	Number	Description	Payment	Deposit	Balance
2			opening balance of 0			0
3	1/2/2010		paycheck		500	500

You can see that it updates the Balance correctly. Enter the following transactions:

- 1/4/2010: check #101 for rent, $120.
- 1/7/2010: check #102 for cable, $40.
- 1/16/2010: deposit paycheck, $500.
- 1/23/2010: ATM withdrawal, $75.

Copy the formula in column F down as you go. Hopefully you'll end up with something like this:

	A	B	C	D	E	F
1	Date	Number	Description	Payment	Deposit	Balance
2			opening balance of 0			0
3	1/2/2010		paycheck		500	500
4	1/4/2010	101	rent	120		380
5	1/7/2010	102	cable	40		340
6	1/16/2010		paycheck		500	840
7	1/23/2010	ATM	cash	75		765

Don't feel bad if this example seems a little bit simple. It is a little bit simple. (If this example seems really, really complicated, then you should feel sort of bad.)

TODAY() is the Greatest

If you don't know what day it is, you can use the TODAY() function, which returns the current date. It's pretty simple, although it's the first function we've seen so far that's nondeterministic. A spreadsheet that uses the TODAY() function will change when you recalculate it tomorrow, even if you don't make any changes to it. The day after that it will be different again. And every day after that.

So you need to be careful. TODAY() will update its value every time you recalculate it. In some cases this might be desired behavior. But sometimes it won't!

If you want to insert today's date as a *value*, you can either type Ctrl-; (you have to type the semicolon) or you can use the TODAY() function and then Paste-Special-Value it.

A Very Good YEAR()

Sometimes you need to extract parts of dates. For instance, if you've built a checkbook register, and you want to count up how many checks you wrote in October, or in 2008, then you'll need a way to turn that date (which, remember, is really a number like 40189) into a month or year.

Excel provides functions for this, with quite unsurprising names. YEAR(), MONTH(), and DAY() will return the three components of a date. If you put the date 1/15/2010 in cell A1, then YEAR(A1) equals 2010, MONTH(A1) equals 1, and DAY(A1) equals 15. These functions are all very simple, but they're very handy, so don't forget them.

Slightly trickier is the WEEKDAY() function, which will let you know what day of the week any given date is. It's trickier because it returns a number that's not obvious how to interpret.

If you give it only one input, for example, WEEKDAY(TODAY()), then it will return a number between 1 and 7, where 1 represents Sunday, 2 represents Monday, up until 7 represents Saturday. You can also give it a second argument to specify the output format. WEEKDAY(TODAY(),1) is the same as WEEKDAY(TODAY()). If you use 2 for the second argument, you'll get 1 for Monday, 2 for Tuesday, all the way up to 7 for Sunday. And if you use 3 for the second argument, you'll get 0 for Monday up to 6 for Sunday.

Don't feel bad if you can't remember all this. Even I have to double-check how the return values work each time I use WEEKDAY(), and probably you will too.

There's also WEEKNUM(), which returns the "week number" of any given date. Like WEEKDAY(), WEEKNUM() takes an optional second argument. If you leave out the second argument or give it the value 1, WEEKNUM() will start new weeks on Sunday. If you give it the value 2, WEEKNUM() will start new weeks on Monday.

Either way, in most years, the first "week" won't have 7 days in it. For instance, 1/1/2010 is a Friday, which means that (according to WEEKNUM) the first "week" of 2010 only contains 2 days. You can check that WEEKNUM(DATE(2010,1,3)) is equal to 2. If you ever use WEEKNUM(), be aware of this.

Adding Months with EDATE()

There are a few more date functions you might find useful. The first is EDATE(), which takes two inputs, a date and the number of months to "add" to it, and returns the resulting date. (If the second input is negative, it subtracts that many months.)

So

EDATE(DATE(2010,1,1),2)

equals 3/1/2010, and

EDATE(DATE(2010,1,1),-2)

equals 11/1/2009. If there aren't enough days in a month, it will go as far as it can. So EDATE(DATE(2010,1,31),1) equals 2/28/2010, since there are only 28 days in February.

It's most common to use this with the first day of each month. In that case EDATE() always outputs the first day of the resulting month.

A similar function is EOMONTH(), which also adds months to your date, but returns the last day of the resulting month. Thus

EOMONTH(DATE(2010,1,1),2)

means "the end of the month that's two months after 1/1/2010," which is 3/31/2010. If you ever need the first day of a particular month, you can get it by adding 1 to the previous EOMONTH().

Right NOW() TIME() Is Having Its Way With You

Although it's less common than working with dates, sometimes you'll want to use times as well. Like dates, times are just numbers with special formatting. Since a numeric difference of 1 represents one day, it also represents 24 hours.

You can enter times by typing them in directly in a variety of formats. To represent "11 in the morning," you could type 11:00, 11 am, 11:00 AM,

11:00:00, or several other formats. You can enter time intervals in the same way. 2:00 means either 2 am or 2 hours. For intervals less than an hour, make sure to use a leading 0. You'd use 0:15 to mean either 12:15 am or 15 minutes. For intervals less than a minute, use two leading zeros. 0:0:10 (or 00:00:10) could mean either 10 seconds after midnight, or just 10 seconds.

Like dates, you can't enter times directly into formulas. Excel will interpret the colon as signifying a range of rows. For instance, in the formula

    =1:15 + 1

Excel thinks your "time" means rows 1 to 15.

Instead you use the TIME() function, which takes as inputs hours, minutes, and seconds. To get 11 am, you'd use TIME(11,0,0), and to get 3:20:49 pm you'd use TIME(15,20,49). Generally speaking, unless you are typing the date in directly and specifying PM, you should be using military (24-hour) time.

There are also HOUR(), MINUTE() and SECOND() functions, which extract the hour, minute, and second from a number representing a time.

How Long Is That Movie?

Suppose a movie starts at 2:45PM and ends at 4:10PM. How many minutes long is it? Well, you can figure out the interval using

    =TIME(16,10,0)-TIME(14,45,0)

This produces the result 1:25AM, which is unfortunate formatting for 1 hour and 25 minutes. But to turn that into minutes requires some extra work.

Here 1:25AM is really just special formatting applied to the number 0.059028, which represents the number of days this time interval lasts. (You can see this by changing the format of the cell to "General".)

Each day has 24 hours, and each hour has 60 minutes. Therefore 0.059028 days is the same as 24 * 0.059028 hours, which is the same as 60 * 24 * 0.059028 minutes. So using this "days to minutes" approach, you'd use the formula

=60 * 24 * (TIME(16,10,0) - TIME(14,45,0))

You can check that this gives 85 minutes. If you needed the length in hours, you would multiply only by 24. And if you needed it in seconds, you'd multiply by 60 * 60 * 24.

You Got Your DATE() in My TIME()

Excel represents 12 am, or TIME(0,0,0), as the number 0. Similarly, it represents 12 noon, which is TIME(12,0,0) as the number 0.5.

This makes it easy to represent date-time combinations. For instance, to represent 1:15pm on 1/1/2010, you could use the formula

=DATE(2010,1,1)+TIME(13,15,0)

You could also type 1/1/2010 1:15 PM directly into the cell. You could type 1/1/2010 into one cell and 1:15 PM into another cell, and then add them together in a third. It's more likely that you'll use date-time combinations than that you'll use time alone.

When you do time arithmetic, you need to be careful about the interplay between dates and times. For instance, if a movie starts at 10:30 PM and ends at 1:15 AM, how many minutes long is it? A naive first approach might be

=24 * 60 * (TIME(1,15,0) - TIME(22,30,0))

Unfortunately, this formula reveals that the movie is -1275 minutes long. That's because Excel considers all times entered using TIME() to be on the same day. So TIME(1,15,0) occurs early in the morning, and TIME(20,30,0) occurs late at night. A movie that started late at night and somehow ended early in the morning on the same day would indeed have a negative run time.

What we're really asking here is "how many minutes from 10:30 PM to 1:30 AM the next day." To add a day, we simply add 1. If our movie starts at TIME(22,30,0), then it ends on the next day at TIME(1,15,0)+1. So the formula should be

   =24 * 60 * (TIME(1,15,0) + 1 - TIME(22,30,0))

which gives the correct answer, 165 minutes.

NOW()

The time analogue of TODAY() is NOW(), which again takes no arguments and returns the current date *and* time when you calculate it. If you just wanted the time, you could subtract out today's date:

   =NOW()-TODAY()

Recall that Ctrl-; inserts the current date as a value. Similarly, Ctrl-Shift-; inserts the current time as a value. If you want the current date *and* time as a value, you have to use Ctrl-; then Space then Ctrl-Shift-;.

Example: A Timesheet

You've just gotten your first gig as a Thinking Spreadsheet consultant. Your client has asked you to build a spreadsheet to track the time you spend working on her spreadsheet-related problems, so she can figure out how much she owes you. You're charging her the discount rate of $20/hour, in the hopes that she'll write a nice recommendation on your LinkedIn page.

What will you need on your timesheet? Well, you'll want each entry to have a Start time and a Stop time. A comment about what you were working on would be nice. Then a column to figure out how many hours you worked, and another column to compute the pay for that line item. Finally, a running total to keep track of how much you've earned so far.

Therefore, we'll have a spreadsheet that looks like this:

	A	B	C	D	E	F
1	Start	Stop	Comment	Hours	Pay	Cumulative

Her problem turns out to be pretty simple. On 4/6/2010 you spend from 1:30pm to 3:45pm trying to understand the error-filled documentation she gave you. On 4/7/2010 you start looking things up in Thinking Spreadsheet at 11:30pm, and you get so enthralled that you don't put the book down until 3:17am. And then on 4/8/2010 you spend from 11am to 2:20pm building a spreadsheet that solves all of her problems.

As a first step, let's enter these data into the spreadsheet:

	A	B	C	D	E	F
1	Start	Stop	Comment	Hours	Pay	Cumulative
2	4/6/2010 13:30	4/6/2010 15:45	reading documentation			
3	4/7/2010 23:30	4/8/2010 3:17	Thinking Spreadsheet			
4	4/8/2010 11:00	4/8/2010 14:20	building spreadsheet			

Remember that to compute hours, we simply multiply the time difference by 24. So our formula for D2 should be

=24*(B2-A2)

Since you're charging $20 per hour, the formula for E2 is

=20*D2

Enter those formulas and copy them down.

Since we'll be showing this to her, let's pretty it up as well. Give the "Hours" column the "Comma" format, and give the "Pay" column the "Currency" format:

	A	B	C	D	E	F
1	Start	Stop	Comment	Hours	Pay	Cumulative
2	4/6/2010 13:30	4/6/2010 15:45	reading documentation	2.25	$ 45.00	
3	4/7/2010 23:30	4/8/2010 3:17	Thinking Spreadsheet	3.78	$ 75.67	
4	4/8/2010 11:00	4/8/2010 14:20	building spreadsheet	3.33	$ 66.67	

Finally, we need to figure out our cumulative pay. How do we compute that? We can use the "running total" technique we learned earlier. In row 2 we just want the value of E2. In row 3 we want the sum of E2 and E3. And in row 4 we want the sum of E2, E3, and E4.

A different way of saying this is that we want to sum the numbers in column E, starting in row 2 and ending in the current row. Since we are clever at $-ing, we know that the formula to put in F2 is

=SUM(E$2:E2)

The missing $ on the last 2 ensures that ending row of the array will increase as we copy the formula down.

F4			f_x	=SUM($E$2:$E4)		
	A	B	C	D	E	F
1	Start	Stop	Comment	Hours	Pay	Cumulative
2	4/6/2010 13:30	4/6/2010 15:45	reading documentation	2.25	$ 45.00	$ 45.00
3	4/7/2010 23:30	4/8/2010 3:17	Thinking Spreadsheet	3.78	$ 75.67	$ 120.67
4	4/8/2010 11:00	4/8/2010 14:20	building spreadsheet	3.33	$ 66.67	$ 187.33

You send her this spreadsheet and a bill for $187.33. Steak dinner on you! And then you realize that you should have planned ahead and built the spreadsheet in a way that would have make it easier for you to raise your rates.

Chapter *12*

TRUE or FALSE

A Boolean is a "truth value" of either TRUE or FALSE. A convenient way to think of Booleans is as answers to yes/no questions. And when we Think Spreadsheet, there are all sorts of yes/no questions we can ask.

Comparisons

A common class of yes/no questions is comparisons. Are two things equal? Is one bigger than the other? Excel makes it easy to ask questions like this.

Equality

Is 1 equal to 1? Excel can tell us:

    =1=1

That looks weird. It's a formula, so it has to start with an = sign, and then it tests for equality, which involves another equals sign. At this point we know that the initial = tells Excel "this cell contains a formula you'll need to calculate." In this case, the formula is 1=1, and if you try it out, you'll find that it's TRUE. (Hopefully you could have figured this out without Excel.)

Is 1 equal to 2? Is 1 equal to "1"? Is "One" equal to "one"? Is DATE(2010,1,1) equal to 40179? You can try them all and see.

If you do, you'll find that Excel is testing whether values are equal, not whether formulas (or formats) are equal. If A1 contains a complicated formula that outputs 1 and B1 contains the value 1, then A1=B1 is TRUE. Equality means equality of values. There's no easy way to test equality of formulas or formats.

What if you want to know whether two things are unequal? Instead of =, you use <>. Since 1 is not equal to 2, the comparison 1<>2 equals TRUE. Similarly, 1<>1 equals FALSE.

One area in which Excel's equality operators behave oddly is when you apply them to text.

These equality operators ignore case, which means that Excel considers "one" equal to "ONE". As we'll see in a later chapter, there is an EXACT() function that only returns true if you give it two strings that are identical including their cases. If you test equality of text using =, then be aware that case doesn't matter.

It's more common to test equality of references or function values. Here are some examples:

Formula	Yes/no question
=A1="one"	Is the value in A1 equal to the text one?
=SUM(A:A)<>0	Is the SUM() of column A different from 0?
=MAX(A1:C3)=3	Is the MAX() of the array A1:C3 equal to 3?
=B4=TIME(12,30,0)	Is the value in B4 equal to (the number representing) the time 12:30pm?
=MOD(A1,5)<>0	Is A1 not divisible by 5?
=A1=B1	Is the value in A1 equal to the value in B1?

This should give you an idea of the sorts of equality tests you can do.

Inequality

Besides testing for equality and "unequality," you can also test for various inequalities.

Inequality	Yes/no question
<	Is the (value of the) left hand side less than the (value of the) right hand side?
<=	Is the left hand side less than or equal to the right hand side?
>	Is the left hand side greater than the right hand side?
>=	Is the left hand side greater than or equal to the right hand side.

If you're good at using = and <>, these shouldn't be difficult to pick up. The only interesting part is what it means for one value to be less than another.

For numbers, it means exactly what you'd expect. For text it's also pretty sensible: one text value is less than another if it comes before it in alphabetical order. As with equality, case doesn't matter. For instance, you'd find the following order:

a < ace < act < actor < ball < BALLOON < BALLoons < car

For Booleans, FALSE is less than TRUE, although you probably shouldn't compare Booleans this way unless you're looking to confuse people.

Mixtures have the same order that we learned when we discussed sorting: any number is less than any text, and any text is less than a Boolean. This means that TRUE is greater than any value (except for TRUE, which it's equal to).

You shouldn't be comparing mixed data very often. If you build your spreadsheets carefully, then cells you expect to have numbers in them will have numbers in them, not text or Booleans. Cells you expect to have Booleans in them will contain Booleans, not numbers or text. Cells that you expect to have text in them might have numbers or Booleans in them – a list of nicknames might include not only Bubba and Books but also (conceivably) 12 or TRUE. If you're careful you'll type them as text, like '12 or 'TRUE, but most people aren't that careful. In this unlikely case, don't be surprised if you get unexpected results.

IF( )s and Buts

The IF() function is one of the most powerful Thinking Spreadsheet tools. In its most typical usage, IF() takes 3 inputs.

The first is a *logical test*, which typically means a Boolean. If the first input is TRUE, then the function output is the *second* input. If the first input is FALSE, then the function output is the *third* input. The formula

    =IF(A1,"A1 is TRUE!","A1 is FALSE!")

will return the correct message if there's a Boolean in A1.

IF() will also work if you give it a number as the first input: 0 will get treated as FALSE, and any other number will get treated as TRUE. However, we'll try not to do this. Part of Thinking Spreadsheet is not confusing people who are trying to understand your work, and using numbers where people expect Booleans is a good way to confuse them.

If you want, you can leave out the third input, in which case Excel assumes you want it to be FALSE. There are circumstances where it's simpler to do so, although it's always acceptable to just specify it as FALSE when that's what you want it to be.

Nested IF()

You can nest IF() functions to deal with conditions that aren't either-or. For instance, the following function will create a text message describing the value in cell A1:

=IF(A1<0,"less than 0",IF(A1=0,"equal to 0","greater than 0"))

It's worth thinking through this one in detail. Although previously we've analyzed complex formulas from the inside out, we'll analyze instances of IF() from the outside in.

The first logical condition to check is A1<0. If this evaluates to TRUE (which means the value in A1 is less than 0) then the IF() takes on the value of its second input, the string "less than 0". If it evaluates to FALSE (which will happen if the value in A1 is greater than or equal to 0), our function will return the value of its third input. Its third input is another function:

IF(A1=0,"equal to 0","greater than 0")

In this inner IF() the logical condition is A1=0. If this evaluates to TRUE (which it will precisely when the value in A1 is 0) then this inner IF() function will take on the value "equal to 0". If A1=0 evaluates to FALSE, then the inner IF() will take on the value "greater than 0".

That is, if A1 is not equal to 0, the inner function will return the value "greater than 0." What if the value in A1 is less than 0? In that case it's also not equal to 0. Won't returning "greater than 0" make our formula wrong?

It won't! Remember that if the value in A1 is less than 0, the outer IF() will return "less than 0", and the inner IF() will never be evaluated at all. So the condition for reaching the "greater than 0" output is really:

- A1=0 evaluates FALSE (necessary for inner IF() statement to take "greater than 0" value), *and*

- A1<0 evaluates FALSE (necessary for inner IF() statement to be evaluated at all!)

This is why we analyze IF() statements from the outside in. Often we need to know which branches we've already gone down ("we're in the A1<0 is FALSE branch") to make sense of the inner conditions.

Technique: The Odometer Pattern

Think about the odometer in an older car. It has a series of dials, each containing the numbers from 0 to 9. As you drive the car, the rightmost dial turns. After it reaches 9, it resets to 0 and the dial to its left increases by 1. After that dial reaches 9, it resets to 0, and the dial to its left increases by 1. This continues until all the dials have 9 on them, at which point the whole odometer resets.

We're going to simulate this "odometer pattern" in Excel. Not because you'd ever actually build an odometer in a spreadsheet. But because – before it resets – the odometer runs over every possible combination of digits exactly once, which is often a useful thing to do.

We'll create a 5-digit odometer, and we'll start it with all zeroes:

	A	B	C	D	E
1	dial 1	dial 2	dial 3	dial 4	dial 5
2	0	0	0	0	0

Let's think about the rightmost dial first. At each row it should increase by 1, until it reaches 9, at which point it should reset to 0. What formula should we put in E3? Well,

=MOD(E2+1,10)

will add 1 to E2, then compute the remainder after dividing by 10. If E2+1 is 9 or less, the MOD() won't do anything to it. And if E2+1 is 10, MOD(E2+1,10) will be 0. This is exactly what we want.

Alternatively, we could use IF(). If E2 equals 9, we want E3 to "reset" to 0. Otherwise we want it to be E2+1. That is, we could have used

    =IF(E2=9,0,E2+1)

or even

    =IF(E2<10,E2+1,0)

This second IF() is probably preferable, as it makes more explicit the idea that we reset once we get to 10. (Also, this second IF() would make it easier to have "number of digits" as a parameter, which we might want to do later.)

The logic in column D will have to be slightly different. The digits in column D don't increase every row. They only increase when the digit in column E resets. What should we test for in column E? One thing we could test for is that the value in column E is equal to zero. Another thing we could test for is that the value in column E has decreased from the previous row.

Either one of these would give the correct condition. However, only one of these tests will also work in columns C, B, and A. It will take 10 rows before the number in column D increases from 0 to 1. Therefore the "dial" in column C can't consider whether column D equals 0; if it did, it would start increasing immediately. To Think Spreadsheet, we should favor the formula that will work in all the remaining columns. Therefore, in D3 we'll use

    =IF(E3<E2,MOD(D2+1,10),D2)

which you should understand as

    If the digit to our right is less than the digit above it (which means its dial has just rolled over to 0), add one to this dial and rollover if it has reached 10. If the digit to our right is not less than the digit above it, then don't change the value on this dial.

If you think about it, you'll see that this formula will work for all the remaining dials, so copy it to the left:

	A	B	C	D	E
1	dial 1	dial 2	dial 3	dial 4	dial 5
2	0	0	0	0	0
3	0	0	0	0	1

The odometer goes from 00000 to 99999, so it contains 100,000 different values. Since the odometer starts in row 2, its 100,000th value will be in row 100001. We'll go even one row further, in order to see the actual rollover, so we need to copy the formulas from row 3 all the way down to row 100002.

Here's one efficient way to do this:

1. Type A100002 into the name bar. (Alternatively, use Ctrl-G to GoTo A100002.)

2. Type Ctrl-Shift-Up. The Ctrl means "go until you find a nonempty cell," which will be A3. The Shift means "select as you go." And the Up Arrow means (obviously) go in the up direction. At this point you'll have the range A3:A100002 selected.

3. Type Shift-Right four times. This will expand your selection to A3:E100002.

4. Type Ctrl-D. This will fill the formula from the top row (A3:E3) down to the rest of the range.

	A	B	C	D	E
99997	9	9	9	9	5
99998	9	9	9	9	6
99999	9	9	9	9	7
100000	9	9	9	9	8
100001	9	9	9	9	9
100002	0	0	0	0	0

And our odometer is finished.

Now, in this example, where we have 5 dials, each with the numbers from 0 to 9, it probably would have been simpler just to look at the numbers 0 to 99,999 in a single column. However, we'll soon see that in situations with differently-sized "dials," we can do all sorts of fancy things.

AND( ) OR( ) NOT( )

Sometimes you need to combine logical conditions. Maybe you want to know whether the value in A1 is between 0 and 10. In other words, you want to check that A1>=0 *and* A1<=10. Perhaps you want to know whether the value is not between 0 and 10. This is the same as checking that either A1<0 *or* A1>10.

Excel provides functions for these, with the not-surprising names of AND() and OR(). Each takes a list of values and references. AND() returns TRUE if all of its arguments are TRUE, and FALSE otherwise. OR() returns TRUE if any of its arguments are TRUE, and FALSE otherwise.

So to check that A1 is between 0 and 10, you could use the formula

    =AND(A1>=0,A1<=10)

To check that it's not, you could use the formula

=OR(A1<0,A1>0)

There's also a NOT() function, which takes one Boolean input and negates it. NOT(TRUE) equals FALSE, and NOT(FALSE) equals TRUE. So an alternative way to check that A1 is not between 0 and 10 would be

=NOT(AND(A1>=0,A1<=10))

It's up to you which one you want to use; the Thinking Spreadsheet bias is always toward formulas that are easier to understand.

Short Circuit

In some cases you don't have to check all of the logical tests in an AND() or an OR() to figure out what its output should be. An AND() is TRUE precisely when all of its inputs are TRUE. Therefore, if its first input is FALSE, the output of the AND() ought to be FALSE regardless of the rest of the inputs. Likewise, if the first input to an OR() is TRUE, the output should be TRUE regardless of the rest of the inputs.

Some computer languages will do what's known as "short circuiting" and completely ignore inputs that they don't need to know. This lets you include possibly impossible conditions like dividing by zero, counting on them never to be evaluated. In such a language, the condition

(A1 > 0) and (1/A1 < 5)

would work when A1 equals zero. Whenever the number in A1 is zero (or less), the first condition is FALSE, which means that whole expression must be FALSE *regardless of the truth of the second expression*, and therefore the second (illegal) expression would never even be evaluated.

Excel doesn't do this. If you try

=AND(A1>0,(1/A1)<5)

when there is a zero in A1, you will get a #DIV/0! error, even though Excel could (in theory) figure out the output is supposed to be FALSE based on just the first condition. What would work is the formula

=IF(A1>0,(1/A1)<5)

(Recall that an omitted third argument is automatically FALSE.)

Every condition in your AND() and OR() functions must make sense for all the inputs you expect to see. If they don't, you need to test your inputs with IF().

Technique: Cleaning Data with IF()

When you import data into Excel, often it's not in the right format. For instance, suppose you want to analyze the locations of all IKEA stores. Their website has a convenient list, but it looks like this:

```
▼ See complete IKEA store list

Arizona               New Jersey
Tempe                 Elizabeth
                      Paramus
California
Burbank               New York
Carson                Brooklyn
Covina                Long Island
East Palo Alto
Emeryville            North Carolina
Orange County Costa Mesa  Charlotte
San Diego
West Sacramento       Ohio
```

To start with, select all of the store listings, Copy, and Paste-Special-Text into Excel.

	A	B
1	.	
2	Arizona	
3	Tempe	
4		
5	California	
6	Burbank	

There's an extra space in front of "Arizona." If this had happened throughout the dataset, we'd use a formula to fix it, but since it just happened once, click in the cell and get rid of it manually.

What we want is to have city in one column and state in another. We already have all the cities in column A, so if we could just add the states in column B (and then get rid of any junk remaining), we'd be done. So let's start by labeling column A "City," column B "State," and column C "Keep?"

	A	B	C
1	**City**	**State**	**Keep?**
2	Arizona		
3	Tempe		
4			
5	California		
6	Burbank		
7	Carson		

Your first instinct might be to get rid of all the blank lines in column A. But those blank lines are the only thing telling us when there's a new state. In fact, except for B2, which (as is often the case with the top cell in a column of formulas) needs its own formula (=A2), the logic in column B needs to be "if the cell in the previous row in column A is blank (i.e. equal to the empty string ""), change the state to the column A value in this row; otherwise, keep the same state from the previous row."

That is, the formula for B3 (and the rest of column B) should be

=IF(A2="",A3,B2)

	A	B	C
1	City	State	Keep
2	Arizona	Arizona	
3	Tempe	=IF(A2="",A3,B2)	

You can't use Double-Click-Fill because it will stop each time there's a blank cell in column A. So use a Drag-Fill or a Copy-Paste:

	A	B	C
1	**City**	**State**	**Keep?**
2	Arizona	Arizona	
3	Tempe	Arizona	
4		Arizona	
5	California	California	
6	Burbank	California	

Now we need to decide which rows we want to keep. We only want rows with proper City-State data. This means we need to throw out row 2 (which again needs its own handling), rows where column A is blank (obviously), and rows below where column A is blank (which have the state appearing as the "city").

Rather than handling row 2 separately, you might have considered throwing out rows where column A and column B had the same value. However, this approach isn't guaranteed to work. If there were a state and a city with the same name (e.g. "New York, New York") then you would be accidentally throwing out good data. That won't happen in this dataset, but it's the sort of thing you should worry about when you're crafting formulas.

So in C2 type FALSE, and then in C3 (and the rest of the column) use

=AND(A2<>"",A3<>"")

Why this way? We wanted to throw out C3 if A2 was blank OR if A3 was blank. That means we want to keep C3 when A2 is not blank AND A3 is not blank. (This rule is called De Morgan's law, and Wikipedia has a nice article on it.) An alternative (logically-equivalent) way of doing the same thing would be

=NOT(OR(A2="",A3=""))

	A	B	C
1	**City**	**State**	**Keep?**
2	Arizona	Arizona	FALSE
3	Tempe	Arizona	TRUE
4		Arizona	FALSE
5	California	California	FALSE
6	Burbank	California	TRUE

We've now reached one of the occasions where sorting data is a good thing. That's because we want to permanently transform this data, and we never plan on updating the pre-sorted data.

A different problem with sorting, though, is that it often breaks formulas. Our formulas in columns B and C both reference "the row above me." Sorting will change each cell's "row above me," which means that sorting will break our carefully constructed spreadsheet. Therefore, in a situation like this, before we sort, we need to Copy-Paste-Special-Value any formulas that have "row above me"-style references. Here, that's all of columns B and C. Copy-Paste-Special-Value them now.

Finally, we're ready to sort our data. Choose "Sort" on the Data ribbon, and make sure "My data has headers" is checked.

Since FALSE sorts before TRUE, we want to sort first by Keep? "Largest to Smallest", then by State "A to Z", and finally by City "A to Z".

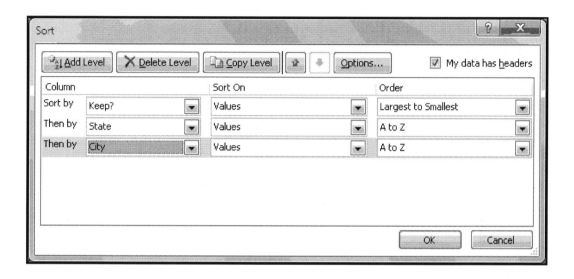

Now we can delete all the data we don't need. First scroll down and delete all the rows where "Keep?" is FALSE. Then you can delete the "Keep?" column, since we don't need it any more. Widen the two remaining columns. And after only a few steps, we finally have our data in a format we can use.

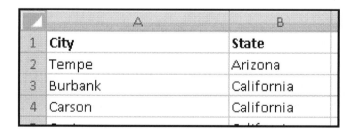

Filling in Blanks

A slightly different (but also common) problem you find in data is that a field might display its value only when it changes:

	A	B
1	**State**	**City**
2	Connecticut	New Haven
3	Florida	Orlando
4		Sunrise
5		Tampa
6	Georgia	Atlanta
7	Illinois	Bolingbrook
8		Schaumburg
9	Maryland	Baltimore
10		College Park

Here, Sunrise and Tampa are also in Florida, which is signified by column A being left blank. We can again use IF() to transform our data to have State in every row:

1. Put a label (e.g. "State2") in C1.

2. Put a one-off formula =A2 in C2.

3. Replace blanks appropriately in C3:

    =IF(A3="",C2,A3)

4. Copy the formula down.

5. Copy the values in column C and Paste-Special-Value them into column A.

6. Delete column C.

Why do we prefer the transformed data? It's much more useful for analysis. If we want to count how many stores are in Florida, we really need each Florida store to be labeled as such. Later, when we learn about Pivot Tables, we'll see that they require their data in this "every value in every column" format, and so it's important to know how to produce it.

Everything ISLOGICAL( )

There are a number of Excel functions that you can use to check that cells have certain types of values. There's two important reasons why you might want to do this:

1. Testing inputs: if the value in A1 might not be a number, you may want to make sure it is before you start using it as one.
2. Testing outputs: sometimes you might not care about the exact output of the formula in A1, you might just want to know whether it produces an error or not.

In our section on errors, we already saw the function ISERROR(), which returns TRUE if its input is an error and FALSE otherwise. Excel has other IS functions:

ISBLANK( ) returns TRUE if its input is a reference to a completely empty cell, FALSE otherwise. Most of the time you'd rather test whether something equals " ", the empty string. If A1 has a formula that produces blank output, ISBLANK(A1) will be FALSE (because of the formula) but A1=" " will be TRUE (because of the blank output). Usually the latter is what you care about.

ISLOGICAL( ) returns TRUE if its input is either TRUE or FALSE, FALSE otherwise.

ISNUMBER( ) returns TRUE if its input is numeric, FALSE otherwise.

ISEVEN( ) returns TRUE if the integer part of its argument is even, FALSE otherwise. This means that =ISEVEN(2.9) returns TRUE, since 2 is even.

ISODD( ) returns TRUE if the integer part of its argument is odd.

It's likely that ISNUMBER() is the only one of these you'll ever find useful, although it's good for you to know the others too.

Careful Counting with COUNTIF( )

COUNTIF() and its brother SUMIF() are two of the best-loved functions in Thinking Spreadsheet.

We'll start with COUNTIF(), the simpler of the two. It takes two inputs, a range and a criterion, and it counts how many of the cells in the range satisfy the criterion. There are several common criteria that we'll see:

Value

The simplest type of criterion is a value, which will make COUNTIF() return the number of cells that have that same value.

Function	Counts cells in A1:A10 that
COUNTIF(A1:A10,TRUE)	Have the value TRUE
COUNTIF(A1:A10,1)	Have the value 1
COUNTIF(A1:A10,B1)	Have the same value as B1
COUNTIF(A1:A10,"one")	Have the text "one" (case-insensitive)
COUNTIF(A1:A10,"ONE")	Same as the previous example.

Cells will be counted if they contain either the value itself or a formula that evaluates to the value.

Wildcard

Text values can also contain wildcards. A ? will match any one character, while a * will match any number of characters (including none at all).

For instance, imagine we have the following values in A1:A5

Then we'd get the following results:

Function	Output	Why
COUNTIF(A1:A5,"ok")	1	Matches A1
COUNTIF(A1:A5,"ok*")	2	Matches A1 and A5
COUNTIF(A1:A5,"o?k")	2	Matches A2 and A3
COUNTIF(A1:A5,"o*k")	4	Matches A1, A2, A3, and A4
COUNTIF(A1:A5,"*y")	1	Matches A5

If you want COUNTIF() to match an actual * or ?, you have to precede it with a tilde ˜. So COUNTIF(A1:A5,"˜*") equals the number of cells in A1:A5 that contain just a *. Because of this, criteria that themselves contain tildes often don't give the results you expect, so be careful if you ever use them.

In practice, the most common use of wildcards is the final *, as in the second example above. For instance, the criterion "A*" would COUNTIF() all words beginning with the letter A. However, you may find some of the other possibilities useful, so keep them in mind.

Comparison

Some of the most interesting uses for COUNTIF() involve comparisons, which need to be described in strings.

Function	Counts cells in A1:A10 that
COUNTIF(A1:A10,">0")	Have a value that's greater than 0.
COUNTIF(A1:A10,"<>ok")	Do not have the value "ok" (case insensitive).
COUNTIF(A1:A10,"<=1")	Have a value that's less than or equal to 1.

The tricky part comes when we want to use a reference in our comparison. You can't put a reference in quotes, because Excel will treat it as text. For instance,

   =COUNTIF(A1:A10,"<>B2")

would count cells whose value doesn't equal the *text* "B2". In order to count cells that don't match the value *contained in* cell B2, you'd have to use

   =COUNTIF(A1:A10,"<>"&B2)

Here & is the concatenation operator, which joins values and references into strings. (We'll learn much more about it in a few chapters.) "<>"&B2 means "the text that results when you join together the string '<>' with the text representation of whatever is in B2."

More Complicated Criteria

The comparison examples above don't cover all the conditions you'd like to be able to COUNTIF(). For instance, you can't use COUNTIF() to count cells that contain values greater than or equal to 0 but less than 1. You can't use COUNTIF() to count cells that contain either the text "thinking" or the text "spreadsheet". You can't use COUNTIF() to count cells that contain only numbers or cells that contain only words that are 3 letters or less.

There are several ways to get around these limitations:

Clever Reasoning

Cells that have values greater than or equal to 0 can be split into two non-overlapping groups:

1. Cells that have values greater than or equal to 0 but less than 1.
2. Cells that have values greater than or equal to 1.

If we COUNTIF() using the criterion ">=0", we can find the total number of cells in both groups. And using the criterion ">=1" we can find the number of cells in the second group. Because the groups don't overlap, the number of cells in the first group is just the difference between the two.

So, to count the cells in A1:A100 that are greater than or equal to 0 and less than 1, we could use

=COUNTIF(A1:A100,">=0")-COUNTIF(A1:A100,">=1")

In general, when we want to COUNTIF() how often a value falls within a range, we can use this method.

Exclusive Or Addition

A cell can't contain both the value "thinking" and the value "spreadsheet". Therefore, to find the number of cells that contain either value, we can just add up the numbers of cells that contain each value:

=COUNTIF(A1:A100,"thinking")+COUNTIF(A1:A100,"spreadsheet")

This method doesn't work if your categories overlap. If you wanted to count values that start with "spread" or end with "sheet",

=COUNTIF(A1:A100,"spread*")+COUNTIF(A1:A100,"*sheet")

would double-count "spreadsheet" (as well as "spread the bedsheet" and anything else that started with "spread" and ended with "sheet").

Extra Columns

If you have only one or two complicated conditions to check, often it's easiest to add them to your data in a new column.

For instance, imagine you need to count how many integers are in A1:A100. To be an integer, first a value must be a number, and then it must be equal to INT() of itself.

So in B1 you could enter the formula

    =IF(ISNUMBER(A1),A1=INT(A1))

and then copy down. (You need to use the IF(ISNUMBER()) so that you don't try to INT() something that's not a number.)

Then you can COUNTIF() on column B:

    =COUNTIF(B1:B100,TRUE)

However, if you have a lot of different conditions to check, you'd have to add a lot of extra columns, which wouldn't be very Thinking Spreadsheet.

Array Formulas

Array formulas can be used to produce the equivalent of really complicated COUNTIF() functions. However, they're very complicated themselves, so we won't discuss them until much later in the book.

COUNTIFS()

In Excel 2007 and later, there is a COUNTIFS() function, which allows you to specify multiple criteria and count cells that meet all of them. We'll discuss COUNTIFS() briefly in a few sections, but I recommend against using it.

Strategic Summing with SUMIF()

SUMIF() is COUNTIF()'s bigger brother. If you understand COUNTIF() pretty well, it won't take you long to understand SUMIF() too.

Whereas COUNTIF() counts cells that meet a certain criterion, SUMIF() adds them up. There's only a slight twist, and that's that you don't have to sum the exact same cells that you're testing your criterion on. This might seem a little bit odd when you first think about it, but it makes a lot of sense.

For instance, if in column A you have a list of names, in column B you have their hometowns, and in column C you have their incomes, you can use SUMIF() to answer questions like "What's the total income of people whose names start with 'J'?" and "What's the total income of people who are from Seattle?" and "What's the total income of people who aren't named 'Bob'?"

To do this, SUMIF() needs 3 inputs. The first two, a range and a criterion, are the same inputs you'd give COUNTIF(). The third is new – it's the sum_range, and it needs to have the same dimensions as the first range.

Then SUMIF() does the following: "for every cell in the first range, if it meets the specified criterion, add up the corresponding value in the sum_range."

For instance, a typical usage might be

    =SUMIF(A1:A10,TRUE,B1:B10)

which means "add up all the values in B1:B10 where the corresponding value in A1:A10 is TRUE." If only A3, A5, and A8 are TRUE, the output will be equal to B3+B5+B8. If all the values in A1:A10 are TRUE, the output will be equal to SUM(B1:B10). If none of the values in A1:A10 are TRUE, the output will be equal to 0.

The sum_range, by the way, is optional, and if you omit it Excel will just use the initial range. This allows you to do things like the following:

    =SUMIF(A1:A10,">7")

which will add up all cells in A1:A10 that have values greater than 7. You could also type =SUMIF(A1:A10,">7",A1:A10) if you like, but the shorter way is shorter.

Criteria for SUMIF() work exactly the same as they do for COUNTIF().

And AVERAGEIF()?

Starting with Excel 2007, there is also an AVERAGEIF() function, which works how you'd expect. It is, of course, wholly unnecessary. An AVERAGE() is a SUM() divided by a COUNT(). So, to find the average of all the cells in A1:A10 that are greater than 7, you could use

    =SUMIF(A1:A10,">7")/COUNTIF(A1:A10,">7")

If column A contained TRUE/FALSE values and column B contained the numbers you want to average, you'd use

    =SUMIF(A1:A10,TRUE,B1:B10)/COUNTIF(A1:A10,TRUE)

to find the average of the numbers in column B with TRUE in column A.

Notice that the COUNTIF() doesn't need to know a thing about column B. It just needs to know how many cells we're including in our sum, which only depends on column A.

Formulas like these will produce #DIV/0! errors if no cells match, so make sure to test if that's a worry.

Example: Lucky Number Seven

A friend of yours has just opened a casino, and he's designed a slot machine themed on his superstitious love of the number seven. He wants the slot machine to have the following features:

- Three reels, each containing the numbers 1 to 5, each number being equally likely on any given spin.
- Each play costs $1.
- If your spin turns up 3-of-a-kind, you win that many dollars. So if you spin 4-4-4, you win $4.
- If the numbers of your spin add up to 7, you win $7. For instance, 1-2-4 would be a winning spin.

He asks you two questions:

1. What percentage of the time will people win?
2. What's the average payout?

A problem this size is amenable to solving via brute force. We can simply use Excel to catalogue every possibility, then use this catalogue to compute the statistics we're interested in.

How many possibilities are there? Each reel can take 5 different values, so there are 5 * 5 * 5 = 125 possible combinations. Based on our assumptions, every possibility is equally likely.

Therefore, if we want to know how frequently a certain condition occurs, we simply count how many times it occurs and divide by the total number of possibilities. To find out how frequently the first dial shows a 3, we count

that there are 25 outcomes where this happens, which means it happens
25/125 = 20% of the time. (We could also have figured this out simply based
on the knowledge that the first dial has 5 numbers, each of which has an
equal chance of showing up.)

To list out all the possibilities, we'll use our odometer technique. Start by
designating a column for each reel, and by filling in the first combination:
1-1-1.

◢	A	B	C
1	reel 1	reel 2	reel 3
2	1	1	1

When we were trying to mimic a car's odometer, we needed the rightmost
dial to "spin fastest" and increase at every step. In general, when we're using
an "odometer" to catalogue possibilities, it doesn't matter which order we
"spin the dials," as long as we produce each possible combination exactly
once. So in this case we'll work left to right. (You could work right to left
again here, and you'd get the same ultimate results, but your "spins" would
get listed in a different order.)

In A3, we'll want to increase the value from the row above, making sure that
after 5 we return to 1. Previously we used MOD(), but that would reset the
reel to 0. Since we want our reel to reset to 1, it will be easier to use IF().
The logic is simple: if the previous value is less than 5, add 1 to it; otherwise
reset to 1.

=IF(A2<5,A2+1,1)

The logic for B3 (and C3) will be slightly different:

- If the value in A3 has just rolled over and the value in B2 is less than 5,
  then add 1 to the previous value.
- If A3 has just rolled over and the value in B2 is equal to 5, then reset
  the value in this column to 1.

- If A3 has not just rolled over, then keep the same value from B2.

There are many ways to write this. But since there are 3 conditions to check, we'll have to use a nested IF().

=IF(A3<A2,IF(B2<5,B2+1,1),B2)

	A	B	C	D
1	reel 1	reel 2	reel 3	
2	1	1	1	
3	2	=IF(A3<A2,IF(B2<5,B2+1,1),B2)		

Convince yourself that this function captures the logic we've described, and then copy it over to C3. Now copy the formulas in row 3 all the way down to row 126. (Since we have one row of headers, our 125 possibilities will go from rows 2:126.) Make sure your slot machine simulation ends with the combination 5-5-5:

	A	B	C
121	5	4	5
122	1	5	5
123	2	5	5
124	3	5	5
125	4	5	5
126	5	5	5

Now, for each row, we need to figure out the payout. If all three numbers are the same, the payout is the number. If all three numbers sum to 7, the payout is 7. And otherwise the payout is 0. Since the two payout conditions are mutually exclusive (if the dials all match, they can't add to 7), we don't have to worry about both being TRUE, but in general we might.

Since there are 3 options, we could capture this using nested IF() functions:

IF(reels all match, reel value, IF(reels add to 7, 7, 0))

Or we could add together two disjoint IF() functions:

IF(reels all match, reel value, 0) + IF(reels add to 7, 7, 0)

You should convince yourself that in every possible case these produce the same answer. We'll add "Payout" in column D, use the second formula in D2, and then copy it down. We just need to translate its conditions into Excel-speak.

First, the test for "reels all match." Once you know what value is in column A, you need the value in column B to be the same, and also the value in column C to be the same. That is, the test can be written as AND(A2=B2,A2=C2).

The only way we'll reach the "reel value" part of the IF() is if the reels all match. So we can look at any of them to find out "reel value." We'll look at A2.

We also need a test for "reels add to 7." This is just SUM(A2:C2)=7. This means our formula in D2 is

=IF(AND(A2=B2,A2=C2),A2,0)+IF(SUM(A2:C2)=7,7,0)

Double-Click-Fill the formula down, and now we're ready to answer your friend's questions. We'll compute them over to the right.

First, he wants to know what percentage of the time a player would win. A player wins precisely when his payout is greater than 0. Therefore we need to know what fraction of the time the value in column D is greater than 0. We'll use COUNTIF() to find how many of the outcomes have positive payout, and we'll use COUNT() to find out how many outcomes there are in all. (We already know there are 125, but as part of Thinking Spreadsheet we prefer not to hardcode numbers that might change if we changed part of our model.)

To count the winning percentage, we'll use the following:

=COUNTIF(D2:D126,">0") / COUNT(D2:D126)

Computing the average payout is even easier, since it's just the AVERAGE() of the payout column:

=AVERAGE(D2:D126)

	A	B	C	D	E	F	G
1	reel 1	reel 2	reel 3	payout			
2	1	1	1	1		Win %	0.16
3	2	1	1	0		Avg Payout	0.96
4	3	1	1	0			
5	4	1	1	0			

So players will win 16% of the time, and the average payout is 96 cents. Since it costs a dollar to play, your friend's average profit will be 4 cents per play. Not a bad business to be in!

Frivolous Example: Brute-Forcing SUBSET-SUM

Does any subset of the numbers 2,5,7,12,19,21 sum to 48? As we'll see, we can use our "brute force odometer" method to check every subset. How many subsets are there? If a set has N elements, then there are $2 * 2 * \ldots * 2$ (N times) possible subsets. Here, there are 6 elements, so there are $2*2*2*2*2*2=64$ possible subsets. That's a small enough number that we can check it by brute force.

First, though, we need to decide how to represent subsets. For instance, {2,19} is a subset (that sums to 21), but is not written in a very Excel-friendly representation. A more Thinking Spreadsheet way begins with the observation that each subset represents a sequence of six yes or no "Include?" decisions. The subset {2,19} corresponds to the decisions {Yes,No,No,No,Yes,No}. If we look at every possible combination of six Yeses and Nos, we'll see every possible subset of {2,5,7,12,19,21}. And if we use 1 and 0 to represent "Yes" and "No," then we just need an odometer with 6 dials, each of which contains only 0 and 1.

To make it even more clear, we'll put the 6 elements in row 1, with "Include?" labels underneath, and with our first subset "None" entered in row 3 as all zeroes:

	A	B	C	D	E	F
1	2	5	7	12	19	21
2	Include?	Include?	Include?	Include?	Include?	Include?
3	0	0	0	0	0	0

At this point you should be pretty familiar with what to do. In cell A4, we'll need the formula

=MOD(A3+1,2)

And in cell B4 we'll need

=IF(A4<A3,MOD(B3+1,2),B3)

Copy this over to the right and then copy all the formulas down to row 66 so that we have all 64 subsets represented.

Now we need to compute the sum of the elements in each subset. One of the benefits of using 1 to represent "this element is included" and 0 to represent "this element is not included" is that we can simply multiply it by the element's value and then sum up to find our result. That is, if there's a 1 in column A ("the 2 is included") then we add 2 (which is 1*2) to our sum. If there's a 0 in column A ("the 2 is not included") then we add nothing (which is 0*2) to our sum.

Therefore, thanks to the way we've set things up, the sum of the elements in the subset corresponding to row 3 is

=SUMPRODUCT($A$1:$F$1,A3:F3)

If we copy this formula down, we'll find the correct sum for each subset:

	A	B	C	D	E	F	G
1	2	5	7	12	19	21	
2	Include?	Include?	Include?	Include?	Include?	Include?	Sum
3	0	0	0	0	0	0	0
4	1	0	0	0	0	0	2
5	0	1	0	0	0	0	5
6	1	1	0	0	0	0	7
7	0	0	1	0	0	0	7
8	1	0	1	0	0	0	9
9	0	1	1	0	0	0	12

And with a quick =COUNTIF(G3:G66,48), we can check that none of the subsets sums to 48.

This sort of brute force approach doesn't scale very well:

# of elements	# of rows required
2	4
6	64
10	1024
20	1048576

If you have more than 10 or so elements in your set, brute-forcing the subsets is probably not an efficient way to solve your problem, and you should try to come up with something more clever.

Technique: Making a Histogram

A histogram is a way of summarizing data by counting how many elements fall into certain "buckets." For instance, if you had a list of 1000 popular vocabulary words, you could create a histogram showing how many start with each letter of the alphabet. Or you might poll the attendees at your family reunion and count how many were born in each decade. You could look at a football roster and count how many players (claim to) weigh less than 200 pounds, how many weigh more than 200 but less than 250, how many weigh more than 250 but less than 300, and how many weigh over 300.

Excel has an add-in that will generate (static) histograms. This means that if you generate a histogram using the add-in and then modify your data, the histogram won't reflect your changes. This makes the histogram add-in not very Thinking Spreadsheet. Fortunately, it's not difficult to build dynamic histograms that update automatically when you change your data.

To start with, we need some data. Let's download the Denver Broncos roster. You can either look for the latest version on denverbroncos.com or (if you want your numbers to match mine) grab the version I used from ThinkingSpreadsheet.com.

The current roster looks like this:

Highlight the active roster and copy it, and then Paste-Special-Text it into Excel. After bolding the headers and resizing the columns, it should look like this:

	A	B	C	D	E	F	G	H
1	#	Name	Pos.	Ht.	Wt.	Age	Exp.	College
2	48	Alexander, Kevin	LB	4-Jun	265	23	R	Clemson
3	82	Arnett, Alric	WR	2-Jun	189	23	R	West Virginia
4	58	Atkins, Baraka	LB	4-Jun	268	25	3	Miami (Fla.)
5	56	Ayers, Robert	LB	3-Jun	274	24	2	Tennessee

To build our histogram, we'll start with the labels:

G	H	I	J	K
xp.	College		Weight	Count
	Clemson		0	
	West Virginia		200	
3	Miami (Fla.)		250	
2	Tennessee		300	

Why did we start with a zero? Well, the way we described most of our buckets was "more than __ and less than __." Our "under 200" bucket can also be described as "more than 0 and less than 200." What about our "over 300" bucket? There we have two options. We could add an unreasonably large number below the 300 to make our bucket "more than 300 but less than 10000." Or we could use a different formula for the last bucket. We'll do the second.

To start with, in K2, we need to count players whose weight is at least 0 but less than 200. Another way of saying this is "greater than or equal to 0, but not greater than or equal to 200." As we've seen, the formula for this is

=COUNTIF($E$2:$E$78,">="&J2)-COUNTIF($E$2:$E$78,">="&J3)

(Your range and results may differ slightly depending on how the Broncos change their roster.)

Copy this formula down twice:

Weight	Count
0	15
200	27
250	15
300	

In K5 we'll need a different formula, since we only want "greater than or equal to 300."

=COUNTIF($E$2:$E$78,">="&J5)

The benefits of doing things this way are immediate. Imagine you decide instead you want the buckets to be "less than 225," "225 to 275," "275 to 325," and "over 325." By changing the labels the formulas will update automatically:

Weight	Count
0	29
225	24
275	21
325	3

And when Robert Ayers puts on an extra 2 pounds and moves into the "275 to 325" bucket, your histogram will adjust *as soon as the data does*. That's Thinking Spreadsheet!

Some Pitfalls of Importing Data

Now that you've got this data in Excel, you can ask all sorts of interesting questions. For instance, what's the average weight of the Broncos quarterbacks? The abbreviation for quarterback is QB, so a good idea seems to be

=SUMIF(C2:C78,"QB",E2:E78)/COUNTIF(C2:C78,"QB")

But if you try this, you'll get a #DIV/0! error, which means that your COUNTIF() must not be finding any matches.

Find one of the QBs and hit F2:

	A	B	C	D
67	14	Stokley, Brandon	WR	Jur
68	15	Tebow, Tim	QB	3-
69	88	Thomas, Demaryius	WR	3

See the space in the formula bar between QB and the cursor? That means there's extra (invisible) spaces in the data. Tim Tebow's position is not stored as "QB", it's stored as "QB ". Our SUMIF() that's looking for "QB" isn't finding any matches.

What can we do? One thing would be to clean the data. If we're going to make a lot of use of the data, we should probably do this. But a simpler fix is to change our criterion to "QB*". This looks for all positions that start with QB, and doesn't mind the extra spaces at the end. (Of course, this only works because there are no other positions that start with QB. If football added a new QBX position we'd start getting wrong answers)

=SUMIF(C2:C78,"QB*",E2:E84)/COUNTIF(C2:C78,"QB*")

This time you'll find that it's 235. When you source data from outside Excel, it's not uncommon to end up with phantom spaces, so check and compute accordingly.

Hang onto this Broncos roster, we'll use it some more later.

SUMIFS( ) and COUNTIFS( )

A few sections ago we discussed some approaches to COUNTIF() and SUMIF() with multiple conditions. In Excel 2007 and later, there are functions COUNTIFS() and SUMIFS() (notice the extra S) that count or sum only cells that meet multiple conditions.

COUNTIFS() behaves largely how you'd expect. You specify your ranges (which all must have the same numbers of rows and columns) and conditions one after another. For example,

    =COUNTIFS(A1:A10,TRUE,B2:B11,"<=3")

counts the number of times a cell in A1:A10 contains the value TRUE and the corresponding cell in B2:B11 also contains a value less than or equal to 3. It will output a number between 0 and 10, depending on how many cells meet both of its criteria.

SUMIFS() is a little different. Recall that the inputs for SUMIF() were a criteria range, then a criterion, and finally an (optional) sum range.

For SUMIFS() you have to specify the sum range first. So the usage would be something like

    =SUMIFS(C3:C12,A1:A10,TRUE,B2:B11,"<=3")

Here the conditions to be checked are in A1:A10 and B2:B11, while the cells to be summed are actually in C3:C12.

As a rule, we will never use SUMIFS() and COUNTIFS(). Array formulas (which we'll get to eventually) can do all the same things and more, and they won't make our spreadsheets unusable by our friends running older copies of Excel. However, you might encounter them, so know how they work.

Data Validation, Revisited

Now that we're experts at Boolean formulas, we can discuss the Custom Data Validation option, which lets you specify an arbitrary formula that has to be true for an input to be valid.

For instance, you could validate that cell A1 is a number greater than zero with

=IF(ISNUMBER(A1),A1>0)

The ISNUMBER() test is necessary because Excel considers any text greater than every number, which means that a test based only on A1>0 would validate text.

You can also validate based on other cells. For example, you could only allow someone to enter a value in A2 if A1 equals TRUE:

=A1

Any formula that produces a Boolean, you can use as your Custom Validation. Just make sure that it does what you want and that you give a helpful error message when the validation fails.

CHAPTER *13*

STRING THEORY

So far we've focused mostly on numbers and Booleans. Now we'll turn our attention to text.

TEXT() Messages

Sometimes you need to create specially formatted text representations of numbers. Conversely, sometimes you need to turn text representations of numbers back into numeric values.

The former can be done with the TEXT() function, which requires two inputs. The first is a value, and the second is a string representing the number format you want.

There are many, many complicated things you can specify using the format string; we'll stick to the simplest and most useful ones.

Digits

A "0" in the text string represents a digit in your number. A period "." represents the decimal point. Digits to the left of the decimal point represent a minimum number of places to display, while digits to right of the decimal point represent an exact number of places to display (with the number rounded if necessary).

The following examples should give you a good sense of how this works:

Function	Output
TEXT(23.45,"00.00")	23.45
TEXT(23.45,"00.0")	23.5
TEXT(23.45,"0.00")	23.45
TEXT(23.45,"0.0")	23.5
TEXT(23.45,"0000.000000")	0023.450000

Each of the outputs listed above is text. If you try to do arithmetic with them, you'll get an error.

If you want the text to represent a percentage, you can include a % sign in the format string. Similarly, if you want your output to be separated by commas, just include them in the format string:

Function	Output
TEXT(23.45,"0%")	2345%
TEXT(23.45,"00.0%")	2345.0%
TEXT(23.45,"00,000.00")	00,023.45
TEXT(23.45,"000,00.0")	00,023.5

Notice that you can be a little sloppy about where you put the comma, and Excel will still use it in the normal way (every 3 digits to the left of the decimal point). Don't take this as license to be sloppy, though. Being sloppy isn't Thinking Spreadsheet at all.

Dates

To convert dates to text, you have even more options.

Format	Example	Output
2-digit year	TEXT(DATE(2010,1,2),"YY")	10
4-digit year	TEXT(DATE(2010,1,2),"YYYY")	2010
Short month	TEXT(DATE(2010,1,2),"M")	1
Zero-padded month	TEXT(DATE(2010,1,2),"MM")	01
Short month name	TEXT(DATE(2010,1,2),"MMM")	Jan
Long month name	TEXT(DATE(2010,1,2),"MMMM")	January
Short day	TEXT(DATE(2010,1,2),"D")	2
Zero-padded day	TEXT(DATE(2010,1,2),"DD")	02
Short weekday	TEXT(DATE(2010,1,2),"DDD")	Sat
Long weekday	TEXT(DATE(2010,1,2),"DDDD")	Saturday

You can also combine these with spaces, commas, dashes, and slashes. For instance,

=TEXT(DATE(2010,1,2),"DDDD, MMMM D, YYYY")

produces "Saturday, January 2, 2010" while

=TEXT(DATE(2010,1,2),"YYYY-DD/M")

produces (the not very useful) "2010-01/2".

Time

There are similar options to convert times to text: H and HH for hours, M and MM for minutes, and S and SS for seconds. If you're astute, you're probably objecting that M and MM are already used for months. This is true. If you use M (or MM) in combination with H or HH or S or SS, you'll get minutes; otherwise you'll get months.

For instance, if in A1, we put the formula

=DATE(2010,1,2)+TIME(8,3,0)

which represents "8:03 am on 1/2/2010", then TEXT(A1,"hhmm") produces "0803", while TEXT(A1,"mm") produces "01". This is not intuitive, so it will probably slip you up at some point. Unless you never use TEXT() with time, in which case it won't slip you up at all.

VALUE()

The opposite of TEXT() is VALUE(), which takes one input, a text representation of a number, and returns the corresponding numeric value. You'll mostly use VALUE() for obvious text representations of numbers, like VALUE("34.58") and VALUE("2"). (Those examples are plainly pointless; in real life the inputs to VALUE() will be formulas that produce such obvious representations.)

If you give VALUE() a number, it returns that same number. And if you give it something that doesn't look at all like a number, you'll get a terrifically appropriate #VALUE! error.

If you give it a string representing a date-time, like "2010-01-01 6:00 AM", it will return the represented number, in this case 40179.25. There's also a DATEVALUE() function that will give you just the number representing the date (here 40179) and a TIMEVALUE() function that will give you just the number representing the time (here 0.8), but it's most common just to use VALUE().

CONCATENATE() & CONCATENATE()

One thing you often need to do with strings is concatenate them, or join them together. Excel provides two different ways to do this.

The first is the CONCATENATE() function, which takes as many arguments as you want to give it (within reason) and returns a string that consists of all of its inputs (or text versions of them) joined together. (It won't always convert numbers to text the way you want them to, so if you care about such things use the TEXT() function.)

The other option is the & operator, which you can use in a similar way to + or *.

Example	Output	Alternative Using &
CONCATENATE(1,"me",3.5)	1me3.5	1&"me"&3.5
CONCATENATE(1+2,"you")	3you	(1+2)&"you"
CONCATENATE("me",",","you")	me,you	"me"&","&"you"

The & operator has very low precedence. If you left out parentheses and used 1+2&"you", you would still get the same result. However, since we are Thinking Spreadsheet, we include them.

Rep[ea]ting Text with REPT()

If you ever need to concatenate the same string to itself over and over again, you can use the REPT() function. It takes two inputs. The first is the string you want repeated, the second the number of times you want it repeated.

There's two somewhat common reasons to use REPT().

The first has to do with TEXT(). If you want the text representation of a number to show 10 decimal places, you can use

    =TEXT(A1,"0."&REPT("0",10))

Our formula concatenates the string "0." with the string "0000000000" to get the format we want.

You could do the same to the left of the decimal point, and you could even make the number of decimal places depend on another cell or the results of some other calculation.

A second use for REPT() is "charts on the cheap." If you have a list of numbers between 1 and 100 in column A, in column B you can use between 0 and 10 "X" characters to represent them:

	A	B	C
1	Number	Hist	
2	87	=REPT("X",INT(A2/10))	
3	44	XXXX	
4	13	X	
5	29	XX	
6	44	XXXX	
7	6		
8	73	XXXXXXX	
9	14	X	

Since we divide by 10 and take INT() of the result, 87 will get 8 X's, 44 will get 4 X's, 13 will get 1 X, and so on.

This is a quick and dirty way of visualizing data without having to create a graph. Recent versions of Excel can do similar (and prettier) things with Conditional Formatting, but you might see (or use) this way as well.

Technique: Concatenating Arrays Using Running Totals

One shortcoming of the CONCATENATE() function is that it doesn't work on arrays. If you have a sequence of items in A2:A101 that you want concatenated, you'd like to be able to use CONCATENATE(A2:A101). However, like other formulas that don't really accept arrays as inputs, CONCATENATE() looks at the top left cell, making this equivalent to CONCATENATE(A2), which is not what you want.

In order to concatenate an array of items like this, we'll need to use our "running total" method.

To start with, let's say we have AFI's original list of the "Top 100 Movies of All Time":

	A
1	**Title**
2	Citizen Kane
3	Casablanca
4	The Godfather
5	Gone with the Wind
6	Lawrence of Arabia

We'd like one string representing all these movies, separated with commas. To get this, we'll build the string one movie at a time. To start with, in B2, we'll just take the first movie with the formula =A2.

Now in B3, we'll want to take the list-in-progress from the cell above, add a comma, and then add the next movie from cell A3:

	A	B	C
1	**Title**		
2	Citizen Kane	Citizen Kane	
3	Casablanca	=B2&","&A3	
4	The Godfather		

Equivalently, we could have used CONCATENATE(B2,",",A3), although that would have involved more typing.

This formula should work for the rest, so we can just double-click-fill it down:

And then the string we want is in B101. The result is too long to visually check, but you could copy B101 and then paste it into (for example) Notepad to see that it worked.

CODE() and CHAR()

Computers don't actually understand words or characters. They only understand numbers. (Really, all they understand are 1's and 0's, but for pedagogical purposes we'll pretend that they understand numbers.)

In particular, your computer actually stores characters as numbers, in a computer-specific way. For instance, on my computer, the character 'A' corresponds to the number 65.

Excel contains a pair of functions to convert back and forth between characters and their numeric representations. CHAR() takes a number between 0 and 255 and returns the character represented by that number. If you give it a number outside this range, you'll get a #VALUE! error.

One possible use of CHAR() is producing characters that aren't on your keyboard. For instance, CHAR(200) is the character 'È'. But you probably won't use crazy characters like this in your spreadsheet, and so you won't use CHAR() this way.

Its converse is CODE() which takes some text as input and returns the number representing the first character of the text. In practice, you'll only ever give it one character, and you'll get back the numeric representation of that character.

This correspondence between characters and numbers varies computer-by-computer. What should always be true, though, is that consecutive characters will be represented by consecutive numbers. Whatever number CODE("A") happens to be, CODE("B") will be the number after it.

This means that if you have a letter in A1, the next letter is

    CHAR(CODE(A1)+1)

This will work as long as the letter in A1 is not Z. CHAR(CODE("Z")+1) could be just about anything! (But if your computer is anything like mine, it's '['.) If Z is a possibility, then test for it.

Example: First Letters of Popular Names

Congratulations! You're having a baby! But your relatives are very superstitious. They want the kid to have a name that starts with a popular letter.

Luckily, the Social Security Administration maintains lists of popular baby names on their website. We can download the 1000 most popular names for 2009 and create a histogram to see which name-beginning letters are currently popular and which aren't.

To start with, go to the website

    http://www.ssa.gov/OACT/babynames/

and in the "Popular Names by Birth Year" section choose the Top 1000 Names for babies born in 2009.

> **Popular Names by Birth Year**
> For a list of the most popular names for a particular year of birth (any
> year after 1879), enter the year and the length of the popularity list.
>
> Enter year of birth 2009   [Go]
>
> Popularity Top 1000 ▼   [Reset]

You'll end up with a big table of names, which you should Copy and Paste-Special-Text into Excel. Resize the columns and bold the headers to make them stand out more:

	A	B	C
1	**Rank**	**Male name**	**Female name**
2	1	Jacob	Isabella
3	2	Ethan	Emma
4	3	Michael	Olivia

We want to count how many male names and female names start with each letter of the alphabet. So a good first step would be to list every letter of the alphabet. Of course, we could type them out, one at a time. But part of Thinking Spreadsheet is using formulas whenever doing so will save us work.

As is frequently the case, we have to type in a starting letter before we can use formulas to continue:

B	C	D	E	F
Male name	**Female name**			**First Letter**
acob	Isabella			A

In F3 we'll need a formula for the next letter. As we saw in the previous section, that formula is

=CHAR(CODE(F2)+1)

Enter that formula and copy it down until we get to Z.

Now, in G2 we'll need a formula to count all the male names starting with A. This is a good job for COUNTIF()'s wildcard functionality. A condition of "A*" will match exactly those names that start with A. We'll need this condition to be a formula as well, so that the row with B uses "B*", the row with C uses "C*", and so on. Our condition, then, should be the value in column F concatenated with the text "*".

This means in G2 we'll use

=COUNTIF(B$2:B$1001,$F2&"*")

Since we didn't $ the B, when we copy the formula one column to the right it will look at column C and count female names. Since we did $ the F, the copied formula will keep looking there for the letters.

Put this formula in G2, and copy it right and down:

F First Letter	G Male Count	H Female Count
A	90	162
B	59	32
C	75	70
D	79	34
E	43	49
F	18	9

You should have found that A is a very popular first letter for girl names, while J is very popular for boy names.

Histograms are usually represented with column (or bar) charts, so let's insert one:

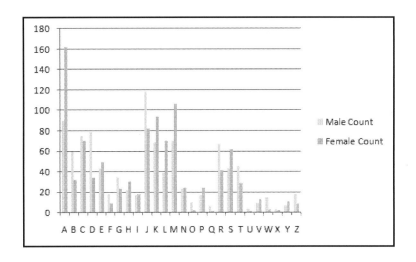

The Curious Case of UPPER() and LOWER() and EXACT()

Despite the herculean efforts of e. e. cummings, most people still use a mixture of CAPITAL and lowercase letters. In the event that you get fed up with that, Excel offers an UPPER() function, which takes some text as input and outputs that same text with all lowercase letters converted to capitals. Similarly, there is a LOWER() function that converts capital letters to lowercase.

These are often useful for cleaning data into a standard format. You might get an array of names like Bob, CHARLES, David, ELLIS and need to make them all look the same. Using UPPER() you could make them all uppercase. Using LOWER() you could make them all lowercase. Using UPPER() and LOWER() and functions we haven't learned yet, you could make the first letter uppercase and the rest of the string lowercase.

As we saw earlier, the standard test for equality ignores case, so that

="UPPER"="upper"

returns TRUE. If you don't want that to be the case, you can use the EXACT() function, which returns TRUE only when its two inputs are exactly the same including case. So

=EXACT("UPPER","upper")

returns FALSE.

Extracting String Parts

When you're working with strings, often you'll want to extract parts of them. For instance, you might have text representation of locations like

	A
1	**location**
2	Seattle, WA 98101
3	Los Angeles, CA 90001
4	Davisburg, MI 48350

and want to break them apart into city, state, and zip. Or you might work in a doctor's office whose filing system uses the first three letters of the patients' last names. Or you might have a bunch of social security numbers in a spreadsheet (although for privacy reasons this is probably a bad thing to do) and need to extract the last four digits.

Excel has functions for this. The simplest are LEFT() and RIGHT(), each of which takes two inputs: some text (or a reference to some text) and a number of characters. The outputs are that many characters from the left or right of the string.

If you specify 0 characters, you'll get an empty string, and if you specify more characters than the string has, you'll just get the string itself:

Function	Value
LEFT("Thinking Spreadsheet",4)	Thin
RIGHT("Thinking Spreadsheet",4)	heet
LEFT("Thinking Spreadsheet",0)	
RIGHT("Thinking Spreadsheet",100)	Thinking Spreadsheet

You can also use a number as the first input. Excel will convert the number to text before taking the LEFT() or RIGHT(), but it won't always convert it into the format you expect, so you probably shouldn't do this. Use TEXT() first to make sure the number is represented the way you want.

If you want to get characters out of the middle of the string, you have to use MID() instead. It takes 3 arguments: the string, the starting position, and the number of characters.

Function	Value
MID("abcdefghij",1,3)	abc
MID("abcdefghij",3,5)	cdefg
MID("abcdefghij",9,2)	ij
MID("abcdefghij",9,10)	ij

If you specify more characters than are actually in the string (as we did in the last example), you get whatever characters are left. Similarly, you can specify a starting position that's too large for the string, and you'll just get an empty string as the result. (If you specify a starting position that's too small for the string, you'll get an error.)

LEN()

Sometimes to extract string parts you need to know how many characters are in the string. (You might want to know this for other reasons, too. For instance, maybe you want to know if your nickname is short enough to fit on the back of your basketball jersey.)

The Excel function LEN() takes a string as its input and returns the number of characters in the string.

Function	Value
LEN("abcdefghij")	10
LEN("abc")	3
LEN("abc"&"def")	6
LEN("")	0

The Missing MID() Case

Sometimes rather than specifying the number of characters for MID(), you'd like to specify the ending point. That is, instead of "return the 3 characters starting at position 6" you'd rather give the instruction as "return the characters from position 6 to position 8."

Why 8? Position 6 is one character, position 7 is the second character, and position 8 is the third character. In general, there are (Start-End+1) characters between Start and End. This means that to get "MID(Text,Start,End)" functionality, you have to use the following (non-intuitive) math:

	A	B
1	Text:	Thinking Spreadsheet
2	Start:	7
3	End:	11
4	Mid:	=MID(B1,B2,B3-B2+1)

We'll see this several times, so stare at it until you understand it.

The Missing RIGHT() Case

Similarly, sometimes rather than specifying the number of characters for RIGHT(), you'd like to specify the starting point. Instead of "return the right-most 3 characters" you'd prefer to specify "return the 7th character and everything to its right." (The analogous use of LEFT() is just its usual usage.)

If you start at (for example) the 7th character of A1 and go to the last character, then (as in the previous section) you'll need LEN(A1)-7+1 characters. Of course, if you use MID() and ask for LEN(A1) characters you'll get the right result too, although you might confuse people trying to understand your work.

Seek and You Shall FIND()

How do you know whether one string contains another? Excel has a FIND() function for answering this question. FIND() takes either 2 or 3 inputs. The first is the substring you're trying to find, and the second is the string in which you're trying to find it. A third optional input tells Excel at what position to start looking. If the third input is 2, for instance, FIND() will start looking at the second character of the string. If you leave the argument out (which you will, usually) Excel will simply start looking at the beginning.

If the string you give FIND() as the second input contains the substring you give FIND() as the first input, the output will be the position where its first appearance begins. If the second string doesn't contain the first, you'll get a #VALUE! error.

Function	Output	Why
FIND("bcd","abcdabcd")	2	First bcd starts at character 2
FIND("bcd","abcdabcd",3)	6	First bcd at or after character 3 starts at character 6
FIND("dab","abcdabcd")	4	First dab starts at character 4
FIND("ba","abcdabcd")	#VALUE!	ba doesn't appear in string
FIND("A","abcdabcd")	#VALUE!	FIND() is case-sensitive!

As you can see in the last example, FIND() is case-sensitive. It expects capital letters to match capital letters and lowercase letters to match lowercase letters.

If you are not interested in case-sensitivity, you can instead use SEARCH().

SEARCH() behaves pretty much the same except that it ignores case when matching. Only the last example above would turn out different. SEARCH("A","abcdabcd") would return 1.

REPLACE() You With a SUBSTITUTE()

Sometimes you don't just want to find one substring within another, you want to swap it out for a different substring. Excel provides a SUBSTITUTE() function for this.

In its simplest form it takes 3 inputs: the text where the substitution is to happen, the "old text" that you want rid of, and the "new text" you want to replace it. When you use it this way, with only 3 arguments, it will replace "every" instance of the old text with the new text, working from left to right.

Why was "every" in quotes? Imagine you have the string ABABAB and you want to replace each occurrence of ABAB with TS. There are two places you can find the substring ABAB within ABABAB. One is starting at the first character, and one is starting at the third. Excel's SUBSTITUTE() will replace only the first.

The way to think about this is that it will replace the first ABAB with TS, at which point the string is now TSAB, and there's no longer a second ABAB.

You can also give it an optional fourth argument. This has to be a number and it will tell Excel to SUBSTITUTE() only a particular occurrence of the "old text." The number 1 means to SUBSTITUTE() the first occurrence, 2 the second, and so on. If there is no such occurrence, you'll get the original string back.

Function	Output
SUBSTITUTE("spreadsheet","spread","bed")	bedsheet
SUBSTITUTE("spreadsheet","Spread","bed")	spreadsheet
SUBSTITUTE("ababab","abab","CDCD")	CDCDab
SUBSTITUTE("abababab","abab","CDCD",2)	abCDCDab
SUBSTITUTE("abababab","abab","CDCD",3)	ababCDCD
SUBSTITUTE("abababab","abab","CDCD",4)	abababab

If you need to do multiple substitutions, you can chain them together by using the output of one as the input of the next.

For instance, if you had a synopsis of *Romeo and Juliet* in A1, you could convert it to a synopsis of *West Side Story* with the formula

=SUBSTITUTE(SUBSTITUTE(A1,"Romeo","Tony"),"Juliet","Maria")

The inner SUBSTITUTE() takes the text in A1 and replaces every instance of Romeo with Tony; the outer SUBSTITUTE() takes the resulting text and swaps out every Juliet for Maria. Move over, Steven Sondheim!

Related but less useful is REPLACE(), which looks for a specific position in the string rather than a specific substring. REPLACE() always takes four inputs.

The first is the source text. (The documentation for SUBSTITUTE() calls this "text," but the analogous documentation for REPLACE() calls this "old text," which meant something entirely different. We'll call it the source text.) After that you need to specify a start position, a number of characters, and some new text.

Function	Output
REPLACE("spreadsheet",1,6,"bed")	bedsheet
REPLACE("spreadsheet",100,6,"bed")	spreadsheetbed
REPLACE("ababab",1,4,"CDCD")	CDCDab
REPLACE("abababab",3,4,"CDCD")	abCDCDab
REPLACE("abababab",5,4,"CDCD")	ababCDCD
REPLACE("abababab",7,4,"CDCD")	ababababCDCD

If you specify a starting point that's after the string ends (as in the second example), REPLACE() will simply append the new text to the end. If there aren't as many characters as you specify (as in the last example), REPLACE() will replace as many as it can.

Example: Checking an ISBN

Every book published in the United States is assigned a 10-"digit" ISBN, which is used to uniquely identify it. While the first nine must indeed be digits 0-9, the last (rightmost) "digit" can also be the letter X.

But not every 10-"digit" string is an ISBN. Only certain combinations represent valid ISBN's. In this example we'll see how to use Excel to check whether an ISBN is valid. Let's use x_1 to mean the left-most digit, x_2 to mean the next digit, and so on.

Then the condition to check for a valid ISBN is that the quantity

$$(10 * x_1) + (9 * x_2) + (8 * x_3) + \ldots + (2 * x_9) + (1 * x_{10})$$

must be divisible by 11. (If x_{10} is X then we give it the value 10.) We're going to build a spreadsheet that checks this.

(If you are a computer programmer, you can probably think of a quicker way to accomplish the same thing in your favorite programming language. But this book is about spreadsheets, and so we're going to solve this problem using a spreadsheet.)

We'll start with the ISBNs of some of our favorite books, which we've sourced from various websites:

	A	B
1	**Title**	**ISBN**
2	*The Da Vinci Code*	0-385-50420-9
3	*The Secret*	1582701709
4	*Dianetics*	088404632X
5	*Left Behind*	0-8423-4270-2
6	*Twilight*	316015849

Curiously, there doesn't seem to be much standardization in their formatting. Some contain hyphens as separators (in an inconsistent manner), others are purely numeric. An important thing to notice is that the displayed ISBN for *Twilight* is only 9 digits, because Excel treated it as a number and ignored the leading zero. We'll need to account for that too.

So our first goal will be to "clean" the ISBNs so they contain only the 10 "digits." This requires two steps. First, we need to get rid of the hyphens. And second we need to tell Excel to print all 10 characters. The following formula should work:

=TEXT(SUBSTITUTE(B2,"-",""),REPT("0",10))

	A	B	C
1	**Title**	**ISBN**	**Clean ISBN**
2	*The Da Vinci Code*	0-385-50420-9	0385504209
3	*The Secret*	1582701709	1582701709
4	*Dianetics*	088404632X	088404632X
5	*Left Behind*	0-8423-4270-2	0842342702
6	*Twilight*	316015849	0316015849

Now we'll need to extract each of the 10 "digits." We'll use 10 columns for this, and (planning ahead) across the top we'll put the factors we're going to want to multiply by.

C	D	E	F	G	H	I	J	K	L	M
Clean ISBN	**10**	**9**	**8**	**7**	**6**	**5**	**4**	**3**	**2**	**1**
0385504209										
1582701709										
088404632X										
0842342702										
0316015849										

Narrow the columns so they don't take up too much space.

In the "10" column, we want the value of the character in position 1 of the ISBN. In the "9" column, we want the value of the character in position 2. In the "8" column, we want the value of the character in position 3. Do you see the pattern? In D2 the character we need will be

MID($C2,11-D$1,1)

If it's a number, we want to compute its value. That seems like a good job for VALUE(). If it's an X, we want to replace it with 10. (We know that an X can only appear in the rightmost position; however, so that we don't have two sets of formulas, we'll pretend it can appear anywhere.)

There are many, many ways to write this logic. I'll use one that allows me to extract the character only once:

=IFERROR(VALUE(MID($C2,11-D$1,1)),10)

If the extracted character is a digit from 0 to 9, VALUE() will return its numeric value. If the character isn't a digit (in which case we know it's X) then VALUE() will produce an error, and the IFERROR() will return 10.

We could have instead (for instance) used IF() to test whether the extracted character was equal to X, but then we would have had to extract the character a second time to use it in the value_if_false.

Notice that we're implicitly assuming that whatever ISBNs we get, they'll consist only of numbers, hyphens, and X's. This is certainly true of our example data, but if we ever get messy data that doesn't conform to this assumption, our formulas will break. Whether we want to worry about this or not depends on whether we expect to ever get bad data or not and how we'd like that bad data handled.

If we copy this formula into all the cells, we'll see our digits:

C	D	E	F	G	H	I	J	K	L	M	N
Clean ISBN	**10**	**9**	**8**	**7**	**6**	**5**	**4**	**3**	**2**	**1**	**Valid?**
0385504209	0	3	8	5	5	0	4	2	0	9	
1582701709	1	5	8	2	7	0	1	7	0	9	
088404632X	0	8	8	4	0	4	6	3	2	10	
0842342702	0	8	4	2	3	4	2	7	0	2	
0316015849	0	3	1	6	0	1	5	8	4	9	

I've also labeled the last column for checking if the ISBN is valid. That means checking that $10 * x_1 + \ldots + 1 * x_{10}$ is divisible by 11. Because of the clever way we've labeled the columns, this quantity is just

SUMPRODUCT($D$1:$M$1,D2:M2)

We need to test that this result is divisible by 11, which is the same as testing that when you MOD() it by 11 you get 0. This tells us how to create our formula:

=MOD(SUMPRODUCT($D$1:$M$1,D2:M2),11)=0

And fill down.

Try checking the ISBN's of some books off your bookshelf. Let me know if you find any that don't pass the test!

Technique: Counting Spaces in a String

Someone has sent you an Excel spreadsheet containing a list of names. Unfortunately, he wasn't Thinking Spreadsheet, and in some cases he put multiple names in the same cell:

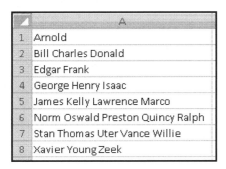

	A
1	Arnold
2	Bill Charles Donald
3	Edgar Frank
4	George Henry Isaac
5	James Kelly Lawrence Marco
6	Norm Oswald Preston Quincy Ralph
7	Stan Thomas Uter Vance Willie
8	Xavier Young Zeek

There's 8 cells with names in them, but there's clearly more than 8 names. How can we count them?

Well, we know that there's a new name whenever we see a space. In fact, if we could count the number of spaces in each cell and add 1, we'd know how many names were in the cell. (We have to add 1 because when there's 1 name there are no spaces, when there are 2 names there's just one space, and so on.)

Excel doesn't have a function to "count spaces," so we'll have to be a little bit clever. What do you get when you SUBSTITUTE() spaces with empty strings? "Arnold" stays unchanged. But "Edgar Frank" becomes "EdgarFrank". If we were to check its length we'd find that it had gotten shorter by exactly 1 character!

If you think about it, when you SUBSTITUTE() spaces with empty strings, the result will be shorter by precisely the number of spaces in the original string. This gives us a way to count spaces, which – if we add 1 – counts words:

=LEN(A1)-LEN(SUBSTITUTE(A1," ",""))+1

And if we copy this formula down, we'll find that there are 26 words in this list.

Note that this method relies on there being only a single space between words. If there were two spaces in "Edgar Frank" then our formula would think "Edgar Frank" represented three words, and we'd have to try to be more clever.

Just a TRIM()

As we've seen before, sometimes when you bring in data from another program into Excel, your text fields end up with extra spaces around them. Excel provides a TRIM() function that removes extra spaces from text. What counts as an "extra" space? Anything that's not a single space between two words. TRIM() gets rid of leading spaces, trailing spaces, and multiple internal spaces, so that, for example

    TRIM(" Thinking   Spreadsheet ")

equals "Thinking Spreadsheet" with only one space between the words and none at the beginning or end.

If you copy and paste data from the web, you'll often end up with text fields with extra trailing spaces. A quick way to fix this is to create a new column that applies TRIM() to the extra-spaces column, Copy-Paste-Special-Value it over the original extra-spaces column, and then get rid of the TRIM() column.

Parsing

One common task people use computers for is parsing data; for example, taking strings that represent certain things and "unpacking" them to get at the meaty components.

Excel is not an ideal tool for parsing things. If you are a somewhat serious computer programmer, you might use a scripting language like Python or Perl to do your parsing. However, most of us are not serious computer programmers, and many parsing problems are actually quite amenable to Excel solutions.

As there are millions of types of data that you might want to parse, we won't list all of them. Instead we'll go over some general principles and work through some detailed examples.

To start with, parsing data in Excel requires cleverness on your part. Excel can easily extract the 10th, 11th, and 12th characters from a string, but it can't figure out that those are the three characters worth caring about. Excel can count commas and tell you their locations, but it won't know that commas are meaningful unless you tell it they are.

Often the data you'll want to parse are "messy" and you'll have to clean them up. Data can contain nonsense characters, extra spaces, odd capitalization, and many other things that you'll want to fix even before you start analyzing.

You'll need to reason through rules for extracting what you care about. Perhaps you want to pull out the first substring in parenthesis or curly braces. Maybe you need everything between the second # sign and the fourth. It will probably be different every time, and it will certainly depend on the idiosyncratic formatting choices of whoever handled the data before it ended up with you.

Example: Pulling Apart Addresses

One of your minions has collected the addresses of companies that might be interested in your new spreadsheet-related book. Unfortunately, he doesn't Think Spreadsheet, and he typed each address into one cell:

A
1 **Addresses**
2 1 Microsoft Way, Redmond, WA 98052-6399
3 1600 Amphitheatre Parkway, Mountain View, CA 94043
4 1 Infinite Loop, Cupertino, CA 95014
5 500 Oracle Parkway, Redwood Shores, CA 94065
6 1801 Varsity Drive, Raleigh, North Carolina 27606

Before we can add these to our marketing database, we need to break each address into its component pieces:

- Street Number
- Street Name
- City
- State
- Zip Code

We just need to come up with the logic to figure all this out.

Street number looks pretty easy – in each case it's everything up until the first space. (Can you think of an address where this might not be the case?) Street name seems to be everything from there until the first comma. City name is whatever is between the commas. State goes until we start seeing numbers, and zip code is what's left.

A good first step in a case like this is to locate the dividers. Here we want to find the first space, the first comma, and the second comma, which we know how to do using FIND().

A	B	C	D
1 **Addresses**	**Space 1**	**Comma 1**	**Comma 2**
2 1 Microsoft Way, Redmond, WA 98052-6399	2	16	25
3 1600 Amphitheatre Parkway, Mountain View, CA 94043	5	26	41
4 1 Infinite Loop, Cupertino, CA 95014	2	16	27
5 500 Oracle Parkway, Redwood Shores, CA 94065	4	19	35
6 1801 Varsity Drive, Raleigh, North Carolina 27606	5	19	28

The only tricky part is starting the search for Comma 2 at the position after the location of Comma 1

=FIND(",",A2,C2+1)

which is what you have to do in order to locate the *second* comma.

The only divider we still need is the space before the zip code. In every case it should be the *last* space in the string. However, it turns out that it's not that easy to find the last space in a string. It requires the use of array formulas, which we won't learn for several chapters. We'll have to find it a different way.

Now, if all zip codes were 5 digits, we'd know that space was at LEN(A2)-5. However, some zip codes are 10 characters (9 digits plus a hyphen). For instance, in Microsoft's address, the character at LEN(A2)-5 is a 2. This gives us a way to test for a 9-digit zip code:

=MID(A2,LEN(A2)-5,1)<>" "

(Alternatively, we could have checked whether that character was a hyphen.)

However, this doesn't produce the expected results:

	A	B	C	D	E
1	Addresses	Space 1	Comma 1	Comma 2	9 digit zip
2	1 Microsoft Way, Redmond, WA 98052-6399	2	16	25	TRUE
3	1600 Amphitheatre Parkway, Mountain View, CA 94043	5	26	41	FALSE
4	1 Infinite Loop, Cupertino, CA 95014	2	16	27	TRUE
5	500 Oracle Parkway, Redwood Shores, CA 94065	4	19	35	TRUE
6	1801 Varsity Drive, Raleigh, North Carolina 27606	5	19	28	FALSE

The Oracle address, for instance, is identified as having a 9-digit zip when clearly it doesn't. This means that when Excel looks at the character in position LEN(A5)-5, it's not seeing a space. How can that be?

It turns out that our worthless minion seems to have included extra spaces at the end of some of the addresses. One solution is to add a TRIM() to any calculation that involves knowing where the address ends. A better solution, however, is to get rid of the spaces altogether.

The simplest way to do this is to insert another column before column A, copy the addresses to it, and replace the old addresses (now in column B) with the formula

    =TRIM(A2)

After making column A narrow, so that we don't have to look at the addresses twice, things are finally behaving how we expect:

	B2	▼	f_x	=TRIM($A2)				
	A	B			C	D	E	F
1		Addresses			Space 1	Comma 1	Comma 2	9 digit zip
2	1 Microso	1 Microsoft Way, Redmond, WA 98052-6399			2	16	25	TRUE
3	1600 Amp	1600 Amphitheatre Parkway, Mountain View, CA 94043			5	26	41	FALSE
4	1 Infinite	1 Infinite Loop, Cupertino, CA 95014			2	16	27	FALSE
5	500 Oracle	500 Oracle Parkway, Redwood Shores, CA 94065			4	19	35	FALSE
6	1801 Vars	1801 Varsity Drive, Raleigh, North Carolina 27606			5	19	28	FALSE

We still need a formula to find the space before the zip code. In G2 that will just be

    =LEN(B2)-IF(F2,10,5)

Convince yourself that 10 and 5 are the correct things to subtract.

Now we're ready to extract our address parts. This will require us to be very, very careful. The important thing to remember is that to extract the characters from Start to End, we use MID(B2,Start,End-Start+1). We're going to apply this with tricky formulas for Start and End, and we'll need to make sure we get it right.

First, in H2 we'll find the street number. Since we're starting at the left, we can take the easy way out and just use LEFT() to get everything before (but not including) the first space:

=LEFT(B2,C2-1)

In I2, we'll extract the street name. It starts at C2+1 (because C2 is the location of the space before the street name) and ends at D2-1 (because D2 is the location of the comma after the street name). This means we need to MID() out (D2-1)-(C2+1)+1, which is D2-C2-1 characters:

=MID(B2,C2+1,D2-C2-1)

Similarly, in J2, we'll find the city. It starts at position D2+2 (because D2 is the position of the comma, and D2+1 is the space after the comma, and we need to skip past both) and ends at position E2-1. In this case we need to MID() out (E2-1)-(D2+2)+1, or E2-D2-2 characters.

=MID(B2,D2+2,E2-D2-2)

In K2, we'll extract the state, which starts at position E2+2 and ends at position G2-1:

=MID(B2,E2+2,G2-E2-2)

And in L2 we can simply use RIGHT() to get the zip:

=RIGHT(B2,IF(F2,10,5))

If we copy down, we've got our parsed data:

	G	H	I	J	K	L
	Zip Space	Num	Street	City	State	Zip
	29	1	Microsoft Way	Redmond	WA	98052-6399
	45	1600	Amphitheatre Parkway	Mountain View	CA	94043
	31	1	Infinite Loop	Cupertino	CA	95014
	39	500	Oracle Parkway	Redwood Shores	CA	94065
	44	1801	Varsity Drive	Raleigh	North Carolina	27606

It's not perfect. North Carolina is written out, while the other states are all abbreviated. Later on we'll learn techniques that can fix this too, but right now we don't know enough.

Looking back, the important steps were

1. check to see if the data needs cleaning (should have done this one first!)
2. reason through the dividing points between fields
3. locate the dividing points between fields
4. carefully extract the fields

This doesn't seem super impressive with only 5 addresses, but if we had hundreds or thousands, then this could save us a lot of time. Of course, if we had thousands of addresses, probably some of them would break our simple assumptions and we'd probably have to make our formulas even more complicated. Such is life.

CHAPTER *14*

THINGS ARE LOOKING UP

Some of Excel's most powerful techniques involve looking up data using some sort of index or key. This is something you should be pretty familiar with from your everyday life. Driving directions often include instructions like "take the third left" and "we're the fourth house on the right." To find dairy products in an unfamiliar supermarket, you look for the aisle labeled "Dairy." To locate the Pottery Barn at the mall, you look for "Pottery Barn" in the mall directory and find the store number listed next to it. Excel is very good at these sorts of tasks.

CHOOSE() Wisely

The CHOOSE() function takes as inputs a number and a bunch of choices and returns the choice specified by the number. So if the number is 1, you'll get the first choice, 2 you'll get the second choice, and so on. If the number has a fractional part, Excel will ignore it. If the number is too big (more than the number of choices) or too small (less than 1) you'll get an error.

Function	Value
CHOOSE(1,"a","b","c")	a
CHOOSE(2,"a","b","c")	b
CHOOSE(2.9,"a","b","c")	b
CHOOSE(3,"a","b","c")	c
CHOOSE(4,"a","b","c")	#VALUE!

CHOOSE() is not a very Thinking Spreadsheet function to use, as it "hides" a lot of information. If we had a spreadsheet with all the examples from the above table and we wanted to change it so that 1 resulted in "d", 2 resulted in "e", and 3 resulted in "f", we would have to go in and change every formula.

There's a very real sense in which the choices ("a", "b", and "c") are *parameters* of our spreadsheet. And one of the huge benefits of using spreadsheets is that they allow us to easily change parameters and see the effects of our changes. Therefore, a more Thinking Spreadsheet approach would be to store just one copy of the choices in (say) A1:A3, and then use the numeric input to tell Excel which cell to look at.

Then if we wanted to change the first output, we'd just change the value stored in A1 and every "choosey" formula would reflect the modification immediately. Thankfully, Excel has a function that does just this.

Look in the INDEX()

The simplest "lookup" is INDEX(), which returns the element from a specific position in an array. There are two ways to use INDEX().

The first involves a 1-dimensional array – that is, an array consisting of either a single row or a single column (or both, but that would not be a particularly clever use of this technique). It requires two inputs: the first is the array, and the second is a number specifying the position of the element you want.

So INDEX(A1:A10,1) would return the value in A1, as would INDEX(A1:J1,1). Likewise, INDEX(A1:A10,5) would return the value in A5, while INDEX(A1:J1,5) would return the value in E1. And INDEX(A1:A10,11) would give you a #REF! error, since there's no 11th element in the specified array.

The number you specify refers to the position in the array, not in the spreadsheet. This means that INDEX(A2:A10,2) returns the value from A3, which is the second element in the array A2:A10. It's a common mistake to expect it to return the value from A2, which is in row 2 of the spreadsheet. But that's not how INDEX() works. Be careful!

A more complicated (and less frequent) usage is to extract items from a 2-dimensional array. In this case you need to specify both a row number and a column number.

For instance, INDEX(B2:E5,1,1) returns the value from B2. INDEX(B2:E5,2,3) returns the value from D3 (that's the second row and the third column). INDEX(B2:E5,3) will give you a #REF! error, since Excel sees a 2-dimensional array and needs both coordinates to know which element to return.

Example: A Deck of Cards

A standard deck contains 52 cards. There are four suits (hearts, clubs, spades, and diamonds), and thirteen ranks (ace, 2, 3, 4, 5, 6, 7, 8, 9, 10, jack, queen, king). One way to represent all possible choices from four suits and thirteen ranks is to use a two-dial "odometer" in which the first dial runs from 1 to 4

    =IF(above_cell < 4, above_cell + 1, 1)

and the second starts at 1 and increases whenever the first dial rolls over

    =IF(left_cell < above_left_cell, above_cell + 1, above_cell)

After 4 * 13 = 52 rows, we'll have covered every possibility.

Number pairs aren't satisfying representations of playing cards, though. After setting up the "odometer" in columns A and B, let's list out the suits and ranks in columns E and F in a readable format.

	A	B	C	D	E	F
1	Suit #	Rank #			Suits	Ranks
2	1	1			Hearts	Ace
3	2	1			Diamonds	Two
4	3	1			Clubs	Three
5	4	1			Spades	Four
6	1	2				Five
7	2	2				Six

Now we can use INDEX() to get a description of each card. We'll use INDEX() once to get the rank, use INDEX() again to get the suit, and concatenate them with "of." The formula in C2 should be

=INDEX($F$2:$F$14,B2) & " of " & INDEX($E$2:$E$5,A2)

	A	B	C
1	Suit #	Rank #	Card
2	1	1	Ace of Hearts
3	2	1	Ace of Diamonds
4	3	1	Ace of Clubs
5	4	1	Ace of Spades
6	1	2	Two of Hearts
7	2	2	Two of Diamonds

Now imagine that you want to pick a random card. Just pick a random number between 1 and 52 (which we'll learn how to do later in the book), and INDEX() that number into C2:C53.

Finding Your MATCH()

Another common use of INDEX() is to retrieve data that meets some complicated condition. In this case, you'll first do some sort of computation to figure out which row (or column or both) you want, and then use INDEX() to retrieve the corresponding data. Quite often this computation involves MATCH().

Exact MATCH()

In some sense MATCH() is the opposite of INDEX(). Whereas INDEX() takes an array and a number and returns the value in the specified position, MATCH() takes a value and a one-dimensional array and (if possible) returns the index where you can find that value.

In order to confuse you, MATCH() takes the value as its first input, and the array as its second input. It also takes a third input, "match type." Initially, we'll always use match type equal to 0, which means "find the first exact match and return a #VALUE! error if there isn't one." Accordingly, we'll call this usage Exact MATCH().

For instance, in A2:A101 you might have a list of 100 people you like.

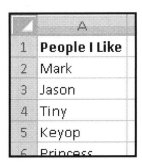

Imagine you want to find Zoltar in the list. The formula

=MATCH("Zoltar",A2:A101,0)

will return a number representing the index where Zoltar first appears in the list, and a #VALUE! error if he doesn't.

If you just want to know whether he's in the list, you could instead use

=ISNUMBER(MATCH("Zoltar",A2:A101,0))

which will be TRUE precisely when MATCH() returns a number, which happens precisely when he's in the list.

Like most other Excel tests for equality, MATCH() isn't case sensitive, so you'd get the same results if you searched for "ZOLTAR" or "zoltar." And MATCH() is happy with the same wildcards we learned for COUNTIF(). So you could check if you like anyone whose name starts with 'Z' using

=ISNUMBER(MATCH("Z*",A2:A101,0))

and you could check if you like anyone who has a 3-letter name starting with 'Z' using

=ISNUMBER(MATCH("Z??",A2:A100,0))

> In every one of these examples, where we didn't care *which* rows matched our criteria but only *whether* any rows did, we could also have checked whether an appropriate COUNTIF() was greater than 0. There's rarely just one way to accomplish something.

Of course you can Exact MATCH() numbers too, although you probably wouldn't use wildcards to do that.

Encyclopedia MATCH()

If your childhood predates the internet, you may remember "encyclopedias," which you can think of as highly-abridged, non-editable, hard-copy versions of Wikipedia. Despite leaving out most topics (my *Little Golden Encyclopedia*, for instance, barely had an article on "Professional Wrestling," let alone biographies of individual wrestlers or descriptions of various kinds of suplexes), these "encyclopedias" still contained too much information to fit in a single book.

The entries were listed in alphabetical order and broken into volumes. The scheme might look something like this:

Volume 1: A
Volume 2: America
Volume 3: Blossom
Volume 4: Chess
...

Each of the above lists the first topic in each volume. (Sometimes you might see the last topic listed as well, but you don't need to know the last topic to figure out which volume the topic you need would be in, so we'll leave it out.)

Now, let's say you need to find the article about "Athens." You'd have to go through a process similar to the following:

1. "Athens" comes after "A", so it's at least in volume 1.
2. "Athens" comes after "America", so it's at least in volume 2.
3. "Athens" comes before "Blossom", so it's before volume 3.
4. Therefore "Athens" has to be in volume 2.

In practice, if you had 50 volumes you'd probably check volume 25, conclude "it has to be before volume 25" then narrow it down by checking next volume 12, then 6, and so on. Nonetheless, the basic task can be described as "find the largest first topic that's still smaller than (or equal to) what we're looking for."

In Excel, if you specify a "match type" of 1 (or if you leave off match type altogether), you'll get precisely this behavior. Accordingly, we'll call this Encyclopedia MATCH().

	A	B	C	D	E
1	First Entry				
2	A		=MATCH("Athens",$A$2:$A$51,1)		
3	America				
4	Blossom				

As before, MATCH() always returns the position in the array, not the row. If you try to Encyclopedia MATCH() something that's less than the first element of the array, you'll get a #N/A error.

You can also Encyclopedia MATCH() numbers. MATCH(10,{1,10,100},1) and MATCH(15,{1,10,100},1) would both return 2, since in each case the second array element is the "largest element that's still smaller or equal to what we're looking for."

For this sort of MATCH() to work, the array you're matching into has to be sorted from smallest to largest. If you expect this array to change often, then use our "Sorting Without Sorting" technique and MATCH() into its result.

There is a third type of MATCH(), which you'll get if you specify a match type of -1. It's what you'd want to call "Reverse Encyclopedia," requires your array to be sorted largest-to-smallest, and finds the smallest array item that's at least as large as what you're looking for. We'll never use this in the book, but you might have reason to someday.

Technique: Sorting Numbers Without Sorting, Part 2

Recall from several chapters ago our "Sorting without Sorting" fundraising spreadsheet:

	A	B	C	D	E
1	**Person**	**$ Raised**		**Ranking**	**$ Raised**
2	Alex	60		1	90
3	Barbara	90		2	80
4	Chris	70		3	70
5	Doug	80		4	60
6	Ellen	40		5	40

At the time we complained that our automatically sorted version didn't include the names of the fundraisers themselves. Now we're ready to add that piece.

We know that 90 is the largest fundraised amount. We just need some way to tie that number back to Barbara. We can do it in two steps:

1. Figure out what row (in our original data) contained the amount 90.
2. Find the name that's in the same row.

For clarity we'll do each step in its own column, although if you were trying to build a presentable spreadsheet you might combine them.

	A	B	C	D	E	F	G
1	**Person**	**$ Raised**		**Ranking**	**$ Raised**	**Row #**	**Person**
2	Alex	60		1	90		
3	Barbara	90		2	80		
4	Chris	70		3	70		
5	Doug	80		4	60		
6	Ellen	40		5	40		

We want to find the row that contains the 90, so we'll be looking for an exact match. Therefore our formula in F2 needs to be

=MATCH(E2,$B$2:$B$6,0)

Copy this down and make sure it gives the correct results.

	A	B	C	D	E	F	G
1	Person	$ Raised		Ranking	$ Raised	Row #	Person
2	Alex	60		1	90	2	
3	Barbara	90		2	80	4	
4	Chris	70		3	70	3	
5	Doug	80		4	60	1	
6	Ellen	40		5	40	5	

Notice that this isn't the row of the spreadsheet, it's the row of the array B2:B6. And now, to find the element in the same row of A2:A6, we can use INDEX():

=INDEX($A$2:$A$6,F2)

and copy down.

	A	B	C	D	E	F	G
1	Person	$ Raised		Ranking	$ Raised	Row #	Person
2	Alex	60		1	90	2	Barbara
3	Barbara	90		2	80	4	Doug
4	Chris	70		3	70	3	Chris
5	Doug	80		4	60	1	Alex
6	Ellen	40		5	40	5	Ellen

Try changing the names and numbers, and you'll find that the sorted list updates automatically!

There's still one problem, though, which you may have discovered. This method doesn't do well with duplicates. In B2, increase Alex's fundraising to 70:

	A	B	C	D	E	F	G
1	**Person**	**$ Raised**		**Ranking**	**$ Raised**	**Row #**	**Person**
2	Alex	70		1	90	2	Barbara
3	Barbara	90		2	80	4	Doug
4	Chris	70		3	70	1	Alex
5	Doug	80		4	70	1	Alex
6	Ellen	40		5	40	5	Ellen

Suddenly, Alex appears in the rankings twice! While the rankings in column E handle the duplicate amounts fine, the MATCH() we used in column F is only smart enough to find the first time an amount occurs. It has no way of knowing that the second time it sees 70 it should find the second row that 70 appears in.

Again we're faced with a problem that we don't yet know enough to solve. Save this example again, because we'll eventually get there, I promise!

Technique: Sorting Strings Without Sorting

"Sorting numbers without sorting" relied on using either LARGE() or SMALL() to generate an automatically updated (and sorted) second version of the list. LARGE(list,1) gave us the biggest value, LARGE(list,2) gave us the second biggest, and so on.

Unfortunately, LARGE() and SMALL() don't work on text.

Think about an alternate approach using RANK() and MATCH(). You could first use RANK() to figure out the proper ordering. The item with RANK() equal to 1 would be the largest element, the item with RANK() equal to 2 would be the second largest, and so on. Then you could MATCH() the item with RANK() equal to 1, 2, and so on.

Unfortunately, RANK() also doesn't work on text. However, we can use

COUNTIF() to create equivalent functionality. Let's say we have a list of the last several presidents. One way of thinking of RANK() is "how many items come before this one"? And that's the sort of thing that's easy to calculate using COUNTIF():

	B2	▼		f_x	=COUNTIF($A$2:$A$7,"<"&A2)	
	A	B	C	D	E	F
1	**President**	**"Rank"**				
2	Carter	2				
3	Reagan	5				
4	Bush	0				
5	Clinton	3				
6	Bush	0				
7	Obama	4				

Notice two things. The first is that we have a duplicate entry in our list, which results in a duplicate "rank." We'll have to remember to account for this when we produce the ranked list.

Second, because we used < and not <=, the "rank" starts at 0. This was done deliberately because of the possibility of duplicates. If our list contained no duplicates, then a "rank" using <= would indeed start with 1. However, in our example the "first" value "Bush" occurs twice, which means that a COUNTIF() using <= would give it a "rank" of 2. If Bush appeared three times in the list, the name would have a "rank" of 3. Because our lives will be much easier if we know that the first element will always have the same value next to it, we used <.

Now we'll put the numbers 1 to 6 in column D for our sorted list. We'll use column E to find the correct row and then column F to look up the corresponding President. (In practice we might combine these steps into one column.)

	A	B	C	D	E	F
1	President	"Rank"		Rank	Row	President
2	Carter	2		1		
3	Reagan	5		2		
4	Bush	0		3		
5	Clinton	3		4		
6	Bush	0		5		
7	Obama	4		6		

As we mentioned above, the first item we want has the "Rank" of 0. Because we started counting at 0, we'll have to subtract 1 from the value in column D before trying to find its MATCH().

Alternatively, we could have used the numbers 0 to 5 in column D, but that would have made the spreadsheet more confusing to look at.

So, we want to exactly match D2-1 in column B. The formula for E2 should then be

=MATCH(D2-1,$B$2:$B$7,0)

and then copy down.

	A	B	C	D	E	F
1	President	"Rank"		Rank	Row	President
2	Carter	2		1	3	
3	Reagan	5		2	#N/A	
4	Bush	0		3	1	
5	Clinton	3		4	4	
6	Bush	0		5	6	
7	Obama	4		6	2	

Notice that there's an error when it tries to find the second item. This is

caused because the previous item appeared a second time. You can check
that if there was a third "Bush" then there would be another #N/A, too.

If you think about it, the error is a signal to repeat the previous item. This
means our formula for F2 can be

=IFERROR(INDEX($A$2:$A$7,E2),F1)

	A	B	C	D	E	F
1	President	"Rank"		Rank	Row	President
2	Carter	2		1	3	Bush
3	Reagan	5		2	#N/A	Bush
4	Bush	0		3	1	Carter
5	Clinton	3		4	4	Clinton
6	Bush	0		5	6	Obama
7	Obama	4		6	2	Reagan

Now we can starting trying some alternate histories. Change A6 to Gore:

	A	B	C	D	E	F
1	President	"Rank"		Rank	Row	President
2	Carter	1		1	3	Bush
3	Reagan	5		2	1	Carter
4	Bush	0		3	4	Clinton
5	Clinton	2		4	5	Gore
6	Gore	3		5	6	Obama
7	Obama	4		6	2	Reagan

And the list re-sorts itself as desired!

Technique: Scenario Analysis

Sometimes you need to create various "scenarios" and analyze them. For instance, you might want to plug various sets of assumptions (e.g. "low growth," "average growth," or "high growth") into the financial model for your alchemy operation and switch back and forth between them. You'd like to be able to somehow choose "low growth" and have the appropriate numbers appear in the model, then choose "high growth" and have all the numbers change.

Excel actually has a built-in scenario analysis tool that does this. It's on the Data ribbon, in the Data Tool section, under What-If Analysis.

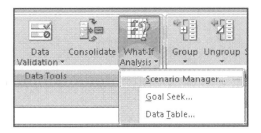

If you dig into its menus, you can name your scenario, specify the cells it changes, and put in the values you want those cells to have. You can construct as many scenarios as you like, and can use the "Scenario Manager" menu to switch between them.

Hopefully at this point you're ready to object that such a procedure doesn't sound Thinking Spreadsheet at all. It makes the scenarios opaque to the spreadsheet user, who has no easy way of knowing that they're there. If your goal is to allow the user to switch between different sets of assumptions, Excel already provides the means to do so in a completely transparent way, which is what we're going to do.

We'll call our scenarios Low, Medium, and High, and we'll assume that each scenario specifies GoldPrice, LeadPrice, Stores, and Employees. We'll write the names of the scenarios in row 1 and the labels for our variables in column A. Over to the right we'll put a cell for selecting the scenario, and for looking up two scenario-specific parameters we need.

	A	B	C	D	E	F	G
1		Low	Medium	High			
2	GoldPrice	500	1000	2000		Scenario:	High
3	LeadPrice	0.9	1	1.2		GoldPrice	
4	Stores	1	2	10		Employees	
5	Employees	1	5	30			

In G3 we want to find the GoldPrice corresponding to the scenario specified in G2. Of course we should create a formula that works in G4 for Employees as well.

All of our parameters are in the array A1:D5. We could use INDEX() to retrieve them if we only knew which row and which column. But of course we want the row that has GoldPrice in column A and the column that has Medium in row 1. That is, we need

```
=INDEX(   $A$1:$D$5,
          MATCH($F3,$A$1:$A$5,0),
          MATCH(G$2,$A$1:$D$1,0))
```

The first MATCH() finds the row corresponding to the parameter in column F, and the second MATCH() finds the column corresponding to the scenario specified in G2.

Copy the formula down to G4, and then try changing G2 to Low or Medium.

At this point you could do any analysis that depended on GoldPrice and Employees by getting them from G3 and G4. Then you could easily switch back and forth between scenarios by changing G2.

Incidentally, this would be a great place to use Data Validation on G2 to make the user select it from a list restricted to B1:D1.

If you need to add rows or columns for additional scenarios or variables, make sure to insert them in the middle, so that the references to A1:D5 will expand appropriately. Otherwise you'll have to modify the formulas.

VLOOKUP() and Friends

As we've seen, a common Excel task is to use MATCH() to figure out what row a certain value is in, then use INDEX() to return the value from a different column in the same row. This is so common that Excel provides a VLOOKUP() function that cuts out the middleman.

VLOOKUP() takes three inputs, with an optional fourth. The first is the lookup value you're trying to find. The second is a rectangular range of values. The third input is a column index number specifying which column you want values from.

The way to think about this is "find the row with the lookup value in the first column of the range and return the corresponding value from the specified column."

The fourth input is a Boolean telling Excel how to do the lookup. If you specify FALSE, Excel will try to find an Exact match. If you specify TRUE (or if you only give Excel three inputs), Excel will try for an Encyclopedia match. In this case the first column needs to be sorted from smallest to largest.

For instance,

    VLOOKUP(10,C3:F102,3,FALSE)

looks in the first column of the range (C3:C102), finds the first cell that exactly matches 10, and returns the corresponding value from the 3rd column (column E). If it can't find a cell that matches the lookup value, you'll get a #N/A error. If you give it a column number that doesn't exist, you'll get a #REF! error.

HLOOKUP()

HLOOKUP() is the transpose of VLOOKUP(). It tries to find the lookup value in the first row of the range you give it, then returns the corresponding value from the specified row. If you understand how VLOOKUP() works and you understand how to turn your head sideways, then you understand how HLOOKUP() works.

It's much, much more common to set up tables of data vertically and therefore it's much, much more common to use VLOOKUP().

There's also a LOOKUP() function, which is included mostly so that spreadsheets created during the Carter administration (back before VLOOKUP was invented) will still function. We won't be using it.

Example: Tax Brackets, Revisited

Being able to VLOOKUP() gives us another way to solve the income tax problem.

	A	B	C	D	E
1				Starting At	Marginal Rate
2	Income:	50000		0	10%
3	Tax Owed:			8,375	15%
4				34,000	25%
5				82,400	28%
6				171,850	33%
7				373,650	35%

Recall that last time we computed how much of our income fell into each bracket, used that to compute the tax from each bracket, and then took the SUM() to find the tax owed.

An alternative approach is to VLOOKUP() which tax bracket the income falls into. That allows us to figure out the marginal tax rate. But we'll also need to know how much tax needs to be paid on earlier brackets. We'll compute that in column F.

In the 10% bracket, there's no earlier income, so the tax Already Owed will be 0.

If you land in any of the other brackets, you Already Owe the tax liability from the bracket above you plus whatever was Already Owed before that bracket. If you land in the 15% bracket, you Already Owe all the tax in the 10% bracket. If you're in the 25% bracket, you Already Owe all the tax in the 15% bracket plus whatever people landing the 15% bracket Already Owe.

So the formula for F3 needs to be

   =E2*(D3-D2) + F2

The first term is the rate for the previous bracket multiplied by the income that falls into the previous bracket, the second term the Already Owed amount from the previous bracket.

Fill this down.

	A	B	C	D	E	F
1				Starting At	Marginal Rate	Already Owed
2	Income:	50000		0	10%	0
3	Tax Owed:			8,375	15%	837.5
4				34,000	25%	4681.25
5				82,400	28%	16781.25
6				171,850	33%	41827.25
7				373,650	35%	108421.25

Now, given any income, we can use VLOOKUP to find out its bracket, its marginal rate, and the amount already owed. Remember that the marginal rate only applies to the amount of income that falls in the bracket, which is why we needed to compute the "Already Owed" amounts. The math we'll need is

Tax = Already Owed + (Income - Start of Bracket) * (Marginal Rate)

We need to do an Encyclopedia match, so we can use the three-input VLOOKUP:

= VLOOKUP(B2,$D$2:$F$7,3) +
  (B2-VLOOKUP(B2,$D$2:$F$7,1))* VLOOKUP(B2,$D$2:$F$7,2)

Try different incomes and make sure you get the same results as before.

Technique: The Join

Using lookup functions, it's possible to "join" multiple datasets together. For instance, imagine that in the 'Friends' worksheet you have a list of your friends, along with the states they live in.

	A	B
1	Friend	State
2	Jenny	Virginia
3	Paul	California
4	Wendy	Massachusetts
5	Jay	Massachusetts
6	Brian	California

In the 'States' worksheet you have a bunch of state-specific data, like state flower and state motto and state boy band.

	A	B	C	D	
1	**State**	**Flower**	**Bird**	**Boy Band**	**Motto**
2	Alabama	Camellia	Yellowhammer	No Mercy	Audemus
3	Alaska	Forget Me Not	Willow Ptarmigan	Busted	North to
4	Arizona	Saguaro Cactus E	Cactus Wren	Ju-Taun	Ditat Deu
5	Arkansas	Apple Blossom	Mockingbird	Plus One	Regnat P

Let's say you'd like to store each of your friends' state flowers in column C, so that you know what to send them on their birthdays. A bad way to accomplish this is to look up that Virginia's state flower is the American Dogwood and then type that in C2.

Why bad? Two reasons. First, Excel is better at looking things up than you are, so this method doesn't play to your strengths. More importantly, if Virginia decides to change its state flower to the Amerika Touch-O-Pink, you'd have to go through your list and find every Virginian friend and change her Flower entry. Similarly, whenever your friends moved, you'd have to manually change their flowers.

A better way is to use VLOOKUP() to "join" the State-specific data to your list of friends using State name as the "key."

In C2 that's the formula

=VLOOKUP(B2,States!$A$1:$E$51,2,FALSE)

which you can then fill down.

	A	B	C
1	**Friend**	**State**	**Flower**
2	Jenny	Virginia	American Dogwood
3	Paul	California	California Poppy
4	Wendy	Massachusetts	Trailing-Arbutus
5	Jay	Massachusetts	Trailing-Arbutus
6	Brian	California	California Poppy

With this new setup, if you need to change a state's flower, you only need to change it in one place (the States worksheet) and your changes will automatically flow to your Friends list. Just as handy, if Wendy moves from Massachusetts to Washington, her State Flower will automatically update as soon as you change her State.

Technique: Multi-Column Lookups

Sometimes you'd like to do a "multi-column" lookup. For instance, maybe you want to find a row that has the value 1 in column A and also the value 5 in column B." (Obviously in this case you're looking for an exact match.)

Excel doesn't immediately allow you to do things like this, but there's an easy way to fake it:

1. Add a new column to the left of your lookup table
2. In this column, CONCATENATE() the two (or more) lookup fields, adding some sort of separator if necessary to avoid collisions
3. VLOOKUP() the concatenated values into the first column

For instance, imagine we have a table of mayors by city and state.

	A	B	C	D	E	F
1	City:	Austin		City	State	Mayor
2	State:	Texas		Atlanta	Georgia	Kasim Reed
3	Mayor:			Atlanta	Texas	Keith Crow
4				Atlanta	Illinois	Fred Finchum
5				Austin	Texas	Lee Leffingwell
6				Austin	Arkansas	Bernadette Chamberlain
7				Austin	Indiana	Doug Campbell

We'd like a formula that takes the city and state we've entered in B1:B2 and returns the appropriate mayor. This means we need to VLOOKUP() both the city and the state. Insert a column between C and D and call it CityState. What should we put in it?

A naive thing to do would be to CONCATENATE() City and State. This potentially causes collisions. You'd like to be able to distinguish between the (fictional) cities of Richmond West, Virginia, and Richmond, West Virginia. If there happen to be errant spaces in your data (always a possibility) both cities could concatenate to "Richmond West Virginia".

For that reason (and also to make things easier to read) it's always a good idea to use some sort of separator that doesn't appear in the original data. For instance, here we could use a comma

=CONCATENATE(E2,",",F2)

and fill down.

D	E	F	G
CityState	**City**	**State**	**Mayor**
Atlanta,Georgia	Atlanta	Georgia	Kasim Reed
Atlanta,Texas	Atlanta	Texas	Keith Crow
Atlanta,Illinois	Atlanta	Illinois	Fred Finchum
Austin,Texas	Austin	Texas	Lee Leffingwell
Austin,Arkansas	Austin	Arkansas	Bernadette Chamberlain
Austin,Indiana	Austin	Indiana	Doug Campbell

Now in B3, we need to VLOOKUP() the concatenated city-state into column D:

=VLOOKUP(B1&","&B2,$D$2:$G$7,4,FALSE)

Of course, you could easily extend this technique to three or more conditions.

Frivolous Example: The Prime Number Sieve

A prime number is a number that's divisible only by 1 and itself. (By convention, 1 is not considered a prime number.) So 2 is a prime number, since it's only divisible by 1 and 2 (itself). Similarly, 3 is a prime number. 4 is not a prime number, since it's divisible by 2.

We're going to use Excel to figure out all the prime numbers that are smaller than 100.

This is a task that you'd never ever ever consider using Excel for in the real world. In fact, it took me a fair amount of thinking before I even figured out a good way to do this. But (like our other frivolous examples) it illustrates lots of interesting concepts and techniques, so we'll press on.

Every whole number greater than 1 can be written as a product of prime numbers. (This is not a math book, so we'll ask you to just take this on faith.) Our method then relies on the following reasoning: if a number is not prime, then it must be divisible by a prime number that's smaller than it. Therefore, if we know all the first several prime numbers, the next prime number is the smallest number that's not divisible by any of them.

For instance, we mentioned above that the first two prime numbers are 2 and 3. This means the next prime number is the smallest number that's not divisible by 2 or 3, which is 5 (since 4 is divisible by 2). Similarly, the next prime number after that is the smallest number that's not divisible by 2, 3, or 5, which is 7. And so on.

This gives us a method to compute prime numbers. We know that 2 is the first prime number. If we make a list of all the numbers up to 100, we can use Excel to figure out the first one that's not divisible by 2, which ends up being 3. Then we can use Excel to find the first number that's not divisible by either 2 or 3. And we'll just keep going.

To start with, we'll put our potential prime numbers (all the numbers from 2 to 100) in column A. I left some space at the top because we're going to keep track of our primes going across to the right. And I filled in 2, which we know is the first prime. (The ... I just typed in to indicate that that's where the next primes will go.)

	A	B	C
1		**Primes:**	
2	**Candidates**	2 ...	
3	2		
4	3		
5	4		

What will we fill in column B? As we mentioned, the next prime (which we already know is 3, but let's pretend we don't) is the first number that's not divisible by 2. So if we use column B to test for "not divisible by 2," we can just look for the first number that passes. Recall that MOD() can test for divisibility. MOD(Number,2) equals zero precisely when Number is divisible by 2. So in B3 we'll use the formula

=MOD($A3,B$2)<>0

and fill down:

	A	B	C
1		**Primes:**	
2	**Candidates**	2 ...	
3	2	FALSE	
4	3	TRUE	
5	4	FALSE	

The first number not divisible by 2 is the first number with a TRUE in column B, which we can find using INDEX() and MATCH(). In C2 replace the dots with

=INDEX($A$3:$A$102,MATCH(TRUE,B$3:B$102,0))

The inner MATCH() function finds that the first TRUE is in the second cell in B$3:B$102 and returns 2. The INDEX() function then returns the second value in $A$3:$A$102, which is 3.

	fx	=INDEX($A$3:$A$102,MATCH(TRUE,B$3:B$102,0))				
	C	D	E	F	G	H
2	3					

Now we want to fill column C with a formula whose first TRUE will be the next prime number after 3. As we discussed above, that formula should be "not divisible by 2 and not divisible by 3." Well, "not divisible by 2" is already in column B. And not divisible by 3 we can compute the same way. So in C3 we'll put

=AND(B3,MOD($A3,C$2) <> 0)

Copy this formula down:

5	4	FALSE	FALSE
6	5	TRUE	TRUE
7	6	FALSE	FALSE
8	7	TRUE	TRUE
9	8	FALSE	FALSE

And now we're set. Copy the formulas in column C over to the right. In every column, the AND() makes our test mean "not divisible by the prime number at the top of this column, and not divisible by any of the smaller prime numbers either," which is exactly the test we need.

	A	B	C	D	E	F	G	H	I	J	K	L	M
1		Primes:											
2	Candidates	2	3	5	7	11	13	17	19	23	29	31	37
3	2	FALSE	FALSE	FALSE	FALSE	FALSE	FALSE	FALSE	FALSE	FALSE	FALSE	FALSE	FALSE
4	3	TRUE	FALSE	FALSE	FALSE	FALSE	FALSE	FALSE	FALSE	FALSE	FALSE	FALSE	FALSE

You can get as far as column Z before you'll start to get an error. (It turns out it's the "no more primes less than 100" error, so it's sort of by design.)

This is quite a bizarre thing to do with Excel. But it's also kind of cool. And if you understand it, you're well on your way to Thinking Spreadsheet.

Chapter 15

Indirection

So far we've been creating formulas with fixed references like "take the sum of the array A1:A10" or "add the value in C3 to the value in D4" or "VLOOKUP the value 'Thinking Spreadsheet' in the array F1:Z1000 and return the value in the 10th column." This is how most people use Excel.

However, Excel can also create references "on the fly." For instance, we can tell Excel to look in A1 to find a number of rows, look in A2 to find a number of columns, look in A3 to find text representing the top left cell, and take the sum of the resulting range. In this chapter we'll see how to do this and think about what it might be useful for.

ROW() and COLUMN()

The ROW() function tells you the row of a cell. If you give it no arguments, it returns the row of its own cell. If you give it a reference, like ROW(A1), it returns the row of the reference. If you give it an array, it (like other functions that aren't expecting arrays) pretends you gave it the top left cell.

There's also a COLUMN() function which behaves analogously.

In order to confuse you, there are also ROWS() and COLUMNS() functions, that expect arrays and return the number of rows and columns.

231

Function	Value	Why
ROW(C2)	2	Cell C2 is in the second row
ROWS(C2)	1	The array C2 contains only one row
COLUMN(C2)	3	Cell C2 is in the third column
COLUMNS(C2:F2)	4	C2:F2 contains 4 columns
ROWS(C2:F2)	1	C2:F2 contains 1 row

Finding an ADDRESS()

The ADDRESS() function takes a row number and a column number and returns the text representation of the cell at that location. So, ADDRESS(1,1) returns the text $A$1, and ADDRESS(3,10) returns the text $J$3.

By default ADDRESS() will $ both the row and the column. An optional third input allows you to change this. A value of 1 (or leaving out the third input altogether) will $ both the row and the column. A value of 2 will just $ the row, 3 will just $ the column, and 4 will $ neither.

An optional fourth input can be set to FALSE to specify the R1C1 style. You will never specify the R1C1 style. Finally, an optional fifth input allows you to specify a different worksheet. For instance, the formula

    =ADDRESS(1,1,4,TRUE,"Sheet1")

would return the text Sheet1!A1. Probably, though, if you ever use ADDRESS() you'll use the simple two-input form. In fact, probably you'll never use ADDRESS() at all.

OFFSET() References

Here's where it starts getting interesting. So far we've dealt with functions that return values. Sometimes numbers, sometimes Booleans, sometimes text, but always values.

OFFSET(), however, is a function that returns a *reference* to a cell or a range of cells.

As its name implies, this reference is *offset* from a different reference by a certain amount.

Getting a Cell

Its simplest usage takes 3 inputs. The first is a starting cell, the second a number of rows to move, and the third a number of columns to move. This usage of OFFSET() returns a reference to a cell.

Function	Refers To	Why
OFFSET(A1,2,3)	D3	D3 is offset 2 rows, 3 columns from A1
OFFSET(F5,-1,-2)	D4	D4 is offset -1 row, -2 columns from F5
OFFSET(A1,-1,1)	#REF!	Can't offset -1 row from A1

Unlike ADDRESS(), which returned a text representation of the cell's location, OFFSET() returns an actual reference to the cell. And whenever you use a reference as the whole of a formula, you simply get back the value of whatever is pointed to by the reference. So if you were to use the formula

=OFFSET(A1,2,3)

you'd get back the value of whatever is in D3, just as if you'd typed =D3.

You can also use this reference *as a reference*. For instance,

=ROW(OFFSET(A1,1,1))

returns the ROW() of B2, which is 2.

Getting a Range of Cells

If you give it two additional inputs, OFFSET() returns a reference to a range of cells. The two additional inputs are number of rows and number of columns, with the original OFFSET() as the starting cell.

For instance,

OFFSET(A1,2,3,2,2)

means "return a reference to the range whose top left cell is 2 rows and 3 columns from A1, and that itself has 2 rows and 2 columns." This means its top left cell is D3, and so the function returns a reference to D3:E4.

In this second usage it's common to use offsets of 0 and 0, like OFFSET(A1,0,0,2,2), which returns a reference to A1:B2.

You can also give it negative rows and columns, which makes the array extend up and to the left.

So

OFFSET(C3,0,0,-3,1)

returns a reference to C1:C3, the array starting at C3 with 1 column and "-3 rows." You should probably think of this as "3 rows, but in the opposite direction."

Technique: Sorting Numbers Without Sorting, Part 3

Recall where we left off last time.

	A	B	C	D	E	F	G
1	Person	$ Raised		Ranking	$ Raised	Row #	Person
2	Alex	70		1	90	2	Barbara
3	Barbara	90		2	80	4	Doug
4	Chris	70		3	70	1	Alex
5	Doug	80		4	70	1	Alex
6	Ellen	40		5	40	5	Ellen

In column E we used LARGE() to find the biggest amount raised, second-biggest amount raised, and so on. Then in column F we used MATCH() to identify which row that amount could be found in. Finally, in column G, we used INDEX() to select the name from that row.

The problem we discovered was that when we had duplicates, MATCH() would choose the same row for each of them. Now we finally know enough to fix this.

If the number in column E is not a duplicate (i.e. it's different from the number above it), then our current formulas work just fine. The only problem is when the number in column E is a duplicate. In that case we need to find the next MATCH() after the one we just found. How can we do this? By giving MATCH() a range that starts after the match we just found.

Look at the example above. The first 70 was found in row 1 (of the range B2:B6). This means that to find another 70, we need to look in the range that we'd get if we skipped row 1. This is a perfect job for OFFSET().

We'll want to OFFSET starting at B2, and we'll need to move by 1 row and 0 columns. The 0 columns will always be the case (since we want to stay in column B), but the 1 row is really because the previous duplicate was found in the first row. If it had been in the second row, we'd need to skip 2 rows. If it had been in the third row, we'd skip 3. And so on.

Since we need to produce an array to feed MATCH(), we'll have to specify a number of rows and number of columns as well. We only want 1 column, because we're only interested in the values in column B, so that's easy.

For rows, we'll need however many are left after the ones we skipped. Since there are ROWS(B2:B6) in all, and we skipped 1, we'll need ROWS(B2:B6)-1 of them. Of course, the 1 is really "the row of the previous match" and our formula needs to account for this.

Finally, when we're looking for the second 70 in what will work out to be B3:B6, we'll find it in the second row of B3:B6, which is the third row of our original array. This means we need to add 1 (again, "the row of the previous match") to our result so that the INDEX() in column G will be looking in the right place.

Let's put that all together. In F2, the formula will be

```
=IF(  E2=E1,
      F1+MATCH(E2,OFFSET($B$2,F1,0,ROWS($B$2:$B$6)-F1,1),0),
      MATCH(E2,$B$2:$B$6,0))
```

In other words, if this amount is equal to the previous amount, find the next time this amount occurs; otherwise, simply find the first time this amount occurs.

	A	B	C	D	E	F	G
1	Person	$ Raised		Ranking	$ Raised	Row #	Person
2	Alex	70		1	90	2	Barbara
3	Barbara	90		2	80	4	Doug
4	Chris	70		3	70	1	Alex
5	Doug	80		4	70	3	Chris
6	Ellen	40		5	40	5	Ellen

And we've done it. This is a difficult solution that involves several complicated concepts, so it might be worth thinking about for a while.

Technique: Dynamic Ranges

Another thing we can use OFFSET() for is creating *dynamic* ranges. For example, imagine that you have a rectangular array of numeric data in A1:D3, but you expect to keep adding more rows and columns of data.

	A	B	C	D	E
1	1	4	7	10	More
2	2	5	8	11	columns
3	3	6	9	12	soon
4	More	rows	later	on	

If you try to sum your data using

    =SUM(A1:D3)

then your formula will be wrong as soon as someone adds another row or column of data. (Unless they *Insert* a new column in the middle of the table, in which case the reference will automatically expand. It's pretty risky to rely on users to always do this, though.)

You could alternatively SUM() the entire worksheet

    =SUM($1:$1048576)

but this will give the wrong result if there's ever any data or analysis elsewhere on the page, and also it *obscures* the idea that the data is really in the top left of the worksheet.

A third alternative is to use OFFSET() starting at A1. How many rows will we need? As many rows as we have data, which we could count with

    COUNT(A:A)

as long as we don't expect any stray data further down in the column.

Similarly, we'd need

    COUNT(1:1)

columns, which means we could SUM() our data with

    =SUM(OFFSET(A1,0,0,COUNT(A:A),COUNT(1:1)))

Try this formula (somewhere that's not in column A or row 1) and see how it adjusts when you add or remove data.

Given the way this formula relies on "no stray data," it's probably best used when you have a worksheet whose only responsibility is storing data, with all analysis happening elsewhere.

Technique: Moving Averages

Sometimes when you're analyzing time series data (like stock prices) you want to smooth out some of the day-to-day volatility. One way of doing this involves "moving averages." Instead of looking at the value each day, you look at the average value over (say) the last 5 or 10 days.

We'll start with a spreadsheet with the daily closing price of the Dow Jones Index from 7/1/2008 to 7/1/2010. You can either collect the data yourself from a site like Google Finance or Yahoo Finance, or you can download it from ThinkingSpreadsheet.com.

	A	B
1		**Close**
2	7/1/2008	11382.26
3	7/2/2008	11215.51
4	7/3/2008	11288.53
5	7/7/2008	11231.96

If we knew that we wanted (for example) the 5-day moving average in column C, then in C6 we could just use the formula

=AVERAGE(B2:B6)

As we copy this formula down the row references will increase. Cell C7 will take the average of B3:B7, cell C8 will take the average of B4:B8, and so on. This is exactly what we want.

However, if we then decide that we'd rather have a 10-day moving average, we'll have to redo every formula. Instead we'll use OFFSET() to create a parameterized moving average that lets us change the average period as we want.

The only question is what we want to do when there aren't enough data points. There's no way to compute a 5-day moving average in C3, because there's only 2 days of data at that point. We have several options for these first few data-deficient points:

- leave them blank
- give them #N/A errors to signify "not available"
- let them have whatever errors the formula produces
- compute an average with as many points as possible
- use the daily value

Since these averages truly aren't available with our data, we'll use #N/A errors.

First, in C1, we'll put the size of our average. We'll start with a 5-day average:

	A	B	C
1		Close	5
2	7/1/2008	11382.26	

If we weren't worried about error-handling, we could simply use

=AVERAGE(OFFSET(B2,0,0,-C$1,1))

which can be understood as "take the average of the array that starts at B2, contains 1 column, and extends C1 rows backward." You can check that this causes a #REF! error in the first few rows (since it's trying to average a range that extends off the sheet) and calculates a 4-day average in row 5 (since AVERAGE() just ignores the text label in B1). As mentioned, we want to replace these with #N/A, so we'll do that.

What we need to check is that the previous 5 values in column B exist (which won't be the case if we're in row 2) and are all numbers (which won't be the case if we're in row 5). As a shortcut, we can just check that the first of those cells is a number. Irritatingly, that's the cell that's offset by -4 rows, not (as you'd naively think) -5 rows. This means we have to look at OFFSET(B2,-C$1+1,0). Putting it all together, our formula will be

=IF(ISNUMBER(OFFSET(B2,-C$1+1,0)),
       AVERAGE(OFFSET(B2,0,0,-C$1,1)),
       NA())

which we can double-click-fill down.

	A	B	C
1		Close	5
2	7/1/2008	11382.26	#N/A
3	7/2/2008	11215.51	#N/A
4	7/3/2008	11288.53	#N/A
5	7/7/2008	11231.96	#N/A
6	7/8/2008	11384.21	11300.49

A potentially simpler approach would have been to notice that the first time we can compute a 5-day moving average is in row 6, the first time we can compute a 10-day moving average is in row 11, and so on. So we could have tested ROW()>C$1. However, this is a fragile test that depends not only on our data but also where our data is located. If we added another row above row 1, then the 5-day moving average wouldn't start making sense until row 7, and our test would be broken! Our slightly more complicated formula is more robust to changes like this.

To quickly change to a 50-day moving average simply change the value in C1 to 50. Then insert a Line Chart to see how the smoothing looks:

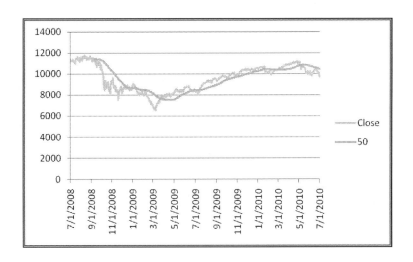

The moving average doesn't start for 50 days, thanks to the #N/A we used for missing values, and the moving average definitely smooths out the volatility. Try changing the period and see how the graph changes.

INDIRECT() References

Whereas OFFSET() created references starting with other references, INDIRECT() creates references directly from *text*. INDIRECT("A1") is a reference to cell A1 (on the current worksheet). INDIRECT("A1:C3") is a reference to the range A1:C3 (on the current worksheet). INDIRECT("Sheet2!A1") is a reference to cell A1 on worksheet Sheet2.

This is a way of creating "unmoveable" references. In general, references move when the cells they refer to move. If I have a formula that refers to cell

A1, then when I insert a row above row 1, my formula automatically adjusts to refer to A2. If I cut-and-paste A1 to C3, my formula automatically adjusts to refer to C3.

However, for cell-movement purposes, Excel sees the A1 in INDIRECT("A1") as text and will never change it. If you wanted to always refer to cell A1, no matter how the spreadsheet was cut and pasted and inserted, you could use an INDIRECT() reference.

Another use for INDIRECT() is to allow references to dynamically refer to different worksheets. The top cell in worksheet Sheet1 is Sheet1!A1, and an indirect way of referencing it would be INDIRECT("Sheet1!A1"). All that's left is to build that string on the fly:

	A	B	C	D
1	Worksheet	Value in A1		
2	Sheet1	=INDIRECT("'"&A2&"'!A1")		
3	Sheet2			
4	Sheet3			

Although it is very difficult to read from the screen shot, before the value from A2 we've concatenated a single quote "'". Similarly, the last string "'!A1" starts with a single quote. The effect of this is that the string we feed into INDIRECT() has the worksheet name single-quoted. If the worksheet name ever has a space in it, this is *required*. Since we want to allow for worksheet names to have spaces in them, we need to include it, even though it makes the formula fiendishly difficult to read on-screen.

An equivalent formula would be

    =INDIRECT(ADDRESS(1,1,4,TRUE,A2))

which uses ADDRESS to generate a text representation of "the cell in row 1 and column 1 of the worksheet named in A2." I find the first method simpler, but feel free to use either.

Technique: Data Segregation

Sometimes your data naturally "splits" itself into different worksheets. The most logical representation might involve a "2008" sheet, a "2009" sheet, and a new sheet for each new year.

In this case often you want a "Summary" sheet. And if each of the sheets has the same structure and an obvious name (for example, if the 2008 sheet is called "2008"), then you can use INDIRECT() to create functions that look at (for example) column A of each year and that naturally extend as you add sheets for additional years.

Big Scenarios

When we discussed INDEX() and MATCH() we saw how to make a table of "scenarios" and dynamically pull values from it. It's possible, though, that you might have really, really elaborate scenarios that don't easily lend themselves to being jammed in a table.

In that case you can give each scenario its own worksheet named after the scenario. As long as the rule to find the data is the same for each scenario-sheet, you can use INDIRECT().

For instance, if each scenario has its field names in A1:A100 and the corresponding values in C1:C100, you might end up doing the following:

	A	B	C	D	E	F	G
1	Scenario:	High					
2	GoldPrice	=VLOOKUP($A2,INDIRECT("'"&$B$1&"'!$A$1:$C$100"),3,FALSE)					
3	Employees						

Again, we single-quoted the sheet name in case it had a space in it.

Frivolous Example: License Plates

You've just landed a consulting gig with the Department of Motor Vehicles. They've decided (over your stern objections) to build a spreadsheet to keep track of license plate data. For each plate, they'll track the registered owner, address, car model, VIN, and lots of other data that will create a ruckus the first time someone loses a laptop containing it.

A license plate consists of 3 letters followed by 3 numbers. This means there are 26 * 26 * 26 * 10 * 10 * 10 = 17.6 million possible license plates, far too many to fit in a single worksheet.

However, only 1 * 26 * 26 * 10 * 10 * 10 = 676,000 of them start with A, the same number start with B, and so on. Therefore you suggest that all the license plates starting with A be tracked in a worksheet called 'A', all with B in a worksheet called 'B', and so on. For instance, the 'A' worksheet might start off like this:

	A	B	C	D	E	F
1	Plate	OwnerLast	OwnerFirst	Address	Brand	ModelYear
2	AAA000	Roberts	Robert	12 Broadway	Honda	2002
3	AAA001	Kennedy	Kenny	8374 112th	Hyundai	2009
4	AAA002	Scalia	Scales	94 Spring St	Oldsmobile	1984
5	AAA003	Bork	Bort	238 La Vista	Ford	1995
6	AAA004	Ginsburg	Ginny	2033 North Ave	Ferrari	2010

Assume that the data goes all the way to column Z. We'll need to create a summary sheet that allows DMV workers to input a license plate number and find out its associated information. Because we're dealing with DMV workers, we'd better first check to make sure what they input is a valid license plate.

What makes for a valid license plate? Well, it has to be 6 characters. The left 3 characters have to be letters. And the right three characters have to be numbers.

B2	▼	*fx*	=AND(LEN(B1)=6,
			LEFT(B1,3)>="AAA",LEFT(B1,3)<="ZZZ",
			RIGHT(B1,3)>="000",RIGHT(B1,3)<="999")

	A	B	C	D	E	F	G
1	Plate #:	CAX736					
2	Valid?	TRUE					
3	OwnerLast						
4	OwnerFirst						

(I put some extra carriage returns (Alt-Enter) in the formula to make it easier to read.) If you want you can Data Validation cell B1 itself using that formula.

Below this we need to retrieve some data.

To get OwnerLast, we'll need to VLOOKUP() B1 into the range 'C'!A2:Z676001. The range part doesn't depend on our license plate, but the worksheet name does. We can get its reference with

INDIRECT("'"&LEFT($B$1,1)&"'!A2:Z676001")

The only remaining issue is which column has OwnerLast in it. We can find this out with MATCH(), by trying to match A3 into the top row of the 'C' worksheet. We can retrieve that row with

INDIRECT("'"&LEFT($B$1,1)&"'!A1:Z1")

This results in the horrific-looking formula for B3

```
=VLOOKUP(  $B$1,
           INDIRECT("'"&LEFT($B$1,1)&"'!A2:Z676001"),
           MATCH($A3, INDIRECT("'"&LEFT($B$1,1)&"'!A1:Z1"), 0),
           FALSE)
```

which can then be copied down to B4 and beyond.

CHAPTER *16*

MATHEMAGIC

You're probably thinking that we already covered mathematics, back when we talked about addition and subtraction and multiplication and division. That's because you're not a mathematician. A mathematician would say what we already covered was arithmetic, and that "real" mathematics consists of other things we haven't learned yet.

At that point we'd punch the mathematician for being a jerk. However, Excel can do a lot of interesting "higher" mathematics that we haven't discussed yet.

I've Got the POWER()

There a mathematical operator we haven't mentioned, and that's the caret ^ which you use to "raise" a "base" to an "exponent." This is less common (and less common-sense) than the other four, which is why it's in the "math" part of the book rather than the "arithmetic" part of the book.

Whole Number Exponents

When the exponent is a whole number, exponentiation is the same thing as multiplying together *exponent* copies of *base*.

So, 2^3 is (by definition) the same as 2*2*2 ("three copies of the number two multiplied together"). Similarly 1.5^4 is (by definition) the same as 1.5*1.5*1.5*1.5 ("four copies of the number one and half multiplied together"). And 7^1 is the same as 7 ("one copy of the number seven multiplied together"). This "raising to a whole number" is the most common type of usage. It's also the easiest to understand.

As is often the case, Excel offers several ways of doing the exact same thing. The POWER() function takes two inputs and raises the first to the second. POWER(2,3) means exactly the same thing as 2^3. Use whichever you prefer.

Other Exponents

Another way of thinking about exponentiation is that you start with 1 and multiply by *exponent* copies of *base*. If you use 0 as the exponent ("multiply by 0 copies of *base*"), then POWER() outputs 1 for every base except 0. (0^0 is not mathematically defined and will give you a #NUM! error.)

Similarly, if the exponent is negative (e.g. "multiply by -2 copies of *base*") exponentiation *divides* by the corresponding copies. So, for instance,

    =POWER(3,-2)

is (by definition) equal to

    =1/POWER(3,2)

That takes care of negative integer exponents.

Finally, we need to worry about exponents that aren't whole numbers. At the risk of taking us too far afield, we'll just say that when the base is positive and the exponent is $1/n$, then the result is the nth root of the base – the number that when multiplied by itself n times gives you the base as a result. So the formula

    =POWER(5,1/3)

outputs the third root (or "cube root") of 5, which is the number that when multiplied by itself 3 times (i.e. "raised to the exponent 3") returns 5. You can check this by trying the formula

   =POWER(5,1/3)^3

Going any further down this path would turn this into a mathematics book. If you're interested in the subject, I suggest the Wikipedia article on "Exponentiation."

Order of Operations

How about order of operations? The convention is that ^ is performed even before multiplication and division. So 2*3^4 means 2*(3^4). As we mentioned before, you should always use parentheses. In the unlikely event that you are chaining together multiple ^ operators, they will be evaluated left to right. However, unlike + and *, the order of operations does matter, and so you should use parentheses here too. 2^3^4 evaluates as (2^3)^4, which (as you can check) is not equal to 2^(3^4). Use parentheses!

Square Roots

The square root of any (non-negative) number x is the number that when multiplied by itself gives the value x. As you just learned, you can find the square root of 5 with

   =POWER(5,1/2)

which you can check with

   =POWER(5,1/2)*POWER(5,1/2)

or

=POWER(5,1/2)^2

or even

=POWER(POWER(5,1/2),2)

Because taking square roots is not an entirely uncommon thing to do, Excel provides a SQRT() function, which takes one (non-negative) input and returns the square root.

Example: Extracting Digits

If you divide a positive integer by 10, the remainder will be the last digit of the number. For instance, 12 divided by 10 is "1 remainder 2." What if we want to extract other digits?

Let's take the example 4321. As we mentioned, the last digit is MOD(4321,10), which is 1. What do we get if take QUOTIENT(4321,10)? We get 432, which is all the digits except the last one. What if we take QUOTIENT(4321,100)? We get 43. And QUOTIENT(4321,1000)? We get 4.

We'll make one more observation that seems odd, but which will make sense in a minute. If you compute QUOTIENT(number,1), you'll always get back the number itself. That's because 1 divides evenly into every number.

Now consider the following formula:

=MOD(QUOTIENT(4321,POWER(10,2)),10)

As usual, we'll work from the inside out. POWER(10,2) raises 10 to the exponent 2, which equals 100.

This makes the next innermost function QUOTIENT(4321,100). As we saw before, when you quotient by 100 you chop off the last 2 digits, so this leaves

43. The last step is MOD(43,10), which we already saw gives us the last digit of 43, which is 3.

To sum up, we're chopping off the last 2 digits of 4321 and then returning the last digit of what's left. If we had used a *power* of 0 instead of 2, then we would have chopped off nothing and returned the last digit. If we had put in a *power* of 1, then we would have chopped off the last digit and returned the next-to-last digit. Each time we increase the value of *power* by 1, we're extracting one digit further to the left.

What if we put in too big a number? Since there are 4 digits in 4321, we should only get meaningful results up until *power* = 3. What if we put in a *power* of 5? Then POWER(10,5) = 100,000. QUOTIENT(4321,100000) equals 0. And then MOD(0,10) also equals zero. So trying to extract extra digits to the left just produces zeroes, which is (if you think about it) what you want to happen.

Exponentially Great

In mathematics there are certain constants that are considered important for some reason or another. One is *e*, which equals approximately 2.718281828. Looking at it, it doesn't look that important, does it? Well, it is, for reasons that you're welcome to explore on Wikipedia.

Usually what people care about is raising *e* to a power, which Excel implements as the function EXP(). It takes one argument, which is the power you want *e* raised to.

If you want just the value *e* itself, that's EXP(1). As you can check, EXP() always outputs a value that's bigger than zero. In fact, any POWER() of any positive number always outputs a value that's bigger than zero.

It's LOG()

The Excel function LN() is the "natural logarithm," which is the inverse of EXP(). That means that whenever EXP(value)=result, it will be the case that LN(result)=value. So, for example, LN(EXP(1)) = EXP(LN(1)) = 1.

Because EXP() only outputs positive numbers, LN() can only take positive inputs. You'll get a #NUM! error if you try to give it non-positive inputs.

LN() has a useful property:

LN(value1 * value2) = LN(value1) + LN(value2)

whenever value1 and value2 are acceptable (positive) inputs. In prehistoric times people used to use "log tables" to multiply numbers.

Percent Changes and Rates of Return

A somewhat common use for LN() is measuring rates of return. This is probably not what you're used to. Imagine that your salary increases from $50,000 to $51,000. Normally you'd think about this in terms of the percent increase, which is

(51000-50000)/50000 = 2%

However, you can instead look at the (similar) "log return," which is computed as

LN(51000/50000) = 1.98%

Why would you want to do this? Well, imagine that the next year your salary increases to $52,000. As a percent change it equals

(52000-51000)/51000 = 1.96%

while the log return is

$$LN(52000/51000) = 1.94\%.$$

Now, imagine that we were interested in the total change. We could compute it as

$$(52000\text{-}50000)/50000 = 4\%$$

But there's no simple way to recapture this from the two individual increases. You'd have to do the unwieldy calculation

$$=(1+2\%)*(1+1.94\%)\text{-}1$$

However, if you instead were working with log returns, you could just add them:

$$LN(52000/50000) = 3.92\% = 1.98\% + 1.94\%$$

If you have lots and lots of changes you want to accumulate, and you use LN() to compute the individual rates of return, then you can just sum them up and then use EXP().

For instance, if you have a sequence of stock prices in A1:A100 and their log returns in B2:B100 (so that B2 equals LN(A2/A1), and so on), then the total return is

$$
\begin{aligned}
A100 / A1 &= EXP(LN(A100/A1)) \\
&= EXP(LN((A100/A99) * (A99/A98) * \ldots * (A2/A1))) \\
&= EXP(LN(A100/A99) + LN(A99/A98) + \ldots + LN(A2/A1)) \\
&= EXP(SUM(B2:B100))
\end{aligned}
$$

where the next to last equality uses the "log of a product equals the sum of logs" rule.

Of course if you wanted to look at the total return over an interval of 100 consecutive days it would be easier to just compare the first price and the last price. But this "log return" trick allows you to easily compute the total return on "just Mondays" or "just dates divisible by 5" or "just the days that my patented stock-trading model says I should be in the market." Just SUMIF() the relevant log returns and use EXP() to convert back.

Log Ten

Why is the log function LN() and not LOG()? Because LOG() returns the *common logarithm*, which gives the inverse of POWER(10,Value). You can use LOG() to find the order of magnitude of a number.

Since POWER(10,0) equals 1, LOG(1) equals 0. Similarly, LOG(10) equals 1, LOG(100) equals 2, LOG(1000) equals 3, and so on. On the other end, LOG(0.1) equals -1, LOG(0.01) equals -2, and so on.

It's very unlikely you'll ever need to use this.

Trigonometry

Trigonometry, in case you've repressed all your memories of high school, is the mathematical study of triangles.

Angles

Most normal people think of angles in terms of "degrees." A right angle is 90 degrees, and a circle is 360 degrees. Mathematicians (and Excel) prefer to think of angles in terms of "radians," which means that (if you use Excel for trigonometry) you'll have to convert back and forth between the two. When you studied trigonometry you probably learned that 180 degrees equals PI() radians (approximately 3.14) and used that data point to do your conversions.

Excel wants to make your life simpler, and has DEGREES() and RADIANS() functions to convert back and forth between the two.

Trig Functions

Trigonometry is most commonly used to study *right triangles*, triangles one of whose angles is 90 degrees (or PI()/2 radians).

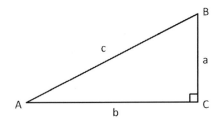

Consider the above triangle. If we have a spreadsheet where cell A1 contains the size (in radians) of the angle at A, then

=SIN(A1)

is the ratio a/c,

=COS(A1)

is the ratio b/c, and

=TAN(A1)

is the ratio a/b. We can produce the inverses by prefacing the functions with 'a'. For instance, if you knew a and c but not the angle at A, you could put the quantity a/c into cell A2 and then use

=ASIN(A2)

to find out the angle (in radians).

Trigonometry is a deeper field than we can do justice to in a section of a chapter in a book about spreadsheets. If you don't already know trigonometry, it's quite unlikely you'd ever want to use these Excel functions. And if you do learn it, they'll be waiting for you.

Counting Things

Surprisingly, *counting things* turns out to be mathematically difficult. Obviously when you can list them all in a spreadsheet, COUNT() can do the job pretty well. Sometimes, however, you'll need to count things that you can't fit into a spreadsheet. For instance, in our earlier license plate example, we "counted" (by reasoning it out) that there were

26 * 26 * 26 * 10 * 10 * 10

license plates consisting of 3 letters followed by 3 numbers. Excel has a number of functions that can help solve complicated counting problems.

The Factorial

The FACT() function computes the *factorial* of its input, which (if the input is a positive integer) is the *product* of all the numbers from 1 up to the input.

So FACT(4) is PRODUCT(1,2,3,4), which equals 24. And FACT(10) is PRODUCT(1,2,3,4,5,6,7,8,9,10), or 3,628,800. These get really big really fast, and if you try to FACT() too big a number, you'll get a #NUM! error.

If the input is not an integer, Excel returns the factorial of its INT(). So FACT(4.9) and FACT(4.1) are both the same as FACT(4). By convention, FACT(0) returns 1. And you can't factorial a negative number. If you try, Excel will give you a #NUM! error.

Sampling Objects

One thing that mathematicians often count is the number of ways to *sample objects from a set*. They'll usually draw two sets of distinctions:

1. Are you allowed to pick the same object more than once? If you are, they'll call it it "sampling with replacement" (because in a sense you "replace" the object after choosing it so it can be possibly chosen again). If not, they'll call it "sampling without replacement."

2. Does order matter? If you're trying to count the number of possible poker hands consisting of five playing cards, you probably don't care what order the individual cards were picked in – it doesn't matter whether the Ace of Hearts was the first card in the hand or the fifth, only whether it's in the hand or not. On the other hand, if you're trying to count how many different 5-song playlists you can make from your MP3 collection, order does matter, since a playlist that segues from "…Baby One More Time" into "Toxic" is (obviously) vastly different from one that does the reverse.

This makes for four possible combinations of "with replacement?" and "ordered?". We won't cover them all because some are difficult (both mathematically and Excel-wise) and not that useful.

We've already seen how to count samples *with replacement* where *order matters*. To count the number of possible 3-letter words, we just observe that there are 26 ways to choose the first letter, 26 ways to choose the second letter, and 26 ways to choose the third letter, which makes

POWER(26,3)

words. More generally, there are

POWER(Elements,SampleSize)

possible samples.

Permutations

The next simplest case is when we sample *without replacement* where *order matters*. These samples are called "permutations," and they're pretty easy to count.

For example, if you have 100 MP3s in your collection, and you want a playlist containing 5 distinct songs, you'd reason as follows:

> There are 100 choices for the first song. After each of those choices, there are 99 choices remaining for the second song. Then there are 98 left for the third song, 97 for the fourth song, and 96 for the last song.

This means the number of playlists is

PRODUCT(100,99,98,97,96)

which also equals

FACT(100)/FACT(95)

since FACT(100) is the product all numbers from 1 to 100 and then dividing by FACT(95) cancels out all the numbers from 1 to 95.

Rather than making you reason this through every time, Excel has a PERMUT() function which takes two inputs: the number of items in your set, and the number of items you want to sample. So you could count playlists simply using

PERMUT(100,5)

It's generally better to use PERMUT(), for two reasons. First, it makes clearer what you're doing, which is an important part of Thinking Spreadsheet. And second, FACT() chokes on large numbers. If you had 200 songs in your MP3 collection, you couldn't use

FACT(200)/FACT(195)

because those numbers are too big to FACT() and will give you #NUM! errors. However, PERMUT() is cleverer, and

PERMUT(200,5)

works.

Combinations

If we wanted to count possible 5-card poker hands (from a standard deck of 52 cards) in such a way that *order mattered*, we just saw there would be

PERMUT(52,5)

which equals

FACT(52)/FACT(47)

of them.

But for poker hands we don't care about what order the cards were dealt in. For example, we'd like to consider

Ace of Clubs, 2 of Diamonds, 5 of Spades, 7 of Hearts, 9 of Hearts

and

2 of Diamonds, 9 of Hearts, 5 of Spades, 7 of Hearts, Ace of Clubs

the same hand, which means that PERMUT() overcounts. By how much?

Well, how many ways are there to order 5 cards? There are

    PERMUT(5,5)

ways, which is the same as

    FACT(5)

Since PERMUT(52,5) counts every 5-card combination FACT(5) times, the actual number of combinations (if we don't care about the order) is

    PERMUT(52,5)/FACT(5)

which is the same as

    FACT(52)/(FACT(47)*FACT(5))

If we were mathematicians, we'd call this "52 choose 5," since we're *choosing* 5 elements from a set of 52. The Excel way of saying this is

    COMBIN(52,5)

More generally, COMBIN(Objects,SampleSize) counts the number of ways to sample *without replacement* when *order doesn't matter.*

Number Theory

You'll be surprised to learn that we've already toyed a bit with number theory, both when we studied the MOD() function and when we built our prime number sieve. Excel contains two more number-theoretical functions that you may someday find useful.

If you have a collection of positive integers, they have a *greatest common divisor*, which is the largest integer that divides all of them. Excel has a GCD() function to compute this:

Function	Value
GCD(2,4)	2
GCD(6,9,12)	3
GCD(4,5)	1

They also have a *least common multiple*, which is the smallest integer that is *divisible* by every one of them. Accordingly, Excel also has a LCM() function:

Function	Value
LCM(2,4)	4
LCM(6,9,12)	36
LCM(4,5)	20

In all likelihood, this is another Excel feature that you'll never use. Or perhaps you'll surprise me.

CHAPTER *17*

FINANCE

Excel is a fantastic tool for financial analysis. Given the tools and techniques we've already discussed, you should have no problems building a spreadsheet that (for example) models your company's sales over the next three years.

Along these lines, Excel contains a huge number of specialized functions for doing more elaborate finance work. There's a NPV() function for computing the Net Present Value of a stream of cashflows. There's a DURATION() function to compute the duration of a bond. There's a YIELD() function to compute a bond's yield.

Unfortunately, exploring these functions would require a substantial detour through the mechanics and mathematics of finance, which would lead us too far astray from the central concepts of Thinking Spreadsheet. If you're a king of finance who needs to use Excel to compute payments for annuities or nominal interest rates, then you'll need to spend a few hours perusing Excel's help documentation on "Financial functions." Luckily, all the principles you've learned here will still apply!

CHAPTER *18*

THAT'S SO RANDOM!

What is randomness? What is probability? These are surprisingly deep and complicated questions, more appropriate for a philosophy book than a spreadsheet book. Nonetheless, before we talk about using Excel to model randomness and probability, we should probably give it a shot.

The Basics of Randomness

When we say **random**, you should think *unpredictable*. Common examples of randomness are flipping a coin, rolling dice, and spinning a roulette wheel.

Although each of these is "unpredictable," that doesn't mean we don't know anything about them. We can quantify them with **probabilities** that indicate the likelihood of certain **events**.

For instance, we consider a coin "fair" if the probabilities of the events "coin flip lands Heads" and "coin flip lands Tails" are both 50%.

In this book we'll take a "frequentist" approach to probability, in which probability represents *the distribution of outcomes you'd see if you repeated the random process a large number of times*. Although there are more modern (and better) approaches, ours has the dual benefits that it's *easy to understand* and *good enough for our purposes*. As always, spend the day with Wikipedia ("Probability interpretations") if you want to know more.

Accordingly, when we say the probability that a coin flip lands Heads is 50%, we mean something along the lines of "if you were to flip the coin an enormous number of times, 50% of the flips would turn up Heads."

There are situations where this interpretation doesn't make a whole lot of sense. When proposing a project to your boss, you might tell her there's a "75% chance of success." Since the project will only occur once, it's hard to apply our frequentist approach. In this case we'll cheat and think of your statement as "if you were to execute a large number of very similar projects, about 3/4 of them would succeed."

Again, this isn't a philosophy book, and we shouldn't spend too much time on the details of "what probability means." But keep these ideas in mind as we talk about randomness.

Random or Pseudo-Random?

As we mentioned when we created our pseudo-random number generator, Excel can't actually generate random numbers. It generates only pseudo-random numbers, numbers that "look" random but are actually completely deterministic. For almost any Excel-sized application, you shouldn't notice the difference, and so we'll refer to what Excel produces as "random numbers," knowing that (in a technical sense) they really aren't.

Volatility and Recalculation

Random functions are volatile – every time you recalculate a spreadsheet that contains random functions, they will pick new (random) values. (We saw this behavior earlier when we discussed the NOW() function.) This means that if you try to recreate the book's examples on your computer, they won't look exactly the same as they do in the book. Anywhere the book shows one random number, your computer will surely show a different one. Don't feel like this means you're doing something wrong (or like the book is doing something wrong).

Generally, whenever you change the contents of a cell, Excel will recalculate your entire spreadsheet. If your spreadsheet contains random-number functions, they'll all generate new random numbers each time you change something in your spreadsheet, even something unrelated.

If you'd like to disable this behavior, there's a setting under Office Button - Excel Options - Formulas:

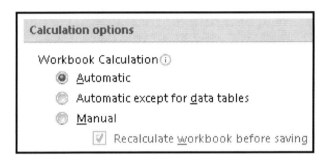

Changing this to manual means that your spreadsheet won't ever recalculate itself unless you tell it to. This is a *dangerous* thing to do, as it breaks the Thinking Spreadsheet assumption that changes in one part of your spreadsheet are automatically reflected in other parts.

It might be the case that you're building a spreadsheet with thousands of random numbers and many formulas depending on them, in which case every change you make to the formulas is accompanied by a severe lag as the random numbers regenerate and your formulas update.

If this is the case, the Thinking Spreadsheet thing to do is to change calculation to Manual while you're building the spreadsheet and then change it back to Automatic as soon as you're done.

When you're in Manual mode, pressing the F9 key will recalculate the entire workbook. Shift-F9 will recalculate only the current worksheet. And editing a cell's formula (which can be as simple as F2 and Enter) will recalculate just that cell.

Typically, though, you'll leave your spreadsheets set to Automatic recalculation, and you'll only use F9 when you want a fresh set of random numbers.

Uniform Randoms

The simplest random function in Excel is RAND(), which takes no inputs and produces a random number uniformly chosen from the interval [0,1). This means that the number will be greater than or equal to 0, that it will be less than 1, and that the probability the number falls within any interval is equal to the length of that interval.

So the probability the number is between 0.5 and 0.75 is 0.25, or one-fourth. According to our "frequentist" understanding, this means that if you generate "a lot" of random numbers using RAND(), about 25% of them should lie between 0.5 and 0.75.

For instance, here's a histogram of 1000 numbers generated with RAND(), bucketed into deciles:

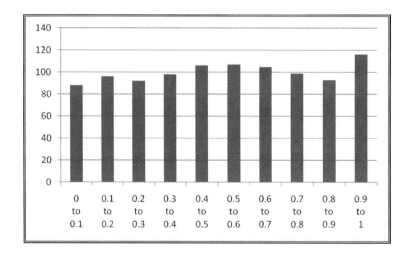

Approximately 100 numbers (10% of 1000) fall into each of the 10 equally-sized buckets. Of course, randomness means that some will contain more and some less. Apparently 1000 doesn't count as "a lot" for these purposes.

By simply multiplying (or dividing) and adding (or subtracting), you can get uniform random numbers from any finite interval. Here's some examples:

Random	Interval
RAND()	0 to 1
5*RAND()	0 to 5
1+RAND()	1 to 2
1+(5*RAND())	1 to 6
RAND()/5	0 to 0.2
RAND()-1	-1 to 0
(RAND()-1)/5	-0.2 to 0

In these cases the probability of falling into a certain interval no longer equals the *absolute* size of the interval, but rather its size as a fraction of the entire interval.

For instance, the output of 5*RAND() will be between 1 and 3 (which represents 40% of the interval from 0 to 5) whenever RAND() is between 0.2 and 0.6, which is 40% of the time.

Random Integers

There's a second basic random function that's frequently useful, and that's RANDBETWEEN(), which takes two integer arguments and returns any integer between them, all with equal probability.

So RANDBETWEEN(1,4) returns either 1, 2, 3, or 4, each with 25% probability. Similarly, RANDBETWEEN(-1,1) returns either -1, 0, or 1, each with probability 1/3.

Example: Rolling Dice

When you roll a (fair) die, you get one of the numbers 1 to 6, with an equal chance of each. Thinking about it this way makes it easy to simulate the roll of a die in Excel:

   =RANDBETWEEN(1,6)

What if you want to roll two dice? The wrong thing to do is

   =2*RANDBETWEEN(1,6)

which is the same as rolling one die and doubling the result. This gives you a 1/6 chance of 2, a 1/6 chance of 4, and so on. The correct way is

   =RANDBETWEEN(1,6)+RANDBETWEEN(1,6)

so that each "roll" is chosen separately from the other. You can check that this always produces a value between 2 and 12, just like rolling two dice does.

Frivolous Example: Dungeons and Dragons

Dungeons and Dragons is a fantasy game where you pretend you're Cruneiros Spiritforge, the level 23 half-dwarf Necromancer, and that you're on a crusade to raid the Hidden Tower of the Lost Spider Queen in order to find some amulet, or maybe a kidnapped princess, or possibly a potion of quickness.

Part of playing this game involves rolling oddly shaped polyhedral dice. The instructions usually say things like "if 2d8+4 is greater than 10, you've slain the dragon." Here 2d8+4 means "roll two 8-sided dice, sum the results, and add four."

Unfortunately, your little brother likes to swallow the dice, which are expensive to replace. Fortunately, you know enough Thinking Spreadsheet to build your own virtual dice.

We're going to build a spreadsheet that accepts criteria like 2d4+8 (roll two 4-sided dice, add the results together, and add 8 more) and d6-1 (roll a six-sided die and subtract one from the result) and produces a random number equivalent to the same roll.

Tackling an open-ended task like this requires making several assumptions, and we'll make the following ones:

- The criterion will consist of the number of dice (which can be omitted if it's 1), the letter d, the number of sides on the dice, and an optional factor to add or subtract
- There's at least one die, but no more than 10.
- All the dice have the same number of sides.

To start with, let's label a cell to enter the criterion:

	A	B
1	Criterion:	2d4+6

I put in a test value of 2d4+6 to work with. As a first step, we'll figure out how many dice there are. Given our assumptions, we want the number (if there is one) to the left of the 'd'. So a good start would be to find the location of the 'd'. Given our assumptions, there's exactly one 'd', so FIND() should work:

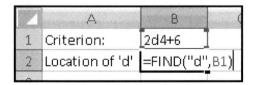

	A	B
1	Criterion:	2d4+6
2	Location of 'd'	=FIND("d",B1)

How do we know if there's anything to the left of 'd'? We can simply check that its location is greater than 1.

	A	B	C	D
1	Criterion:	2d4+6		
2	Location of 'd'	2		
3	# of dice	=IF(B2>1,VALUE(LEFT(B1,B2-1)),1)		

This seems like a mouthful, but it's not too bad if we think about it. If 'd' is not the first character of the criterion, compute the numeric value of everything to its left. (We have to subtract 1 from the location of 'd' so that the LEFT() function doesn't grab the 'd' as well.) Otherwise (according to our assumptions) there's only one die.

Next we need to figure out how many sides the dice have. That's the numeric value of everything after the 'd' until we see a '+', a '-', or the end of the string.

So a good next step is to check if there's a plus or a minus in the criterion. If there is, we'll also want to know where it is. First, we'll check for the location of '+'. If we can't find it, we'll check for the location of '-'. If we can't find that, we'll keep the error. (Recall that FIND() will return an error if it can't find what you ask it to.)

	A	B	C	D	E
1	Criterion:	2d4+6			
2	Location of 'd'	2			
3	# of dice	2			
4	Location of +/-	=IFERROR(FIND("+",B1),FIND("-",B1))			

Now we're ready to extract the size of the dice. We'll start at position B2+1. If there's a number in B4, we'll go until we get to B4-1, which means extracting (B4-1)-(B2+1)+1 or B4-B2-1 characters. If there's an error in B4 (which means no plus or minus), we'll go until we get to LEN(B1), which means

LEN(B1)-(B2+1)+1 or LEN(B1)-B2 characters.

> Recall that the +1 is because we need to include both the starting and stopping points. If you take characters 2 to 4, that's 4-2+1 characters. If you take just character 3, that's 3-3+1 characters. It's always good to double check your formulas by reasoning through them like this.

We can handle this again using IFERROR():

	A	B	C	D	E	F
1	Criterion:	2d4+6				
2	Location of 'd'	2				
3	# of dice	2				
4	Location of +/-	4				
5	Dice size	=VALUE(MID(B1,B2+1,IFERROR(B4-B2-1,LEN(B1)-B2)))				

At last we have to figure out what to add. If there's an error in B4, we add nothing. Otherwise, we have to add the numeric value of the rest of the string starting at the position in B4.

We can use RIGHT() for this. But how many characters? Just as above, we'll need LEN(B1)-B4+1 characters, since we want all characters starting at the position in B4, ending at the last position LEN(B1), and including both starting and stopping points:

	A	B	C	D	E
1	Criterion:	2d4+6			
2	Location of 'd'	2			
3	# of dice	2			
4	Location of +/-	4			
5	Dice size	4			
6	What to add:	=IFERROR(VALUE(RIGHT(B1,LEN(B1)-B4+1)),0)			

To check we've got everything correct so far, let's try changing the criteria to cover our different use cases:

	A	B
1	Criterion:	3d12-6
2	Location of 'd'	2
3	# of dice	3
4	Location of +/-	5
5	Dice size	12
6	What to add:	-6

	A	B
1	Criterion:	d145
2	Location of 'd'	1
3	# of dice	1
4	Location of +/-	#VALUE!
5	Dice size	145
6	What to add:	0

Now we're ready to simulate our dice. The number of dice can vary, but we've assumed it's never more than 10. So we'll simulate 10 dice and then ignore the ones we don't need.

Each die is a RANDBETWEEN(1,$B$5), so put this formula in D2:D11.

Finally, we'll need to add up B3 of them and add an extra B6. This is a perfect use for OFFSET().

	A	B	C	D
1	Criterion:	2d4+6		
2	Location of 'd'	2		1
3	# of dice	2		4
4	Location of +/-	4		4
5	Dice size	4		1
6	What to add:	6		1
7				4
8	Roll:	=SUM(OFFSET(D2,0,0,B3,1),B6)		

And we're done! Try changing the criteria around and refreshing the sheet.

Technique: Discrete Distributions

Both RAND() and RANDBETWEEN() assign equal probability over their ranges. RAND() is equally likely to return any number in $[0,1)$, and RANDBETWEEN() is equally likely to return any integer between its bounds. But sometimes you don't want equal probabilities.

Bernoulli Trials

The simplest example is a **Bernoulli Trial**. It equals 1 with some probability p and 0 with the remaining probability $1 - p$. If $p = 0.5$ (which means there's a 50% chance of a 0 and a 50% chance of a 1) that's the same as

RANDBETWEEN(0,1)

However, if we want a 90% chance of 1 and a 10% chance of 0, this won't work. Instead, observe that RAND() has a 90% chance of being less than 0.9. This means that

IF(RAND()<0.9,1,0)

has probability 0.9 of equaling 1 and probability 0.1 of equaling 0, as desired. By replacing the 0.9 with any other number (between 0 and 1) we can get Excel to produce a Bernoulli Trial with whatever probability we want.

More Elaborate Discrete Distributions

Imagine you want to generate random numbers that behave as follows:

Value	Probability
1	50%
2	25%
3	15%
4	10%

Notice that the probabilities add up to 100%, which is necessary for something to be a random variable. It turns out that with a little cleverness we can generate this distribution using RAND().

The key observation is that RAND() has a 50% probability of being between 0 and 0.5, a 25% probability of being between 0.5 and 0.75, a 15% probability of being between 0.75 and 0.9, and a 10% probability of being between 0.9 and 1. This allows us to use VLOOKUP() to turn a number chosen with RAND() into a number from this (or any other) distribution with only finitely many outcomes.

Because Excel can't store arbitrarily many decimal points, it turns out that even RAND() has only finitely many possible outcomes, since there are only finitely many numbers between 0 and 1 with fewer than (say) 15 decimal places. Nonetheless, because RAND() is intended to approximate a uniform distribution that can pick any of the uncountably many numbers between 0 and 1, we pretend that the random numbers produced by RAND() are not from a discrete distribution.

To start with, let's input our probability table into Excel. Because we're going to VLOOKUP() into it, and VLOOKUP() looks for matches in the first column, we'll leave an extra "Lookup" column to start:

	A	B	C
1	Lookup	Value	Probability
2		1	50%
3		2	25%
4		3	15%
5		4	10%

What should we put in the lookup column? We're obviously not counting on exact matches (since RAND() can produce all sorts of numbers) which means we'll need to use Encyclopedia-match in our VLOOKUP(), which (you remember) will find the row with the largest value less than or equal to the key.

As a first guess, you might think the value in A2 needs to be 50%. But think about what happens when RAND() produces 0.1. We'll want VLOOKUP() to choose the first row, which means that the value in A2 has to be *less than or equal to* 0.1. If you think about it further, you'll realize that the value in A2 has to equal 0. For Encyclopedia-match to work, each Lookup value in column A has to mean "smallest value of RAND() that corresponds to this outcome."

Since we want a 50% probability of choosing value 1, the value in A3 needs to be the value in A2 plus 50%. Similarly, the value in A4 needs to be the value in A3 plus 25%.

So after inputting a 0 in A2, we'll need the formula

=A2+C2

in A3, which we can then copy down:

	A	B	C
1	Lookup	Value	Probability
2	0	1	50%
3	50%	2	25%
4	75%	3	15%
5	90%	4	10%

We'll put our RAND() numbers in column E and our discrete randoms in column F.

First, in E2 put the formula

=RAND()

In F2 we'll want to VLOOKUP() the value from E2 into the lookup table A2:C5, returning what's in column B, which is the second column. For Encyclopedia-match, we omit the fourth variable:

=VLOOKUP(E2,$A$2:$C$5,2)

In practice you'd probably do both the preceding steps at the same time using VLOOKUP(RAND(),$A$2:$C$5,2).

Fill down to row 101 so that we've got 100 discrete randoms, and then we can use COUNTIF() to look at their distribution.

fx	=COUNTIF($F$2:$F$101,H2)				
D	E	F	G	H	I
	RAND()	**Discrete**		Output	Count
	0.284291	1		1	46
	0.912219	4		2	27
	0.988535	4		3	16
	0.75988	3		4	11

You can see that they roughly correspond with our specified probabilities. Your numbers won't be exactly the same as these, but they should be close.

Try changing the parameters of the discrete distribution, making sure the probabilities still add up to 100%.

Technique: Random Ordering

You have five students with book reports to present, and you want to choose a random order for them to present in.

There's a simple way to do this. Just use RAND() to generate a random number for each student. Whoever gets the largest number goes first, the second-largest goes second, and so on. Since everyone is equally likely to have the largest number, everyone has an equal chance of going first.

To start, we'll list the names in column A, and put random numbers in column B.

	A	B
1	**Name**	**RAND()**
2	Alex	0.311113
3	Bob	0.760859
4	Charles	0.150459
5	David	0.972352
6	Eddie	0.853863

Then in column C we can use RANK() to figure out the order:

=RANK(B2,B$2:B$6)

	A	B	C
1	**Name**	**RAND()**	**Order**
2	Alex	0.368924	4
3	Bob	0.184471	5
4	Charles	0.940452	2
5	David	0.624107	3
6	Eddie	0.982307	1

(Notice how the random numbers all recalculated when I entered the RANK() formula.)

While it's technically possible that RAND() might produce duplicates and create a tie, it's so astronomically unlikely that it's not worth worrying about.

Sampling Without Replacement

This technique also is a way to "sample without replacement." Imagine that you want to randomly choose three of your ten students to clean the erasers. You can't simply use RANDBETWEEN(1,10) three times, because you might choose the same student twice (or even three times).

Instead you can randomly order them and then take the first three. That is, give each student a RAND() and choose the three students with the largest ones. Obviously this method can be used for any number of samples.

Technique: Fake Data

One simple use for random functions is to make up fake data for testing. For example, let's say you're building a spreadsheet to model a bank's "Keep the Pennies" program. You'd like to test it with lots of data, but you don't want to type out hundreds of grocery bill amounts.

If you're anything like me, your (rounded) grocery bill could be anything from RANDBETWEEN(45,95), depending on what's on sale that week. If you wanted cents too, you could use RANDBETWEEN(4500,9500)/100.

You can also choose random dates

    =DATE(2010,1,1)+RANDBETWEEN(0,365)

random Christmases

    =DATE(RANDBETWEEN(1950,2050),12,25)

random times

    =TIME(0,0,0)+RAND()

random grade point averages

=RANDBETWEEN(0,40)/10

and pretty much anything else you can imagine. Of course, nothing can substitute for well-thought-out test cases, but fake random data is quick and can even point out cases you might not have considered.

CHAPTER *19*

STATISTICS

Rather than trying to figure out our own definition of statistics, we'll crib Wikipedia's:

> Statistics is the formal science of making effective use of numerical data relating to groups of individuals or experiments. It deals with all aspects of this, including not only the collection, analysis and interpretation of such data, but also the planning of the collection of data, in terms of the design of surveys and experiments.

This is not a book about statistics, so we won't go into as much detail as we would if I were training you to be a statistician, which I'm not. Instead, we'll cover some of the most useful basics and point you in the right directions to go deeper if you're so inclined.

The Basics of Descriptive Statistics

The simplest use of statistics is to *describe* data, which we'll give the unsurprising name "descriptive statistics." We've already seen many examples of this, when we learned how to take the SUM(), the AVERAGE(), the MAX(), and the MIN() of large datasets.

Obviously, in each case the "most descriptive" way to communicate the data is to provide the entire dataset. However, this is usually impractical, both because large datasets aren't easily communicated (for example, a collection of millions of survey responses doesn't fit well into the body of an email) and because large datasets aren't easily comprehended (for example, it's hard to make sense of a raw collection of millions of survey responses).

Statistics solve both of these problems. Where thousands of raw surveys might be too much information, "percent of respondents who rated their care good or excellent" is easily communicated and understood. While you'd probably never want to know every SAT score in the country, you might want to know how many test-takers got perfect scores and how many got the lowest score possible.

One Set of Data

First we'll look at statistics for describing one set of data in isolation.

Measures of Central Tendency

Perhaps the most common descriptive statistics are used to identify a value that's in some way "central" to your data. One popular statistic is the **mean**, which you probably know as the AVERAGE(). It's the SUM() of your data divided by the COUNT() of your data.

Its less common cousin is the **median**. If you line your data up from smallest to largest, the MEDIAN() is the *middle* value. If you have an even number of data points, in which case there are *two* "middle" values, the median is halfway between them.

The median is better than the mean at ignoring "outliers." For instance, if you have the five data points

1,2,3,4,5

then (as you can check) the mean and median are both equal to 3. If the data were instead

   1,2,3,4,50

then the median would still be 3 but the mean would jump to 12. Which is a better description of the data depends on the phenomenon the data are supposed to capture. If you're trying to estimate the "typical" value (for instance, if you had data representing people's incomes) then you'd probably want to use the median (so that, for instance, a city's handful of billionaire playboys doesn't throw your measure totally off). On the other hand, if the amounts represented by the outliers really matter (for instance, if you had several years of sales data and wanted the holiday season included in your per-month summary) then you'd need to use the mean.

There's a third "typical" statistic, the **mode**, which measures the *most frequently occurring value* in your data. If there are multiple "most-occurring" values, it looks like MODE() returns whichever one occurs first, although I wouldn't count on this always being the case.

Function	Value
MODE(1,2,3,3)	3
MODE(1,2,2,1)	1
MODE(2,1,1,2)	2

MODE() isn't super useful, but you might as well know about it.

Measures of Dispersion

It's also good to know how *dispersed* your data are. Are they tightly clustered or are they spread all over the place?

One way to measure this dispersion is with the **sample variance**, which is computed according to the formula

$$\frac{1}{n-1}[(x_1 - \bar{x})^2 + \ldots + (x_n - \bar{x})^2]$$

where n is the number of data points you have, $x_1 \ldots x_n$ are the data points themselves, and $\bar{x}$ is the mean of your data. If that doesn't make the slightest bit of sense, don't worry about it (or check out the Wikipedia article on Variance). If you ever compute the variance, you'll use the VAR() function.

For example, imagine that you time five commercial breaks during "Charles in Charge," and their lengths are 1, 2, 3, 4, and 5 minutes. Then the variance is

=VAR(1,2,3,4,5)

which equals 2.5 minutes * minutes. One problem with the variance is that (as you can see from the formula) its units are the *square* of the original units, which makes them hard to interpret. What's a minute * minute? No one knows!

Accordingly, we'll more frequently use the **sample standard deviation**, which is the *square root* of the sample variance, and which has the same units as the original data. Excel computes it with the STDEV() function:

=STDEV(1,2,3,4,5)

equals 1.581139 minutes, which is the square root of 2.5, as you can check.

For various technical reasons that are out of scope for this book, the STDEV() and VAR() functions are appropriate whenever you have data that represents a *sample* of some population. If your data represent the *entire* population in question (for example, if you have the lengths of every commercial break during every episode of "Charles in Charge," then you should use the **population variance** and **population standard deviation**, which are computed by the Excel functions STDEVP() and VARP().

In practice this won't usually be the case, and almost always you'll use the *sample* versions. Once you have more than a handful of data points, the two versions are pretty much equal anyway.

If you've never worked with standard deviation before, it's probably not obvious why it's useful. Stick around for a few sections and learn.

Quantiles

One way of thinking about the median is that it's the 50%-ile of the data – it's the number that the bottom 50% of the data are less than or equal to. You could just as easily ask for the 25%-ile (the number that the bottom 25% of the data are no greater than) or the 10%-ile or the 1%-ile or any other number. Excel computes these with the PERCENTILE() function, which takes two inputs: the first is an array of values, the second a number specifying the percentile you want. For instance, if your data were in A1:A1000, then

    PERCENTILE(A1:A1000,0.1)

would give you the 10%-ile. You can use quantiles to get a fuller picture of how your data is distributed. Consider the two datasets

    100,150,200,250,300

and

    88,200,200,200,312

The mean (and the median) of each data set is 200, and the standard deviation of each is approximately 79. And yet it's plain that those two sets of data are quite different from each other, which (if the datasets were too big to compare by eyeballing) you could see by looking at quantiles:

Percentile	First Dataset	Second Dataset
1%	102	92
10%	120	133
25%	150	200
50%	200	200
75%	250	200
90%	280	267
99%	298	308

This shows you that the "middle half" of the second dataset is clustered more tightly (in fact, all at 200) than the "middle half" of the first dataset, while the extremes of the second dataset are more extreme than the extremes of the first. These are differences that you wouldn't know just by looking at mean and median and standard deviation.

You might be wondering how the 10%-ile of the first dataset can be 120 when that's not even in our dataset. The answer is that PERCENTILE() *interpolates* to find its answer, in the following way.

The smallest value (here 100) is the 0%-ile, and the largest value (here 300) is the 100%-ile. Excel then divides the range 0% to 100% evenly into a number of pieces that's *one less than the number of data points*. Here we have 5 data points, so 100% gets divided into *four* pieces that are necessarily 25% each. Then the second value (150) is the 25%-ile, 200 is the 50%-ile, 250 is the 75%-ile, and (as we already said) 300 is the 100%-ile. If we need a percentile that's not one of our data points (like 10%-ile), Excel performs the following interpolation:

10% is 2/5 of the way from 0% to 25%, so the 10%-ile is 2/5 of the way from the 0%-ile (100) to the 25%-ile (150), which is 120.

If you have a large dataset, you'll probably never even notice this interpolation happening, but with small amounts of data you should be aware of it.

Quantiles in Reverse

Sometimes instead of wanting to know what value represents a certain %-ile, you instead want to know what %-ile a hypothetical value would represent. You can do this with the PERCENTRANK() function. Its first input is your original array of data, and its second is the hypothetical value you want ranked. It does the same interpolation as PERCENTILE(), so that

> PERCENTRANK({100,150,200,250,300},110)

is 0.05 (or 5%), since 110 is 1/5 of the way from 100 (the 0%-ile) to 150 (the 25%-ile). By default PERCENTRANK() returns only three decimal places of output; if you want more (or less) you can give it an optional third input specifying how many you'd like. Probably three should be enough for anybody.

If you try to PERCENTRANK() a value that falls outside the range of your dataset, you'll get a #N/A error. If there's a possibility that your value is too big or too small to PERCENTRANK() properly, you should probably test for that.

Correlation

The statistics we've looked at so far have all been for summarizing one dataset at a time. (We sometimes used them to *compare* multiple datasets, but the statistics themselves each depended on only set of data.)

Correlation is a way of measuring how much two paired datasets *vary in tandem about their means*. We measure this with the *correlation coefficient*, a number between -1 and +1.

Roughly speaking, when this number is close to +1, it means that large values of the first variable tend to be paired with large values of the second variable (and small values of the first with small values of the second, and average

values of the first with average values of the second). A correlation equal to
1 means there's an exact linear relationship between the two variables. If the
correlation is close to -1, it means that large values of the first variable tend
to be paired with *small* values of the second variable. And a correlation near
0 means that large values of one variable don't predictably correspond to
either large or small values of the other.

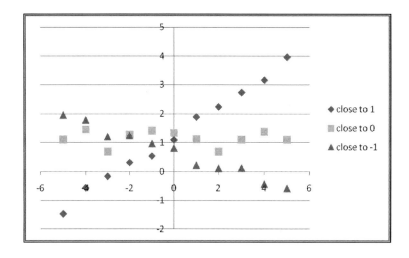

Excel computes correlations with the CORREL() function, which takes two
equally-sized arrays as inputs and outputs their correlation. For example,

CORREL({1,2,3,4,5},{6,7,8,9,10})

equals 1, because there is a perfect linear relationship between the two arrays.
Similarly,

CORREL({1,2,3,4,5},{10,9,8,7,6})

equals -1, and it turns out that

CORREL({1,2,3,4,5},{10,6,7,8,9})

equals 0.

However, a correlation near 0 doesn't mean there is no relationship between the two variables, only that there's not a relationship *of the type we described.* For example, you can check that

CORREL({-10,-5,0,5,10},{10,5,0,5,10})

equals 0, even though in every case the second variable is ABS() of the first! Knowing the first variable allows you to *exactly* predict the second; however, knowing *how the first variable differs from its mean* doesn't allow you to predict *how the second variable differs from its mean*, which is what correlation measures.

Correlation is not causation

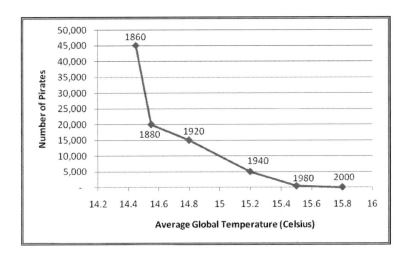

If you have two datasets A and B, there are several reasons why they might be correlated. If they have very little data, the correlation might be *spurious*, caused by picking the "wrong" data points. It might be that the phenomenon captured by dataset A causes the phenomenon captured by dataset B. Or it might be that B causes A, or that each causes the other, or that some third factor causes both.

In the above graph, the correlation between "number of pirates" and "average temperature" is -0.89. And yet it's apparent (I hope) that neither causes the other.

In short, knowing that two variables are correlated is not sufficient to conclude that either causes the other. Nonetheless, all else being equal, correlation should be *stronger evidence* for causation than a lack of correlation would be.

Autocorrelation

Sometimes when you have a sequence of data that varies over time, you want to check whether it's correlated with a *time-lagged* copy of itself. For instance, if you had a series of stock returns, you might want to know if large positive returns tended to be followed by large positive returns. If these returns were in A1:A100, you could look at

    =CORREL(A1:A99,A2:A100)

where the first range can be thought of as "current day's return" and the second range as "next day's return," since A1 (in the first) is paired with A2 (in the second), and so on.

Covariance

For various technical reasons that you'd find boring, statisticians often prefer to look at the **covariance** between two datasets, which is just their correlation multiplied by their standard deviations.

In fact, probably if you were taking a statistics course you'd start with covariance and then define correlation using the above relationship. Excel computes covariance with the COVAR() function. But unless you already know why you'd want to use COVAR(), you probably don't want to use COVAR().

Example: A Pseudo-Random Number Generator, Revisited

Recall the pseudo-random number generator we built and used to produce 10,000 "random" numbers. At the time we couldn't really test "how random" these numbers were. We checked their AVERAGE(), but that was it.

Now we can check more properties. If the numbers were really uniform random from [0,1), their median should be 0.5. Their 5%-ile should be 0.05 and their 90%-ile should be 0.9. Their standard deviation should be SQRT(1/12). (Just take my word for it.) The correlation between each number and the next should be zero, since if the numbers were "truly" random then there would be no relationship (and in particular not a linear one) between each number and the next. Let's check all these things:

    MEDIAN(C7:C10006)

equals 0.4978, which is pretty close.

    PERCENTILE(C7:C10006,0.05)

equals 0.0529, and

    PERCENTILE(C7:C10006,0.9)

equals 0.8978. The standard deviation is

    STDEV(C7:C10006)

which is 0.2894 (while SQRT(1/12) is 0.2887). Finally,

    CORREL(C7:C10005,C8:C10006)

is -0.0113, which is also good. Along all these dimensions, our numbers look "pretty random," although that's not to say that there aren't some other measures we don't know that would reveal us as frauds.

The Bell Curve

If you start looking at statistical data, you'll often notice that your data has a "bell" shape.

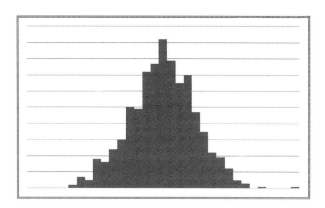

Most of the data is concentrated right around the average, with smaller and smaller amounts of data as you move further away. This "bell curve" pattern is most frequently modeled using the family of **normal distributions**.

Every normal distribution can be described by two parameters:

1. The *mean* (i.e. average) specifies the center of the distribution

2. The *standard deviation* specifies how dispersed the data is. A small standard deviation means that most values are close to the mean; a large one indicates that many values are not.

For example, the below graph shows two normal distributions, one of which (the lighter one) has twice the standard deviation of the other. While they are both centered at the same point, the low-standard-deviation one has much higher probability of being close to that center, while the high-standard-deviation one spreads its weight across a wider range.

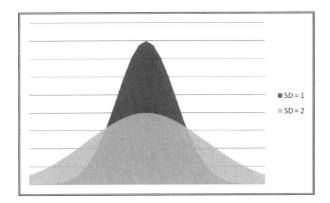

Any variable described by a normal distribution has the following probabilities of being within the specified distance of the mean:

Value between	Probability
-0.5 SD and +0.5 SD	38%
-1 SD and +1 SD	68%
-1.5 SD and +1.5 SD	86.6%
-2 SD and +2 SD	95.5%

For instance, the distribution of adult male heights is roughly normally distributed, with a mean of 70 inches and a standard deviation of 3 inches.

One possible problem with using normal distributions is that no matter how far away you get from the mean, you still have some non-zero probability. This means that if you model height using a normal distribution, you'll find some (very small) probability that height is negative (which is plainly impossible) and some (very small) probability that someone is 10 feet tall (which is in practice impossible). Generally you'll accept this as a reasonable tradeoff for the modeling benefits you get from using normal distributions.

Using the above table, approximately 68% of adult men should be between 67 inches (5'7") and 73 inches (6'1") tall. Similarly, approximately 95.5% of adult men should be between 64 inches (5'4") and 76 inches (6'4").

Rather than using the above table, we can use Excel. The NORMDIST()
function takes four inputs: a value to find in the distribution, the mean of
the distribution, the standard deviation of the distribution, and a Boolean
that we'll always specify as TRUE. It returns the cumulative distribution, the
probability that the specified normal distribution takes on a value *less than
or equal to* the first input. (If you gave it FALSE as the fourth input, you'd get
the *marginal* distribution, which indicates how likely you are to see values
near the first input.) For instance,

    NORMDIST(76,70,3,TRUE)

is the probability that a normal random variable with mean 70 and standard
deviation 3 is less than or equal to 76. Using a now familiar trick, we can
subtract one NORMDIST() from another to find the probability the variable
lies in a certain range. To estimate the number of adult men who are between
64 and 76 inches tall you'd use

    NORMDIST(76,70,3,TRUE)-NORMDIST(64,70,3,TRUE)

which is 95.5%, as we saw in the table above.

It's common to want a "standard normal" with a mean of 0 and a standard
deviation of 1, in which case you can use NORMSDIST(), which takes only
one input: the value you want to check the probability of being less than.
For instance,

    NORMSDIST(2)-NORMSDIST(-2)

is the probability that the standard normal is between -2 and 2, which is the
same as the probability that *any* normal is within 2 standard deviations of
its mean, which we already know is 95.5%.

If you need to work in the other direction, you can use the NORMINV() function, which takes as inputs a probability, a mean, and a standard deviation,
and outputs the value from the specified normal distribution to which there
is the appropriate probability of being less than or equal.

For instance, to find the 99%-ile of adult male height (the height that only 1% of males are taller than) you could use

    NORMINV(0.99,70,3)

and find that it's 77 inches, or 6'5".

It's a little bit trickier to find *intervals* containing specified probabilities. Let's say you want to find the symmetric range about 70 inches that contains 60% of all adult males. This means you want 40% of them *not* to fall into the range, and since you want it symmetric you'll need 20% too tall and 20% too short. So the upper bound needs to be the height above which only 20% fall, which is the height below which 80% fall:

    NORMINV(0.8,70,3)

Similarly, the lower bound needs to be

    NORMINV(0.2,70,3)

which gives the interval 67.5 inches to 72.5 inches.

Again, if you have a standard normal with mean 0 and standard deviation 1, then Excel provides a simpler function, NORMSINV(), which only takes one input, a probability, and returns the corresponding value.

For instance, a variable that follows the standard normal distribution will 90% of the time lie between NORMSINV(0.05) and NORMSINV(0.95), or -1.64 and +1.64.

Example: Closing the Honors Gap

You're the superintendent of a school system that gives a final graduation exam, scored out of 100. Historically the system has granted graduation honors to students scoring 90 or higher on the exam.

A group of community activists has noticed that every year the students at Washington High School always are honored at a much higher rate than the students at Jefferson High School, and they insist you do something to remedy this unfairness.

You set your district statisticians on the problem, and they report back with the surprising news that the average score at Jefferson is in fact higher than the average score at Washington! They tell you that the distributions of scores within each school are approximately normal. At Washington the mean is 84 and the standard deviation 5. At Jefferson the mean is 85 but the standard deviation is only 3.

Sure enough, this means that at Washington we honor

    1-NORMDIST(90,84,5,TRUE)

or 12% of the class, whereas at Jefferson we honor only

    1-NORMDIST(90,85,3,TRUE)

or 5% of the class.

Why did we subtract the NORMDIST() from 1?   Because NORMDIST(90,84,5,TRUE) tells you what percentage of students scored *less* than 90. To find out what percentage scored *at least* 90, we have to subtract that result from 100%, or 1.

Your advisors suggest all sorts of expensive remedies like smaller class sizes and tutoring and rewriting the test. Unfortunately, you don't have budget for any of them. Finally, your Thinking Spreadsheet instructor suggests lowering the honors threshhold.

By experimenting with the numbers, he discovers that at a cutoff of 86.5, you'd be honoring 31% of the students at Washington and 31% of the students at Jefferson, completely eliminating the honors gap. Congratulations, you're a hero of education reform!

The Central Limit Theorem

Why is the normal distribution so important? There's a result in mathematics, called the Central Limit Theorem, that says that whenever you have some source of randomness and you start taking *averages*, the results will start to look sort of normal. (Its actual statement is more precise and technical, of course, and references neither "some source of randomness" nor "sort of normal.")

To see this, we'll take averages of random numbers generated by RAND() and look at how the distribution changes as we add more numbers to the average. We'll look at 1000 averages of between 1 and 5 random numbers.

To start with, put the formula

=RAND()

in cells A2:E1001. For each row we'll compute 5 averages in columns F:J, and for histogram-ing purposes we'll round them to one decimal place. In F2 we can just use the formula

=ROUND(AVERAGE($A2:A2),1)

and copy it down and over all the way to J1001.

D rand4	E rand5	F avg1	G avg2	H avg3	I avg4	J avg5
0.772084	0.509865	0.2	0.6	0.4	0.5	0.5
0.489637	0.086881	0.4	0.7	0.6	0.5	0.5
0.701887	0.717554	0.8	0.6	0.5	0.5	0.6

Label the columns, and then let's build a histogram. In L2:L12 we can put the labels 0, 0.1, ..., 0.9, 1.0 (since we rounded to one decimal place), and then we can just use COUNTIF(). If we put in M2

=COUNTIF(F$2:F$1001,L2)

and then fill down and across, we'll get the histograms we want. In an example like this, a nice line chart could help illustrate:

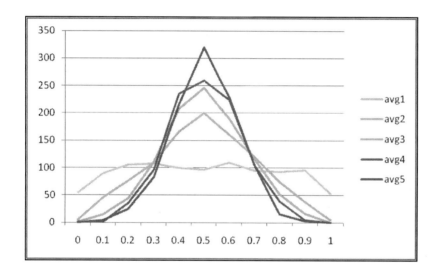

You can see that "Avg1" – which is just a single RAND() – is distributed pretty uniformly across [0,1] like you'd expect, and as you add more RAND()s to the average, you get more and more of a bell-curve shape. Because of this, normal distributions show up in real-world data even when there's no obvious reason that they should, which is why you should understand them.

Technique: Random Normals

In an earlier section we saw that we could generate random numbers from discrete distributions by using RAND() and then transforming the output in a specific way.

It turns out that in fact you can generate any random variable by cleverly transforming RAND(). For a number of common distributions, Excel has functions to do the transformations.

For instance, think about what happens when we feed RAND() into NORMSINV(). Well, 25% of the time, RAND() will be less than or equal to 0.25, which is precisely when NORMSINV(RAND()) will be less than or equal to -0.67. And 50% of the time RAND() will be less than or equal to 0.5, and NORMSINV(RAND()) will be less than or equal to 0. Similarly, 97.5% of the time RAND() will be less than or equal to 0.975, which is exactly when NORMSINV(RAND()) will be less than or equal to 1.96.

In other words, NORMSINV(RAND()) produces a random variable that is distributed the same as a standard normal random variable. Therefore it *is* a standard normal random variable.

This is no accident. For any random variable if you have a FUNCTION() that takes a probability and returns the value that the variable is less than or equal to with the specified probability, then FUNCTION(RAND()) has the same distribution as the random variable. In fact, in the "Simulating a Discrete Random Variable" section, this is actually what we were doing. We just didn't know it.

Simple Linear Regression

We've seen how to use CORREL() to test to what extent there's some sort of linear relationship between two variables. But even when we saw a correlation close to 1 (meaning "perfect linear relationship"), CORREL() didn't tell us anything about the *details* of that linear relationship.

The statistical tool of *linear regression* finds the "best" linear relationship between two datasets. For various technical reasons, "best" means "the linear relationship that minimizes the sum of the squares of the differences between corresponding elements of the array of observed values and the array of predicted values."

In this section we'll look at *simple* linear regression, the case when each dataset contains only one variable. One of the datasets will contain the values of our **independent variable**, which we'll call x, and one will contain the values of our **dependent variable**, which we'll call y.

Our procedure finds the parameters m and b so that the linear equation

$$y = m * x + b$$

"best" predicts the observed values of y.

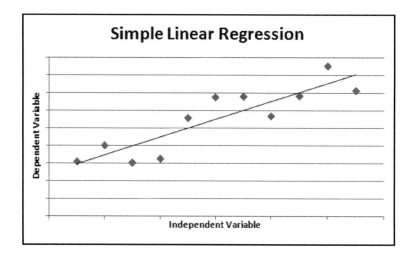

The above picture graphically illustrates a regression line that best fits the relationship between two datasets. You can see that it's not a perfect fit but it generally captures how the two variables are related. (If you want more mathematical details, check out the Wikipedia article "Simple linear regression.")

Excel computes m with the SLOPE() function and b with the INTERCEPT() function. Each takes the array of y variables as its first input and the array of x variables as its second input.

Goodness of Fit

SLOPE() and INTERCEPT() find the *best* linear relationship between x and y, but they don't say anything about how good this relationship is. It could be terrible!

One measure of the goodness of the fit is the *R-squared* of the regression, a number between 0 and 1 that measures the fraction of variation in the y variable that can be "explained" by variation in the x variable.

Why is "explained" in scare-quotes? Because (as we saw when we discussed correlation) the *existence* of a strong relationship between two variables doesn't mean that one *causes* the other. This is not the sort of "explanation" that would necessarily convince a judge or an angry parent or a jealous lover. Here we mean "explain" only in the purest *mathematical* sense.

If the R-squared is close to 1, then there's a strong linear relationship between x and y, which means that almost all the variation in y can be "explained" by the variation in x; if it's close to 0, then almost none of the variation in y is "explained" by the variation in x.

Excel provides the RSQ() function to compute the R-squared. Following form, it takes two inputs, an array of y values and an array of x values. If your x data is in A1:A100 and your y data in B1:B100, then you'd compute

    RSQ(B1:B100,A1:A100)

It turns out that the R-squared also equals the square of the correlation between x and y. Technically you should probably think of it as the correlation between $m * x + b$ (the predicted values of y) and y, but since the predicted values are (by definition) a linear function of x, they have the exact same correlation with y (or any other variable) as does x.

So you could also compute it as

CORREL(B1:B100,A1:A100)^2

and you'd get the same result.

Another measure is the "standard error of regression," which is the standard deviation of the prediction errors, the differences between the predicted values of y and the actual values of y. We compute this with the Excel function STEYX(), which takes the same two inputs as the other regression functions

=STEYX(B1:B100,A1:A100)

A common assumption when doing regression is that the prediction errors are *normally distributed*. To the extent this is a good assumption, then (from what we already know about the normal distribution) the predicted values of y should be within STEYX() of the actual values of y approximately 68% of the time.

Forecasting

One reason we might perform a regression is in order to *forecast* what values our dependent variable would take on for hypothetical values of the independent variable.

One way of doing this is to use SLOPE() and INTERCEPT() to estimate m and b and then to plug hypothetical x values into the equation

$$y = m * x + b$$

to estimate the corresponding y values.

An alternative approach is to use the Excel function FORECAST(), which takes three inputs: a hypothetical value of x, an array of the known y values, and an array of the known x values. Behind the scenes Excel will compute the SLOPE() and the INTERCEPT() and then output the predicted y value correponding to the first input.

If you only need to predict one new data point, this might be a preferable approach – it's much simpler, which decreases the chance you'll make some sort of error. On the other hand, each time you use FORECAST(), it computes a SLOPE() and an INTERCEPT() behind the scenes. Using more than one FORECAST() on the same x and y data means doing a lot of unnecessary work, which can really slow your spreadsheet down!

Instant Scatterplot Regression

If you've made a Scatter Chart of your data, you can actually "run" the regression *in* the chart. Just right-click on one of the data points and choose Add Trendline. In the menu that pops up, make sure the Regression Type is "Linear," check the boxes for "Display Equation on Chart" and "Display R-squared value on chart," and click Close. Excel will add a label to the chart with the equation for the best fit line and the R-squared value.

Now, because all these values are in chart labels instead of cells, you can't actually *use* them. Nonetheless, this gives you a quick way to inspect how good a simple regression would be.

Multiple Regression

In practice, "simple" linear regression isn't always useful. Most "dependent" variables depend on a lot of things, and most useful linear models take more than one of them into account.

When you're computing a multiple regression, you'll still have an array of dependent variables y, but now you'll have several arrays of dependent variables $x_1, x_2, \ldots, x_n$. And you'll be looking for a linear relationship

$$y = m_1 * x_1 + \ldots + m_n * x_n + b$$

by again choosing $m_1, \ldots, m_n$ and b to minimize the sum of the squares of the prediction errors.

There are two ways to use Excel for multiple regression. One is through a menu item that calculates the regression and then stores the results as static numbers. Just as we eschewed a similar method of generating histograms as not Thinking Spreadsheet, we'll avoid this way of running regressions.

The second way involves the function LINEST(), which must be used as part of an *array formula*. Accordingly, we'll postpone discussing it until the chapter on array formulas.

Example: Predicting Football Wins

All things being equal, a football team that scores more points throughout the season will probably win more games, as will a football team that allows its opponents to score fewer points.

The file FootballWins.xlsx on ThinkingSpreadsheet.com contains, for each of the 32 NFL teams, how many points they scored, how many points they allowed, and how many games they won during the 2009 season.

	A	B	C	D
1	Team	Scored	Allowed	Wins
2	Arizona	375	325	10
3	Atlanta	363	325	9
4	Baltimore	391	261	9
5	Buffalo	258	326	6

If you check the correlation between Scored and Wins with

CORREL(B2:B33,D2:D33)

you'll find that it's a healthy 0.88, which indicates a strong linear relationship between the two. The correlation between Allowed and Wins is a weaker -0.68. The sign is negative because (in general) teams that allow their opponents to score *more* points win *fewer* games.

It's often a good idea to inspect the data visually with a scatterplot. Here the x-axis is Scored and the y-axis is Wins:

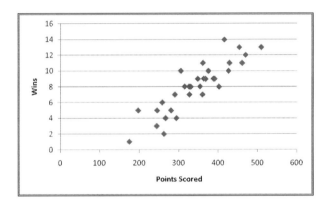

First we'll compute the slope with

=SLOPE(D2:D33,B2:B33)

and then we'll do the same for INTERCEPT(), RSQ(), and STEYX().

H	I
Slope	0.035272
Intercept	-4.11475
R-squared	0.778279
Steyx	1.542662

The best fit line tells us that if we know how many points a team scored, we predict their win total with

Wins = 0.035272 * Scored - 4.11475

Obviously this is not an exact relationship. First, the number of Wins needs to be an integer between 0 and 16 (the number of games in a season), but this formula doesn't in general produce integers, is less than zero when the number of points scored is very small, and is greater than 16 when the number of points scored is very big.

Nonetheless, it gives us an estimate of how much points matter. Each additional point scored (on average) counts for 0.035 wins, which means that every 28 points you score during the season earns you (on average) an additional win.

You could also find this best fit by adding a Trendline to the scatter plot

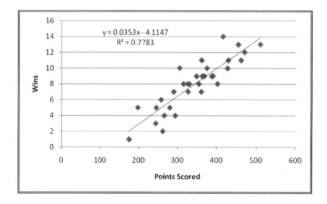

although this wouldn't give you the regression outputs in a usable format.

Starting in E2, let's compute the predicted number of wins according to our model:

$$=B2*\$I\$1+\$I\$2$$

and fill down. Then in F2 we'll compute the error in our prediction:

$$=E2-D2$$

and fill down again:

	A	B	C	D	E	F
1	Team	Scored	Allowed	Wins	Predict	Error
2	Arizona	375	325	10	9.112163	-0.88784
3	Atlanta	363	325	9	8.688901	-0.3111
4	Baltimore	391	261	9	9.676511	0.676511
5	Buffalo	258	326	6	4.985367	-1.01463
6	Carolina	315	308	8	6.995857	-1.00414

Where are the biggest errors? The biggest *positive* errors (which means we predicted too many wins) are for Detroit, Kansas City, and NY Giants, all of which Allowed a lot more points than average. Similarly, the biggest *negative* errors (which means we predicted too few wins) are for Indianapolis, Cincinnati, and Dallas, all of which Allowed a lot fewer points than average.

This suggests that our model would be even better if it could also take points Allowed into account. One way of doing this would be to look at the point differential (Scored - Allowed). Indeed, if you do so, you'll find an even better fit than just looking at wins. Why give them equal weight, though? Why not look at (Scored - 0.5 * Allowed)?

This is where *multiple regression* would be handy, as regressing Wins on both Scored and Allowed would find the optimal weights for prediction. We'll get there, I promise!

CHAPTER *20*

MONTE CARLO

Monte Carlo is a powerful technique that uses random numbers to simulate complicated phenomena in order to analyze the results. Excel turns out to be a surprisingly capable tool for small-scale simulations.

What is Monte Carlo?

We know (or rather, we assume) that if you flip a coin you'll get heads half the time and tails half the time. But what if we didn't know that? What if someone handed you an unfair coin and asked you to figure out how frequently it ended up heads?

Probably you'd start flipping it and counting how many heads you got. If after 1000 flips you'd seen 250 heads, you would estimate that the unfair coin landed heads about 25% of the time.

Some probability problems we can quickly get exact answers for, either through careful reasoning or brute force. For instance, if you roll two dice, the probability that their sum is at least 11 is 1/12, which you can check by listing out all 36 possible (and equally likely) rolls and observing that 3 of them add up to 11 or 12.

Not all problems are amenable to this kind of solution, though. If you roll 10 dice, what's the probability the sum is at least 40? Since there are POWER(6,10) possible rolls, you'd have to look at more than 60 million

311

outcomes. You could write a computer program to do this, but you probably couldn't do it in a spreadsheet.

But if you didn't need an exact answer, you could estimate it just like you did with the unfair coin. You could repeatedly roll (virtual) sets of 10 dice and keep track of how often their sum was at least 40. If you did this a lot of times, the observed probability would "converge" to the true probability. (How many times? We'll punt on that question for now.)

To demonstrate this, let's roll 10 dice in A2:J2. Each die is just a RANDBETWEEN(1,6). Then in K2 we'll take their sum:

=SUM(A2:J2)

And in L2 we'll record whether it's greater than or equal to 40.

=IF(K2>=40,1,0)

Your spreadsheet should look like this:

	A	B	C	D	E	F	G	H	I	J	K	L
1											sum	sum >= 40
2	1	6	2	1	6	5	5	5	1	3	35	0

but with different rolls.

Why did we use 1 and 0 instead of TRUE and FALSE? Because if we use to 1 to mean "success" and 0 to mean "failure" then the AVERAGE() is exactly the observed probability of success.

AVERAGE() = (1 * # of TRUE + 0 * # of FALSE) / (# of OBSERVATIONS)

Copy the formulas down 1000 rows, and in M2 take the average of everything in column L. (Recall that AVERAGE() will ignore the text label in M1.)

	A	B	C	D	E	F	G	H	I	J	K	L	M
1											sum	sum >= 40	average
2	6	4	3	1	3	3	1	6	2	1	30	0	0.209
3	5	4	2	5	5	6	3	1	3	1	35	0	
4	2	5	4	6	6	5	1	5	5	5	44	1	

I see an estimated probability of 0.209. If I refresh with F9, it drops to 0.198. (Your numbers will differ, of course.)

So it looks like the probability is around 20%, but we'd like a more precise estimate. When I copy it down another 4000 rows, I see 0.2054, and when I go to 10,000 rows I get numbers that seem mostly between 0.2 and 0.21.

Finally, extend what's left all the way down to row 100,001. It probably takes a while to compute, but I get numbers between 0.204 and 0.206.

This tells us that the actual probability of getting the dice to add to 40 or greater is right around 20.5%. (In fact, to four decimal places, the exact probability is 20.4968%.) The more rows you add, the more precise your estimates will become.

Frivolous Example: Estimating PI() by Throwing Darts

Imagine a square whose side has length 1. We can pick "random" points in the square by choosing an x-coordinate with RAND() and a y-coordinate with a second RAND().

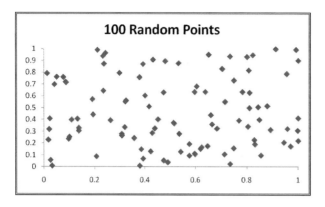

If we have some subset of the square that takes up half the area of the square (for instance, the left half), then we expect that half the points we "randomly" pick will end up in that subset. If the subset takes up 1/10 the area of the square, then we expect that 1/10 of the points we pick will end up in that subset.

What's interesting is that we can do this in reverse. If we have a subset whose area we don't know, we can randomly pick points in the square and keep track of what fraction of them land in the subset. If we're picking points in a way that everywhere in the square is equally likely, and we find that about 25% of the points we pick land in the subset, then we estimate that the subset takes up 25% of the area of the square.

We'll call this the "throwing darts" method, since one way of doing this without a computer would be to throw darts at the square and count how many land in the subset we're interested in.

The mathematical constant PI() is equal to the ratio of a circle's area to the square of its radius. (There are other ways to define it, but this is the one we'll stick with.) Its value is approximately 3.14. Excel happens to come with a PI() function that will give you its value, but back in antiquity people had to come up with clever ways to approximate it. Here's one.

The circle with radius 1, you might remember from geometry, is the set of points whose x and y coordinates satisfy $x^2 + y^2 = 1$. Points with $x^2 + y^2 < 1$ are inside the circle, those with $x^2 + y^2 > 1$ are outside the circle. (If you don't remember this from geometry, you might want to read through the Wikipedia article "Circle.")

Notice that 1/4 of the circle lies inside the square where x is between 0 and 1 and y is between 0 and 1:

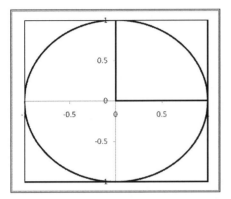

Since the area of the whole circle is PI(), the area of the part of the circle inside the square is PI()/4. That means that if we pick points at random in the square and look at the fraction that satisfy x^2 + y^2 < 1, that fraction should be approximately PI()/4. If we multiply that fraction by 4, the results should be approximately PI().

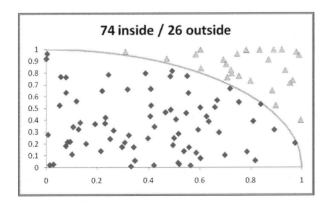

So, in A2 and B2, let's start by picking x and y-coordinates with RAND(). In C2 we can compute (A2^2)+(B2^2), and in D2 we'll check whether it's inside the circle:

=IF(C2<1,4,0)

Why 4? If we'd used 1 to represent "inside the circle" and 0 to represent "outside the circle," then the average would approximate PI()/4. Using 4 (=4*1) and 0 (=0*1) means that the average will approximate PI().

Now, copy these formulas down 10,000 times and in E10001 let's check the average

=AVERAGE(D2:D10001)

In F10001, let's put =PI() for comparison.

	A	B	C	D	E	F
9997	0.283539	0.302003	0.1716	4		
9998	0.925547	0.668218	1.303152	0		
9999	0.61021	0.104202	0.383215	4		
10000	0.428613	0.097046	0.193127	4	**Average**	**PI()**
10001	0.034036	0.082232	0.00792	4	3.1408	3.141593

Refresh it a few times. How good a job did we do?

Technique: Using a Data Table

One little known feature of Excel is the "Data Table," which you shouldn't confuse with the more recent "Table" feature.

If you remember when we first introduced the use of $, we gave the example of building a multiplication table, with one factor down the first column, another factor across the top row, and each cell containing their product.

	A	B	C	D	E	F
1		1	2	3	4	5
2	1	=$A2*B$1				
3	2					
4	3					
5	4					
6	5					

A data table allows us to do the same thing with more complicated formulas that can't just be entered into one cell. For simplicity, we'll illustrate it by rebuilding our multiplication table (which plainly can be built without using Data Table functionality).

To start, put the value 1 in both A1 and A2. (It doesn't actually matter what values you use, but let's put 1.) Now recreate the multiplication table labels in C2:C6 and D1:H1. Here's the tricky part: enter the multiplication formula only in the top left corner in cell C1, and have it multiply A1 and A2:

	A	B	C	D	E	F	G	H
1	1		=$A$1*$A$2			3	4	5
2	1		1					
3			2					
4			3					
5			4					
6			5					

Now select the whole range C1:H6, and on the Data Ribbon in the Data Tools section under What-If Analysis choose Data Table:

You'll get a pop-up window asking for "row input cell" and "column input cell." The "row input cell" means "where do you want Excel to plug in the values from the top row?" We'll want them plugged into A1, so input A1 there. Similarly, the "column input cell" means "where do you want Excel to plug in the values from the first column?" We'll want those in A2, so input A2 there and click OK.

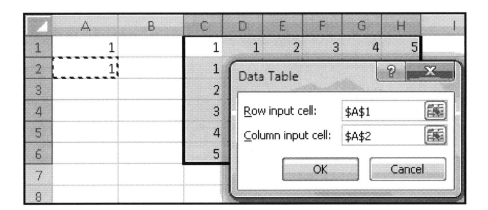

In each cell of the table, Excel has applied the formula at the top left ("multiply A2 by A1") after substituting the value from the top row into A1 and the value from the first column in A2. You can change the values in the first row and first column and you'll see that the table values change accordingly.

Of course, we could have done the same thing by putting the formula

$$=D\$1*\$C2$$

in D2 and filling the table, but that wouldn't have illustrated how to use Data Table.

If you click anywhere in the Data Table, you'll see a fake array formula

{=TABLE(A1,A2)}

which is how you can see that it's a Data Table and where its values are getting plugged in. If you try to clear one of the cells, you'll get a popup informing you that you can't change part of a Data Table, which you can't.

Data Tables and Monte Carlo

What on earth does this have to do with Monte Carlo simulations? All of our simulations so far have involved repeated sampling of quantities that can be easily computed in a few cells, like the x and y-coordinates for a point in a square, or the rolls of ten dice.

Yet you can imagine wanting to use Monte Carlo to simulate some quantity that you can't simply fit into one row. Maybe it takes most of a worksheet to compute, but it's not feasible to create 1000 (or 10000 or more!) identical worksheets in order to get lots of samples.

However, what you can do is use the quantity you want simulated as the formula for a Data Table. Just put descriptive labels along the rows and columns. The key idea is to use nonsense values for "row input cell" and "column input cell" – you should specify cells that aren't even used!

Then Excel will populate the Data Table by plugging each of your meaningless row and column labels into the unused cells and recalculating the spreadsheet. And although your meaningless labels won't affect the Data Table's formula, the recalculation will cause the random variables in your model to be regenerated. The effect is that each cell in the Data Table represents one simulation of your random variable.

This is not to say that you have to specify meaningless cells. You might want only the column values to be meaningless and have the row values actually feed into the model.

To see how this works, let's simulate 10 rolls of a die.

In A1 enter the formula for the Data Table:

=RANDBETWEEN(1,6)

Then in B1 put the nonsense value "Rolls" and in A2:A11 put labels 1 through 10. (The labels aren't a necessary part of the process, and nothing bad would happen if you used different labels or none at all.) Select A1:B11, and insert a Data Table using the empty cells D1 and D2 as "row input" and "column input". You'll see the table populated with random dice rolls, and if you recalculate the sheet, you'll see them change.

	A	B
1	4	Rolls
2	1	
3	2	
4	3	
5	4	
6	5	
7	6	
8	7	
9	8	
10	9	
11	10	

	A	B
1	5	Rolls
2	1	4
3	2	6
4	3	3
5	4	3
6	5	3
7	6	2
8	7	5
9	8	1
10	9	5
11	10	1

	A	B
1	5	Rolls
2	1	6
3	2	6
4	3	1
5	4	2
6	5	3
7	6	2
8	7	2
9	8	2
10	9	6
11	10	4

Of course, in this simple example, you could have just used RANDBETWEEN(1,6) ten times. But more complicated models might need this Data Table approach.

Because of the way Excel calculates them, Data Tables can really slow your spreadsheets down. Try not to use them unless they're necessary, and try to avoid using more than one in a spreadsheet.

Data Tables and Graphing

Another thing Data Tables can be useful for is graphing unwieldy functions. If you have some output that takes all of cells A1:A100 to compute, it can be hard to generate a graph showing how it changes as cell A1 changes.

A Data Table makes this simple. Put the values you want to plug into A1 down the column and a dummy label in the top row, then make a Data Table and graph the results.

Again, Data Tables will slow down your spreadsheet tremendously, so after you produce your graph you might consider using Copy-Paste-Special-Value.

Example: Catching the Cheaters

As part of your classroom lesson on probability and statistics, you tell your students to flip a coin 100 times and bring you the sequence of results. Over the years you've learned that most students are too lazy to do the assignment and instead just write down a sequence that "seems like" the results of flipping a coin 100 times.

However, they never seem to put enough long streaks in their flips, which gives you an easy way to catch them. We'll use Monte Carlo to estimate the size of the longest streak (of either Heads or Tails) we should expect to see.

If we use 0 for Tails and 1 for Heads, we can simulate the flips in A2:A101 with

    =RANDBETWEEN(0,1)

and then in B2:B101 keep track of the current streak of Heads or Tails. In B2 the streak length is just 1. And in B3 (and below) the streak is either 1 (if the flip is different from the previous flip) or one more than the previous streak (if the flip is the same):

=IF(A3=A2,1+B2,1)

and then fill down:

	A	B
1	Flip	Streak
2	1	1
3	1	2
4	0	1
5	0	2
6	0	3
7	1	1

Now in D1 find the longest streak with

=MAX(B2:B101)

and in D2:D501 put the labels 1 to 500 for our simulations. Select D1:E501 and insert a Data Table with the (nonsense) values C1 and C2 for Row input cell and Column input cell.

D	E
7	
1	7
2	4
3	7
4	7
5	7

It might take a while to compute. Once it finishes, we'll add a histogram to summarize the distribution. In G2:G21, we'll have buckets from 1 up to 20 representing the longest streak in a sequence. Then in H2, we'll count how many simulated sequences had the corresponding longest streak:

=COUNTIF($E$2:$E$501,G2)

And in I2 we'll convert this to a percentage by dividing by 500, the number of simulations:

=H2/500

Finally, we fill down to see the results:

LongestStreak	Count	Pct
1	0	0%
2	0	0%
3	0	0%
4	17	3%
5	76	15%
6	115	23%
7	131	26%

We can see, for instance, that if a student turns in a sequence that doesn't even have 4-in-a-row at some point, then probably she didn't generate it by flipping coins.

If a phenomenon is truly random, then some fraction of the time it will necessarily behave in ways (like streaks) that "appear" non-random. Paradoxically, if the phenomenon never appears (to the human eye) "non-random" then probably it isn't random.

Example: The Birthday Problem

Your friend, who just took a probability class, insists that if you have 23 people in a room, there's a more than 50% chance that at least two of them have the same birthday. This seems pretty incredible to you, so you decide you'll check it using Monte Carlo.

After a little bit of thought, you come up with the following steps:

1. Simulate the birthdays of 23 people.

2. Check whether any two of the birthdays are the same.

3. Use Data Table to repeat and collect statistics.

The first is easy. If we ignore leap years and assume that all birthdays are equally likely, then we can simulate birthdays using

=RANDBETWEEN(1,365)

which we'll put in A2:A24. In B2 we need to find out if the birthday in A2 is a duplicate. In other words, does the value in A2 match any of the values in A3:A24? That suggests using MATCH(), but if you play around a bit you'll see that – because of the "every row but this one" construction – it's hard to craft a single formula that works for all 23 people.

A more Thinking Spreadsheet way of asking the same thing is "does the value in A2 match any of the values in A2:A24 *more than once*?" The "more than once" is important because the value in A2 will certainly match the value in A2. This suggests the formula

=COUNTIF($A$2:$A$24,A2)>1

which can then be copied down without incident.

	A	B
1	Birthday	Duplicate?
2	334	FALSE
3	123	TRUE
4	199	FALSE
5	312	FALSE
6	123	TRUE
7	225	FALSE

Now in D1 we can test if there are *any* duplicates using

=OR(B2:B24)

In D2:D101 let's label our simulations 1 to 100, and in E1 add the label Duplicate. Select D1:E101, and create a Data Table with the unused C1 and C2 as Row input cell and Column input cell. This will give you 100 Booleans indicating whether each group of 23 had a duplicated birthday or not.

Then in G2 you can estimate the probability of duplicate birthdays:

=COUNTIF(E2:E101,TRUE)/100

and you should get an answer not too different from

	A	B	C	D	E	F	G
1	Birthday	Duplicate?		FALSE	Duplicate		Probability
2	268	FALSE		1	TRUE		0.56
3	312	FALSE		2	TRUE		
4	109	FALSE		3	TRUE		

To feel really confident you'd want to simulate a lot more than 100 groups of people, but your friend's claim certainly seems reasonable!

You show this spreadsheet to your friend, who promptly accuses you of making things unnecessarily difficult. If you have a list of 23 people, she points out, there are

POWER(365,23)

possible combinations of birthdays. And "no duplicates" amounts to choosing the birthdays *without replacement*, which means that

PERMUT(365,23)

of the choices have no duplicates. Therefore the exact likelihood of duplicates is

1-PERMUT(365,23)/POWER(365,23)

or 50.7%.

Example: A Poker Hand Simulator

Poker is a popular card game played with a standard deck of 52 cards consisting of all possible combinations of four suits (hearts, clubs, diamonds, and spades) and thirteen ranks (ace, two, three, four, five, six, seven, eight, nine, ten, jack, queen, and king). The ace plays a dual role in that it can either be "the rank below two" or "the rank above king."

A poker hand consists of 5 cards, and the player with the highest-ranked hand wins. The rankings are as follows, from best to worst:

1. Straight Flush: All five cards have the same suit, and their ranks are consecutive. As mentioned above, {ace,two,three,four,five} would count as "consecutive" but so would {ten,jack,queen,king,ace}.
2. Four of a Kind: Four of the five cards have the same rank.

3. Full House: Three of the cards have the same rank, and the other two also have equal rank (but obviously different from that of the first three).
4. Flush: All five cards have the same suit.
5. Straight: The cards have consecutive ranks.
6. Three of a Kind: Three of the cards have the same rank, but the other cards have different (unequal) ranks.
7. Two Pair: Two cards share a rank, two other cards share a second rank, and the fifth card has a third rank.
8. One Pair: Two cards share a rank, while the other three cards have three different ranks.
9. Nothing: None of the above.

There are various rules for breaking ties between two identically ranked hands, but we're not going to go into them. Also, we'll pretend that the suits are {1,2,3,4} and the ranks are {1,...,13}. We've already seen how to use INDEX() to convert them to more descriptive names if we wanted to.

To start with, we'll create a "deck" of cards, using our time-tested odometer pattern. In column A, we'll put the Card #, which runs from 1 to 52. In column B, we'll put the Rank, starting with a 1 in B2. And in column C, we'll put the Suit, starting with a 1 in C2.

Then one way of setting up the odometer is simply

=MOD(B2,13)+1

in B3 and

=C2+IF(B3<B2,1,0)

in C3 and filling down. Finally, since we'll want to simulate drawing five cards at random, we'll need to put RAND()s in column D for the "sampling without replacement" technique.

Your spreadsheet should start out like this

	A	B	C	D
1	Card #	Rank	Suit	RAND()
2	1	1	1	0.631159
3	2	2	1	0.032914
4	3	3	1	0.082039
5	4	4	1	0.083168
6	5	5	1	0.83599

but with different random numbers, of course.

Now in columns F:I, let's find the five cards in our hand. We'll start simply with the numbers 1 to 5.

	F	G	H	I
		Card #	Rank	Suit
1				
2				
3				
4				
5				

To sample without replacement, G2 needs to find the card with the largest RAND(), G3 the card with the second largest, and so on. This means the formula for G2 should be

=MATCH(LARGE($D$2:$D$53,F2),$D$2:$D$53,0)

which you can then fill down. (Technically this gives the index of the cell in D2:D53 that contains the largest value, but its first cell D2 contains card #1, its second cell D3 contains card #2, and so on, which means this does what we need.)

Given a card number in G2, we can find its rank with

=INDEX(B$2:B$53,$G2)

Not $-ing the B and $-ing the G means that if we Copy-Paste this same formula into the Rank column, its references will move appropriately:

=INDEX(C$2:C$53,$G2)

Fill these down and you'll have your five cards.

F	G	H	I
	Card #	Rank	Suit
1	25	12	2
2	5	5	1
3	49	10	4
4	35	9	3
5	23	10	2

Yours will be different because of randomness, of course.

Now we need to think about how to categorize our hand. How do we know if it's a Full House or a Flush? Well, a Flush means you have five cards of the same suit, so if you were to count how many of the cards were of each suit, you could just look for a five. Similarly, if you were to count how many cards were of each rank, you could look for a 4 to find a Four-of-a-Kind, and you could look for a 3 and a 2 to find a Full House.

Therefore, it seems like a good start would be to count the cards of each rank and of each suit. We'll set this up in columns K:O.

K	L	M	N	O
Suit	**Count**		**Rank**	**Count**
1			1	
2			2	
3			3	
4			4	
			5	

This is just a simple job for COUNTIF(). In L2 the formula should be

=COUNTIF($I$2:$I$6,K2)

and in O2

=COUNTIF($H$2:$H$6,N2)

Every poker hand can be easily read off from these numbers, with the exception of a Straight, which we'll have when there are five consecutive ones in column O. In order to determine this, we'll label column P "Straight?" and add in a Boolean telling us whether there's a straight ending at a certain rank.

In cell P6, we can check if there's a straight ending at a 5 with

=COUNTIF(O2:O6,1)=5

which is TRUE when every cell in O2:O6 contains a 1, which happens precisely when our hand contains one ace, one 2, one 3, one 4, and one 5. If we fill this down, it will cover all Straights except for the weird special case of "aces high," which will need its own formula in P2

=AND(O2=1,COUNTIF(O11:O14,1)=4)

which checks that there's one ace *and* one ten, one jack, one queen, and one king.

Suit	Count		Rank	Count	Straight?
1	2		1	0	FALSE
2	1		2	0	
3	0		3	0	
4	2		4	0	
			5	2	FALSE

You should sanity check that your cards are all being counted correctly and refresh a few times with F9.

At this point we're ready to judge our hand. Let's put the rankings in column S, leaving room in column T for a Boolean identifying what we dealt.

Hand	Judgment
Straight Flush	
Four of a Kind	
Full House	
Flush	
Straight	
Three of a Kind	
Two Pair	
One Pair	
Nothing	

Our first possible hand is a Straight Flush, which we have precisely when we meet the conditions for both a Straight *and* for a Flush. This means we can use in T2 the formula

=AND(OR(P2:P14),COUNTIF(L2:L5,5)=1)

The first condition in the AND() checks that one of the Straight tests is TRUE.

The second checks that all five cards belong to a single suit, which is the Flush test. The AND() will be TRUE exactly when both are TRUE, that is, exactly when the hand is a Straight Flush.

In T3 we need to identify Four-of-a-Kind, which is the case exactly when there's a 4 in one of the cells O2:O14

   =COUNTIF(O2:O14,4)=1

In T4 we have Full House, which means that one of the ranks appears three times in our hand and a different rank appears twice. That's the same as saying that there's a 3 in O2:O14, and that there's also a 2.

   =AND(COUNTIF(O2:O14,3)=1,COUNTIF(O2:O14,2)=1)

Next is Flush. We can't just look for a 5 in L2:L5, because we don't want to include Straight Flushes, which we've already counted. That means in T5 we'll have to exclude them:

   =AND(COUNTIF(L2:L5,5)=1,NOT(T2))

Similarly, we need to exclude Straight Flushes when counting Straights in T6:

   =AND(OR(P2:P14),NOT(T2))

A hand is a Three-of-a-Kind if there's a 3 in O2:O14 and there's not a 2 (which would mean Full House instead). We can check this in T7 with

   =AND(COUNTIF(O2:O14,3)=1,COUNTIF(O2:O14,2)=0)

We have Two Pair if there are two 2's in O2:O14

   =COUNTIF(O2:O14,2)=2

and we have just one One Pair if there's one 2 and three 1's.

=AND(COUNTIF(O2:O14,2)=1,COUNTIF(O2:O14,1)=3)

The only case left is Nothing, which should be TRUE precisely when all the other possible Rankings are FALSE:

=NOT(OR(T2:T9))

Again refresh the spreadsheet several times to make sure it's judging your poker hands correctly.

Finally, if we want a cell to contain the judgment, we can simply use

=INDEX(S2:S10,MATCH(TRUE,T2:T10,0))

which looks for the TRUE in T2:T10 and returns the corresponding Hand from S2:S10.

At this point you could use the last output as the start of a Data Table to simulate thousands of poker hands and ask questions like "how frequently does a flush appear?" Excel is almost certainly not the best tool for this task, but this example ties together many of the things we've learned and makes a nice ending to the "easy" part of the book. (That's right, this was the easy part.)

Chapter *21*

Array Formulas

Array formulas are an advanced technique that most spreadsheet users never learn. That's too bad, as there are many things that are easier to do if you use array formulas, and there are many other things that are impossible to do without using array formulas. Before writing this chapter, I used array formulas sparingly. Since writing this chapter, I use them all the time.

The Basics of Array Formulas

What is an array formula? An array formula is

- a formula
- that uses an array
- as an array
- somewhere where Excel doesn't usually expect an array.

At this point you know what a formula is, so we won't dwell on that part of the definition.

You know what an array is too. It's a rectangle of values, specified either explicitly (like {1,2,3;4,5,6}) or by reference to its containing range (like C3:D4). We won't dwell on that part of the definition either.

The "as an array" piece is important. You can always use an array as a value; Excel will just use the value in the top left cell. For instance, if you enter the formula =(A1:A3)+1, you'll get the same result as if you'd used =A1+1.

The "where Excel doesn't expect an array" is also important. =SUM({1,2,3})
is a formula that uses an array as an array, but SUM() is perfectly happy to
take arrays as its arguments. For our purposes, this makes SUM({1,2,3}) not
an "array formula."

The Idea Behind Array Formulas

When Excel gets a formula that has an array where it's expecting a single
value, you can specify that it should apply the formula to each value in the
array and return the array of results.

For instance, in an array formula, Excel will understand ABS({-1,0,1}) as
"apply ABS() to each of the elements in the array and return the results in a
new array," which in this case will be {1,0,1}.

Similarly, if you use {1,2} * {3,4} in an array formula, multiplication will be
done component-wise, and will result in the array {1*3,2*4}, or {3,8}.

Now, if you type one of these formulas in as is, you won't see an array result.
The formula

    =ABS({-1,0,1})

will just produce the value 1, because Excel doesn't know it's supposed to be
using array formulas and just looks at the first element.

Entering an Array Formula

In order to specify an array formula, you need to hold down both Ctrl and
Shift when you press Enter. If you don't Ctrl-Shift-Enter, your formula won't
work.

You'll know you have an array formula because in the formula bar you'll see it in curly braces.

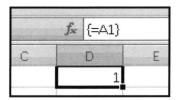

Accordingly, when we write down array formulas, we'll also surround them in curly braces. **You should *never* type these curly braces.** This is just a signal to remind you that these are array formulas and that you should use Ctrl-Shift-Enter when you input them.

The only time you actually type curly braces is when you're specifying constant arrays.

Putting One Formula in One Cell

Most commonly we'll use array formulas that return a single output. We'll do this by finishing with functions like SUM() and AND(), which can take arrays as inputs and return just a single value.

For instance, if you wanted the sum of the absolute values of the contents of cells A1:A100, you could use the array formula

{=SUM(ABS(A1:A100))}

(The curly braces show that it's an array formula and that you have to use Ctrl-Shift-Enter.)

What's going on here? ABS(A1:A100) is the 100x1 array whose values consist of ABS() applied to cells A1:A100. Then SUM() adds up the values of that array, as you'd expect. Because ABS() doesn't normally take an array as an input, this is an array formula that needs to be input with Ctrl-Shift-Enter.

If you forget Ctrl-Shift-Enter, ABS() will only look at the *first cell* of A1:A100, and you'll get the same results as if you'd typed =SUM(ABS(A1)).

Technique: Using Constant Arrays

It's often useful to create array formulas using constant arrays. For instance, if you want to check whether a cell matches any one of several values, you could use

   {=OR(A1={1,2,3})}

Here A1={1,2,3} creates the 3x1 array {A1=1,A1=2,A1=3}. Then OR() tests whether any of these is TRUE. If you forget Ctrl-Shift-Enter, you'll only be testing whether A1 equals 1, and you'll get the wrong answer.

Of course, in this case it wouldn't be substantially more difficult to use the non-array formula

   =OR(A1=1,A2=2,A2=3)

A more interesting example is checking whether the text in a cell contains swear words:

   {=OR(ISNUMBER(SEARCH({"heck","darn","gosh","shoot"},A1)))}

Here the inner SEARCH() creates an array consisting of position numbers (for the swear words that SEARCH() finds) and #VALUE errors (for the swear words that it doesn't). The ISNUMBER() converts this to an array of TRUE and FALSE values, and the OR() checks that at least one of these is TRUE. If you forget Ctrl-Shift-Enter, the formula only checks for "heck."

Another solution is

   {=COUNT(SEARCH({"heck","darn","gosh","shoot"},A1))>0}

since COUNT() counts any position numbers and ignores any #VALUE errors.

Again you could do this as a non-array formula, but you'd have to include a separate SEARCH() for each swear word. And when you realized that you needed to also test for "golly" and "flip" and "jeez," you'd have to add an additional SEARCH() for each of these as well. With our approach, you just have to add them to the constant array.

Technique: Abusing SUM()

Although we mentioned it a long time ago, we haven't really used the fact that you can do arithmetic with Booleans. TRUE counts as 1, and FALSE counts as 0. So, for instance, TRUE+1 will be 2, and FALSE*3 will be 0. TRUE+TRUE+FALSE equals 2.

SUM() ignores Booleans in cells, you'll remember, so if A1 contains TRUE, then SUM(A1) equals 0. However, SUM(A1*1) equals 1, because A1*1 is evaluated as TRUE*1, which equals 1, before SUM() gets a hold of it. Similarly, SUM(A1*A1) equals 1, since A1*A1 is evaluated as TRUE*TRUE, which equals 1.

We can use this trick to make SUM() behave like SUMIF() and COUNTIF().

To start with, put the numbers 1 to 10 in A1:A10.

Imagine we want to count how many of those values are less than 5. The array (A1:A10<5) is a 10x1 array with TRUE values in the first 4 cells (which contain values that are less than 5) and FALSE values in the last 6 cells. Since it only consists of TRUE and FALSE, if we SUM() it using an array formula

    {=SUM((A1:A10<5))}

we'll get 0. However, the array 1*(A1:A10<5) contains 1 in the first 4 cells (from 1 * TRUE) and 0 in the last 6 cells (from 1 * FALSE), so the array formula

{=SUM(1*(A1:A10<5))}

behaves equivalently to COUNTIF(A1:A10,"<5"). Probably you'd never do this with an array formula, since using COUNTIF() is simpler.

What if we wanted SUMIF() functionality?   Consider the array (A1:A10<5)*(A1:A10). The first element is TRUE * 1, which equals 1. The second element is TRUE * 2, which equals 2. The third element is TRUE * 3, which equals 3, and the fourth element is TRUE * 4, which equals 4. The fifth element is FALSE * 5, which equals zero, and similarly all subsequent elements equal zero. So the array formula

{=SUM((A1:A10<5)*(A1:A10))}

equals 1 + 2 + 3 + 4, and is the equivalent of SUMIF(A1:A10,"<5"). Again, you'd probably never do this, since it's easier just to use SUMIF(). But we can extend this method to do things that SUMIF() can't. For example, we can easily add extra conditions to the IF().

The array (A1:A10<5) * (A1:A10>2) will be TRUE precisely for those cells whose value is *both* less than 5 and greater than 2. Therefore

{=SUM((A1:A10<5)*(A1:A10>2)*(A1:A10))}

equals 3 + 4, since 3 and 4 are the only numbers having both conditions TRUE. And this is something you *can't* do with SUMIF. (You could do it with SUMIFS(), except that I made you promise never to use SUMIFS().)

Example: The Histogram, Revisited

Recall our histogram of Denver Broncos by weight:

E	F	G	H	I	J	K	L
Wt.	Age	Exp.	College	How Acq.		Weight	Count
265	22	R	Clemson	CFA- '10		0	33
189	22	R	West Virginia	CFA- '10		225	25
212	27	5th	California	UFA (Arz)-'09		275	21
268	25	4th	Miami	FA-'10		325	4

Previously we used a pair of COUNTIF() functions to figure out each bucket. With array SUM() we can just use one function.

In L2 we want to count the weights in E2:E84 that are greater than or equal to K2 but less than K3. This is just

$$\{=SUM((\$E\$2:\$E\$82>=K2)*(\$E\$2:\$E\$82<K3))\}$$

We can copy and paste this formula down to to L3 and L4. In L5 we don't want an upper bound, so there's just one condition to meet. We can either use the "multiply by 1" trick

$$\{=SUM(1*(\$E\$2:\$E\$82>=K5))\}$$

or just use SUMIF().

Example: A Case-Sensitive SUMIF()

Recall that the SUMIF() function isn't case sensitive. The formula

=SUMIF(A1:A100,"TS",B1:B100)

will include cells in column B that have any of "TS", "Ts", "tS", or "ts" in column A. We know that the EXACT() function returns TRUE only when its arguments are equal including case. Using EXACT() and array formulas, we can get a case-sensitive SUMIF().

What will we need to SUM()? Well, we'll need an array that's TRUE or FALSE depending on whether we should include the row. We can get this array with the formula EXACT(A1:A100,"TS"). Then we can just multiply this by B1:B100.

{=SUM(EXACT(A1:A100,"TS")*(B1:B100))}

Of course we could get a case sensitive COUNTIF() using "multiply by 1."

Example: Working Around Errors

Imagine you want to compute the AVERAGE() of the numbers in cells A1:A100, but some of those cells have errors in them. This means your AVERAGE() computation will also return an error. But you can use array formulas to tell Excel to ignore cells with errors in them.

First, recall that IFERROR() returns its first input unless that's an error, in which case it returns its second input. We can use this to get an array of error-less values. What should we replace errors with? Not 0, since AVERAGE() would treat those as actual zeros, and we want to simply ignore them. Instead, we'll use FALSE, which AVERAGE() will indeed ignore.

So IFERROR(A1:A100,FALSE) represents the array that contains values where A1:A100 contains values and contains FALSE where A1:A100 contains errors. We can find its average with the array formula

{=AVERAGE(IFERROR(A1:A100,FALSE))}

You could handle errors in more complicated ways if you like.

Example: COUNTIFS() with OR() Conditions

When we discussed COUNTIFS() and SUMIFS() (which, of course, you should never use) we pointed out that they worked for AND() conditions but not for OR() conditions. If you want to COUNTIF() cells that meet an OR() condition, you'll have to use array formulas. You have two options, depending on your conditions.

Exclusive OR()

If your conditions are mutually exclusive (which means that at most one of them can be TRUE for any given cell) then you can simply add your Boolean arrays. For instance, to count how many cells in A1:A100 contain values less than 5 or greater than 10, you could use the array formula

   {=SUM((A1:A100<5)+(A1:A100>10))}

For each cell that's less than 5, the two elements in the sum will be TRUE and FALSE, and they'll add up to 1. For each cell that's greater than 10, the two elements will be FALSE and TRUE, and again they'll add up to 1. And for each element between 5 and 10, they'll be FALSE and FALSE and will add up to 0.

The end result is that we'll be adding a 1 each time we meet one of the conditions and a 0 each time we don't, which gives us the count we're looking for.

If we wanted to SUMIF() the corresponding elements in B1:B100, we'd use

   {=SUM(((A1:A100<5)+(A1:A100>10))*(B1:B100))}

Notice the extra parentheses around the original terms, so that Excel adds them first, then multiplies.

Non-Exclusive OR()

If your conditions aren't exclusive, you can't add them the way we did above.
If you do, you'll double-count when both are TRUE.

For instance, if you wanted to count how often there's a 1 in A1:A100 or a 2
in the corresponding cell in B1:B100, you could naively try

> {=SUM((A1:A100=1)+(B1:B100=2))}

For each row that has either a 1 in column A or a 2 in column B but not
both, this will work correctly. Likewise, if a row has neither, this will work.
However, any row that meets both conditions will evaluate as TRUE+TRUE
which equals 2, and such a row will get double-counted, which is wrong!

Instead, we'll have to count whether this sum is greater than 0.

> {=SUM(1*((A1:A100=1+B1:B100=2)>0))}

With array formulas, there are often many ways of doing the same thing. For
instance, you could also use OR():

> {=SUM(1*OR(A1:A100=1,B1:B100=2))}

Or you could use IF():

> {=SUM(1*IF(A1:A100=1,TRUE,B1:B100=2))}

Or you could use two IF()s:

> {=SUM(IF(A1:A100=1,1,IF(B1:B100)=2,1,0)))}

There's rarely just one way to solve a problem!

Technique: Using ROW() to Generate Sequences

If you give the ROW() function a cell, it will return the row number of the cell. If you give it an entire row (like 1:1 or 15:15) it will also return the row number. This means that if you give it multiple rows in an array formula, ROW() will produce the corresponding array of row numbers. ROW(1:3) is the array {1;2;3} and ROW(24:30) is the array {24;25;26;27;28;29;30}. This is an easy way to generate arrays of consecutive numbers.

For instance, you can easily sum all the numbers from 1 to 100 with an array formula:

    {=SUM(ROW(1:100))}

You can even parameterize the array with INDIRECT(). For example, imagine you want to add up all the numbers from 1 to whatever value is in A1. You can represent the correct number of rows with INDIRECT("1:"&A1) and then use the array formula

    {=SUM(ROW(INDIRECT("1:"&A1)))}

Similarly, if you need a variable-sized array of constant values, you could use IF() (which treats positive numbers as TRUE) to transform the row numbers into constants.

For instance, IF(ROW(INDIRECT("1:"&A1)),1) would produce an array with A1 elements all equal to 1.

Example: Finding the Last Occurrence

We've seen that MATCH() and FIND() can find the *first* time a given value or substring occurs. We can use array formulas to find the last occurrence.

The Last MATCH()

MATCH() is the easier of the two. Let's say we want to find the last 1 in cells A1:A100. It's simply in row

$$\{=\text{MAX}(\text{IF}(A1:A100=1,\text{ROW}(A1:A100),0))\}$$

Wherever column A contains 1, the IF() array will contain the row number; wherever column A doesn't contain 1, the IF() array will contain 0. So if the MAX() of this array is 0, 1 wasn't in A1:A100; otherwise, the MAX() of the array is the largest row number where 1 was found.

The Last Character

We can use a similar technique to find the last occurrence of a certain character in a string. Our first step is to turn the string into an array of characters. Now, to get just one character, we'd use MID(). For example, MID(A1,5,1) is the 5th character of the string in A1.

If instead you give MID() an *array* of positions, you can get back an array of characters. For instance, MID("think",{1,2,3,4,5},1) is the array {"t","h","i","n","k"}. To do this to an arbitrary string, we'll need to generate the array of positions based on its length.

So if our string is in A1, we'd need an array of LEN(A1) characters, which we could produce with

$$\text{MID}(A1,\text{ROW}(\text{INDIRECT}("1:"\&\text{LEN}(A1))),1)$$

Then if we want to find the position of the last 'E' in the string in cell A1, we can use IF() to create a new array that contains the character number anywhere there's an 'E' (which requires a second ROW-INDIRECT) and a 0 everywhere else. Then MAX() gives us the largest character number, which is the position of the last 'E'.

```
{=MAX(  IF(  MID(A1,ROW(INDIRECT("1:"&LEN(A1))),1)="E",
             ROW(INDIRECT("1:"&LEN(A1))),
             0))}
```

Obviously you can enter the formula all on one line, but it wouldn't fit in the book that way.

You could find the last occurrence of a longer substring by asking MID() for more than 1 character at time.

Example: Converting Column Names to Numbers

We know that column A is the first column. Since column Z is the 26th, it must be that AA is the 27th, AZ is the 56th, and so on. But what's column TS? Column BOB? When Excel 2023 adds support for four-letter and five-letter columns, what will column JOEL be? Incredibly, we can find out using an array formula.

First, we'll figure out how to turn single letters into column numbers. We know the function CODE() turns single letters into some sort of numbers; however, we need to turn A into 1. We'd also like to deal equally well with upper and lowercase characters. A formula that does this to the character in A1 is

```
=CODE(UPPER(A1))-CODE("A")+1
```

You can check that this turns 'A' into 1, 'B' into 2, and so on. As a next step, we'll turn a sequence of characters (again in A1) into an array of numbers. Instead of feeding the above formula A1, we'll need to feed it the array of the characters that make up A1:

```
MID(A1,ROW(INDIRECT("1:"&LEN(A1))),1)
```

For instance, this turns AZ into {1,26}, as required.

When a column name contains only one letter, the column number is just the letter value itself. J is the 10th letter, and column J is the tenth column. When a column is two letters, increasing the rightmost letter still increases the column number by 1; for example, AJ is one column after AI. However, increasing the second-to-last (first) letter increases the column number by 26. BI is 26 columns after AI. Likewise, if the column name contains three letters, increasing the third-rightmost (first) letter increases the column number by 26 * 26.

In other words, when we have a single-character column name, we want to multiply the array of letter-values by {1}. If it's two characters, we want to multiply the array by {26,1}. If it's three characters, we want to multiply it by {26 * 26, 26, 1} which (suggestively) is

{POWER(26,2),POWER(26,1),POWER(26,0)}

or (even more suggestively)

{POWER(26,3-1),POWER(26,3-2),POWER(26,3-3)}

This suggests how to generate the array:

POWER(26,LEN(A1)-ROW(INDIRECT("1:"&LEN(A1))))

All that's left is to assemble the mess of an array-formula that SUM()s the product of these two arrays.

```
{=SUM(   (CODE(UPPER(MID(A1,ROW(INDIRECT("1:"&LEN(A1))),1)))
         -CODE("A")+1)*
         (POWER(26,LEN(A1)-ROW(INDIRECT("1:"&LEN(A1)))))
      )  }
```

Example: Multi-MATCH()

The formula MATCH(10,A1:A100,0) finds the index of the first cell in A1:A100 with value equal to 10. Imagine that we need to find the first row where the value in A1:A100 is 10 and also the value in B1:B100 is 20. We can use an array formula.

An incorrect (but correct-looking) solution would be

$$\{=\text{MATCH}(10\&20,(A1:A100)\&(B1:B100),0)\}$$

Here, (A1:A100)&(B1:B100) returns the 100x1 array each of whose elements is the value in column A concatenated with the corresponding value in column B.

What makes this solution incorrect? Well, MATCH() is trying to find the string 10&20, or 1020. However, 10 and 20 are not the only values that concatenate to 1020. For instance, if A1 contained 102 and B1 contained 0, then A1&B1 would also equal 1020! To be safe, we should add some sort of separator that doesn't appear in our data.

If columns A and B contain only numbers, we could separate them with an underscore:

$$\{=\text{MATCH}(10\&"\_"\&20,(A1:A100)\&"\_"\&(B1:B100),0)\}$$

Now the 10 20 row will get concatenated to 10_20 while the 102 0 row will get concatenated to 102_0.

Cross Products

In the array formulas we've looked at so far, Excel has applied some sort of formula to each element of an array, creating a new array with identical dimensions.

You can also combine row arrays with column arrays to create multi-dimensional arrays. As we've seen many times, the array formula

   {=SUM({1,1,1}*{1,1,1})}

will array-multiply the two (identical) row arrays to get again {1,1,1} which will then sum to 3. However, the similar formula

   {=SUM({1,1,1}*{1;1;1})}

needs to array-multiply a row of 1's by a column of 1's, which it does by multiplying the row by the first column, by the second column, and by the third column, which creates a 3x3 array of 1's, which sums to 9. It's not likely you'll find this useful, although you might.

One Formula, Multiple Cells

So far all the array formulas we've used have managed to produce only a single cell worth of output, using SUM() or MATCH() or some other function that happily takes arrays as inputs but returns only one value.

You can also use array formulas to return multiple outputs. With most formulas this doesn't add a whole lot of value. For instance, if you select cells A1:A5 and enter the array formula

   {=ROW()}

with Ctrl-Shift-Enter, Excel thinks of this as one formula applied to all five cells, producing 5 different outputs. If you try to get rid of the formula from just A5, you'll get stopped with a "cannot change part of an array" message. Some people consider this a feature, although most people consider it a nuisance and prefer to just place the non-array formula

   =ROW()

in each of the cells A1:A5. We won't ever use array formulas this way.

But there are some Excel functions whose normal usage produces multiple outputs, in which case this technique becomes necessary. To properly use a function which produces a column of 5 outputs, you have to select a range like A1:A5 and enter the function as an array formula.

Technique: Building Histograms with FREQUENCY()

We've already seen how to build histograms using COUNTIF() or array SUM() formulas. Because Excel usually contains many ways to do the same thing, it turns out there's a FREQUENCY() function which returns the entire histogram as an array.

FREQUENCY() requires two arrays as inputs. The first is the array of values you want to histogram, the second an array of buckets. The output of FREQUENCY() is an array with one column, and one more row than the number of buckets. If you give FREQUENCY() four buckets, then it will return (up to) five outputs, and you should enter it as an array formula into 5 cells to capture all of them.

Buckets in Order

If your buckets are in increasing order, for instance

    {10,20,30,40}

then FREQUENCY() will use each as an *upper bound* and tack on an extra bucket for everything that's too big. The function

    {=FREQUENCY({4,10,16,22,28,34,40,46},{10,20,30,40})}

would return the array

$\{2;1;2;2;1\}$

understanding the buckets as "less than or equal to 10," "more than 10 but less than or equal to 20," and so on, with the fifth bucket meaning "more than 40."

Buckets Out of Order

It's not immediately apparent what FREQUENCY() does when its buckets are not in ascending order. The one case where it does behave reliably is when every data point exactly matches a bucket. For instance,

$\{$=FREQUENCY($\{1,2,3,4,5,2,3,4\},\{5,1,2,3,4\}$)$\}$

will return the array

$\{1;1;2;2;2;0\}$

as you'd hope. Whenever you have an array formula like this, you can always request *fewer* cells and just not get the data you left out. If you used FREQUENCY() this way, you might not ask for the contents of the last "everything else" bucket. Or you might.

Duplicate Buckets

If you specify a bucket more than once, its first occurrence gets completely filled and its later occurrences all get zeroes. Why would you specify a bucket more than once? You probably wouldn't. But what if the buckets were generated on the fly?

Example: Counting Unique Items

Counting Unique Numbers

The array

{5,2,6,3,4,1,5,5,3}

contains 9 elements, but it only contains 6 *unique* elements. We can count elements with COUNT(), but to count unique elements we need a clever use of FREQUENCY().

Think about

FREQUENCY({5,2,6,3,4,1,5,5,3},{5,2,6,3,4,1,5,5,3})

which uses the same array for both the data and the buckets. Although the buckets are out of order, it will still count exact matches. This means the resulting array will be

{3;1;1;2;1;1;0;0;0}

since there are three 5's, one 2, one 6, two 3's, one 4, and one 1, at which point we've already seen the last three elements 5, 5, and 3.

If you look at the output, each element that's greater than 0 represents the first occurrence of an element in the original array; each entry that equals 0 represents a repeat occurrence. This means that the number of unique elements in the original array is exactly the number of nonzero elements in the self-FREQUENCY() array.

So to find the number of unique elements in A1:A100, you could use the array formula

{=SUM(IF(FREQUENCY(A1:A100,A1:A100)>0,1,0))}

which – since it uses SUM() – returns only a single value.

Counting Unique Non-Numerics

If you have instead a list of names in A1:A100 this won't work, because FREQUENCY() only works on numbers. Fortunately, there's a simple way to map text to numbers using MATCH(). Think about the array

    MATCH(A1:A100,A1:A100,0)

Since MATCH() expects an array as its second input, the "array formula" aspect of this involves expanding the array supplied as the first input.

The first element of the resulting array is then MATCH(A1,A1:A100,0), the first time A1 occurs in A1:A100, which is necessarily 1. Its second element is MATCH(A2,A1:A100,0), which is either 1 (if A2 equals A1) or 2 (if it doesn't). In essence, it takes the array A1:A100 and replaces each element with *the index number of the first time that value occurs.* This means that if two cells have equal values in A1:A100, they'll have equal values in this new array, and if they don't then they won't.

Necessarily, then, this new array has the exact same number of unique elements as the original array, which means we can count them with the somewhat unwieldy

    {=SUM(IF(FREQUENCY(MATCH(A1:A100,A1:A100,0),
                          MATCH(A1:A100,A1:A100,0))>0,1,0))}

Technique: Multiple Regression with LINEST()

As we saw earlier, SLOPE() and INTERCEPT() found the best-fit linear relationship between a dependent variable and a single independent variable.

But in many situations you'll want to look at variables that depend on multiple factors. That is, you'll have multiple independent variables $x_1, \ldots, x_k$, and you'll want to find the best relationship

$$y = m_1 * x_1 + \ldots + m_k * x_k + b$$

When we performed simple regression, we used different functions to compute the SLOPE() and the INTERCEPT() and the RSQ() and the STEYX(). For multiple regression, we have one function that does it all: LINEST().

LINEST() takes four inputs. The first is the array of dependent y values. The second is the (rectangular) array of independent x variables. If there are k different independent variables, then this array should have k columns, and it should always have the same number of rows as the first input. The third input is a Boolean allowing us to insist that the intercept b equal zero, which we could specify with FALSE. Don't ever do this unless you know you have a good reason to. The last input is another Boolean that specifies whether LINEST() should output a lot of information (TRUE) or not much information (FALSE).

The last two inputs are optional, and if you omit them they'll be TRUE ("don't assume b is zero") and FALSE ("don't output extra information"). Since we'll always want the detailed outputs, we won't ever leave them off.

The detailed output will require 1 column more than the number of dependent variables and 5 rows, and will have the following format:

	A	B	C	D	E	F
1	m_k	m_{k-1}	...	m_2	m_1	b
2	se_k	se_{k-1}	...	se_2	se_1	se_b
3	r^2	se_y				
4	F	df				
5	ss_{reg}	ss_{resid}				

Notice that if you have more than one independent variable, the output won't fill an entire rectangular array. Nonetheless, you need to enter it into a rectangular array big enough to hold its outputs, which means that you'll get a bunch of #N/A errors everywhere there's nothing to output. It's ugly, but it doesn't hurt anything.

The top row contains the regression coefficients, which (irritatingly) are in the reverse order as the independent variables. The leftmost column contains the coefficient for the rightmost variable, and so on, with the constant term all the way at the right. If you ever ignore my advice and request that Excel not return detailed outputs, you'll only get this first row.

Standard Errors

The second row contains the *standard errors* for each of the coefficients (and of the constant term). Roughly speaking, each indicates how confident we should feel about the estimate of the corresponding coefficient. A standard error that's much smaller than the coefficient indicates confidence that our estimate is a good one. If a coefficient is small compared to its standard error, you might consider removing that variable and redoing the regression.

One way this might arise is if two of your independent variables are highly correlated with each other. If x_1 and x_2 take on very similar values, then (for instance) $2x_1 + x_2$ and $x_1 + 2x_2$ also take on very similar values, which makes it hard to confidently decide that one is the "best-fitting" linear combination. In the most extreme case, when some of the independent variables are perfectly correlated, regression won't even work.

The third row contains the R-squared, which you already know is the square of the correlation between the *predicted y* values and the *actual y* values. And it contains the standard error of regression, which you previously knew as STEYX().

In multiple regressions, R-squared is harder to use, because adding extra variables always increases the R-squared. For instance, the "best-fit" regression of y on x_1 and x_2 has to be at least as good the "best-fit" regression of y

on x_1 alone, simply because the best x_1-only model is one of the candidates when we choose a model involving both x_1 and x_2. So a high R-squared value doesn't mean you have a good model, it could just mean that you've added lots of unnecessary variables that happened to reduce your errors. You should *always* look at the standard errors of the coefficients to make sure they're meaningful, which means that you should always use LINEST() with the "show extra statistics" option.

Analysis of Variance

The fourth row contains the F-statistic of the regression and its "degrees of freedom." These indicate how likely it is that the regression represents an actual relationship rather than a chance one. Large values of the F-statistic hint at meaningful regressions. If you want to make this concept mathematically precise (which we won't do), you'll need to know the degrees of freedom as well.

Finally, the fifth row shows the Sum of Squares of the Regression (that is, the sum of the squares of the differences between the predicted values of y and the average value of y) and the Sum of Squares of Errors (that is, the sum of the squares of the differences between the predicted values of y and the actual values of y).

It turns out that if you add these together, you get the Sum of Squares Total, which equals the sum of the squares of the differences between the actual values of y and the average value of y. What does it all mean? Well, each observed value of the y variable differs by some amount from the overall average y value. The SSR and SSE break down the overall difference into the part that's accounted for by the regression model and the part that's not.

If you are statistically inclined, you might find these useful.

TREND()

Because the output of LINEST() is not in an easy to use format, Excel provides a TREND() function that calculates the linear model and uses it for predictions, all in one step.

It takes either three or four inputs. The first, as we're used to at this point, is the array of dependent y variables, and the second is the array of independent x variables. The third is another (possibly identical) array of x variables that you want to make predictions for. The last input is a Boolean specifying whether you want the regression to have a constant term. If you leave it out (which we'll always do) or set it TRUE, a constant term will be included.

If the third argument contains only one row, then you can enter the formula normally. But if it contains multiple rows, the output will also contain the same number of rows, which means you'll need to enter it into multiple cells with Ctrl-Shift-Enter.

Although it's possible to use TREND() without LINEST(), that would require you to have an immense amount of faith that your model is good. We don't operate on faith in Thinking Spreadsheet, and therefore you should always first use LINEST() to make sure that the model looks good, and only then use TREND(). The effect of this is that Excel will be computing your regression twice, which might slow things down.

One possible problem with using TREND() is that once you have a multi-cell array formula somewhere, you can't sort or delete from its outputs. This may or may not be a limitation.

Multiple Dependent Variables

Imagine you have a set of independent variables $x_1 \ldots x_k$, just as before, but you want to find linear models to predict two different dependent variables y_1 and y_2. Well, the best-fit linear model to predict y_1 in terms of the x variables doesn't depend on y_2 at all, and vice versa.

So the thing to do is simply use LINEST() once to find a model for y_1 and a second time to find a model for y_2. Each will have its own coefficients, standard errors, and so on. For each additional dependent variable, you can just add another instance of LINEST().

Example: Predicting Football Wins, Revisited

We left off our "Predicting Football Wins" example frustrated that we couldn't use *both* points Scored and points Allowed to predict the number of Wins. Now we can.

	A	B	C	D
1	Team	Scored	Allowed	Wins
2	Arizona	375	325	10
3	Atlanta	363	325	9
4	Baltimore	391	261	9
5	Buffalo	258	326	6

We always need 5 rows for the output, and since we have two independent variables, we'll need 3 columns. So we'll enter the formula in H2:J6

	E	F	G	H	I	J	K
	Predict	Error					
				=LINEST(D2:D33,B2:C33,TRUE,TRUE)			

and use Ctrl-Shift-Enter:

H	I	J
-0.019095	0.028911	4.628752
0.0041217	0.002985	2.105826
0.8725839	1.189436	#N/A
99.300382	29	#N/A
280.97202	41.02798	#N/A

This gives us a model of

Wins = -0.019095 * Allowed + 0.028911 * Scored + 4.628752

which we can enter in E2 with

=$H$2*C2+$I$2*B2+$J$2

and then fill down. (I told you that the reverse order of the regression coefficients was going to be an irritation.) Alternatively (and equivalently) you could enter the array formula

{=TREND(D2:D33,B2:C33,B2:C33)}

into cells E2:E33. (Although if you did so, as mentioned above, the multi-row array formula would subsequently prevent you from sorting the data, say, by error.)

Then in F2 we can compute the error as E2-D2:

	A	B	C	D	E	F
1	Team	Scored	Allowed	Wins	Predict	Error
2	Arizona	375	325	10	9.264263	-0.73574
3	Atlanta	363	325	9	8.917334	-0.08267
4	Baltimore	391	261	9	10.94895	1.948947
5	Buffalo	258	326	6	5.862605	-0.13739

As is necessarily the case when we add more variables, the R-squared increased, and the standard error of the regression went down. Each of the coefficients is a good bit larger than its standard error, which suggests they all "belong" in the regression.

Our model still isn't perfect. You can check that we most underpredict wins for Indianapolis, Cincinnati, and Oakland, and that we most overpredict wins for Baltimore, Washington, and New England.

If you wanted to continue, you might look for a statistic that (at a minimum) distinguishes these two sets of teams. If you find one, let me know!

CHAPTER 22

THE PIVOT

Pivot tables are a form of magic.[1] Actually, they're pretty simple, but no one ever understands them, so that when you get good at pivot tables (which you will, if you read and understand this chapter) people will think you can work magic. If you're clever, perhaps you can parlay this into a series of performances in Vegas, where (I'm told) what happens stays.

Pivot tables are a Microsoft-Excel-only feature, and our treatment will be pretty Excel-2007-or-later-centric.

What Is a Pivot Table?

Over the course of the book you've become adept at using tools like SUMIF() and COUNTIF() to answer quantitative questions about datasets, like

- What fraction of male babies born in 2009 had names starting with J?
- How popular are different browsers among the visitors to my web site?
- What's the average weight of the quarterbacks on the Denver Broncos roster?

Once you learn pivot tables, you'll be able to answer questions like these both *quickly* and *without writing complicated formulas*.

---

[1] Magic doesn't really exist.

At a high level, we'll say that a pivot table is a way to dynamically aggregate, bucket, and filter data. Let's take that description apart.

Aggregating Data

By *aggregate* we simply mean producing summary statistics that describe the data. For instance, if you had a football roster, some aggregates might be "the average weight," "the number of players," "the length of the longest name," and "the largest uniform number"

Pivot tables only aggregate *numeric* data. For instance, you can't use them to find the largest (i.e. last alphabetically) *name* the same way they find the largest uniform number. Usually this won't be a problem.

Bucketing Data

Once you know what aggregates you want, pivot tables allow you to compute and re-compute them by placing your data into *buckets*. For instance, you might want to know the average weight *by position*, so that you'd see the average for quarterbacks, the average for running backs, and so on. You might want to know the largest uniform number *by years of experience*, so that you'd see the largest number for rookies, the largest for second-year players, and so on.

You might want to bucket by multiple fields; for instance, you might want to know the number of players by position and by year (e.g. "there are 3 defensive ends with 5 years of experience"). And you might want to group buckets into larger ones; rather than bucketing by "years of experience" you might want your buckets to be "less than 4 years of experience" and "at least 4 years of experience." Rather than bucketing by position, you might want your buckets to be "offensive positions" and "defensive positions."

Pivot tables allow you to do all these things.

Filtering Data

Pivot tables also make it easy to compute aggregates on only *some* of your data. For instance, you might want to know the average weight by position *excluding rookies*. It's easy to specify that a pivot table should ignore (for instance) all players with zero years of experience.

In a Dynamic Way

What makes pivot tables really special is that all the aforementioned features are *dynamic*. Want to change your aggregate from "average weight" to "maximum weight"? Want to change your buckets from "position" to "college"? Want to change your filter from "exclude rookies" to "exclude players older than 30"?

If you'd used formulas for your computations, you'd have to go in and laboriously change them all. But if you'd used a pivot table, you could make each of these changes *instantly*. (OK, maybe each would take you several seconds, but it would still be faster and easier than modifying lots of complex formulas.)

This makes pivot tables an ideal tool for quickly *exploring* data. Once you're certain that the quantity you care about is "average weight of non-rookie quarterbacks," probably the Thinking Spreadsheet thing to do is to create a formula that automatically updates as the data changes. However, when you're initially trying to figure out what features of the data you even care about, pivot tables are an invaluable alternative to crafting and re-crafting complex formulas in a trial-and-error fashion.

A Quick Detour: Tables

Excel 2007 and later has a "Table" feature (not to be confused with the "Data Table" feature we learned in our Monte Carlo chapter or the "Pivot

Table" feature we'll learn about shortly) which is sometimes convenient when working with pivot tables. For instance, imagine we have some data we want to explore with a pivot table.

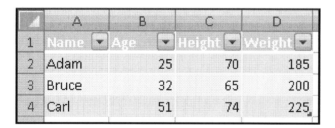

Click somewhere in the data range and then on the Insert ribbon choose "Table". Make sure "My data has headers" is checked (and before that, make sure your data has headers, i.e. column names in the top row) and click OK. Your data will be highlighted in a clever every-other-row way, with the row of headers in bold and with dropdown arrows.

What does this table do? A couple of things. First, Excel has given it a name that we can use to refer to it. If you click anywhere in the table, a new Table Tools - Design ribbon appears, and if you click on it you'll see the name Excel has given it.

You can change the name, and you can use it in formulas. So far this is pretty uninteresting. One thing that makes tables nice is that they'll *automatically grow*. For instance, let's say we need to add Darren, who's 40 years old, 68 inches tall, and 175 pounds. As soon as you type Darren into A5, the table will automatically add another row.

	A	B	C	D
1	Name	Age	Height	Weight
2	Adam	25	70	185
3	Bruce	32	65	200
4	Carl	51	74	225
5	Darren			

This means the name Table1 (or whatever you changed it to) will instantly refer to the new, larger table, and any formulas that reference Table1 will also refer to the larger table.

Tables will grow columns too, and will even automatically fill formulas. For instance, let's say we want to add in column E age in "Dog Years".

One estimate is that the first two dog years are 10.5 human years each, and that every subsequent dog year is 4 human years. This means that if your human age is less than 21, you divide it by 10.5. If it's more than 21, you start with 2 dog years and add 1/4 of all the years above 21.

First, type Dog Years in E1. The table will automatically grow. Then in E2, enter the formula for dog years:

=IF(B2<21,B2/10.5,2+(B2-21)/4)

Excel automatically fills your formula down.

	A	B	C	D	E
1	Name ▼	Age ▼	Height ▼	Weight ▼	Dog Ye ▼
2	Adam	25	70	185	3
3	Bruce	32	65	200	4.75
4	Carl	51	74	225	9.5
5	Darren	40	68	175	6.75

And if you add another row to the table (try it!), Excel will fill the formula down into the new row as well.

Excel may try to replace the B2 in your formula with an ugly expression involving the table name. This is undesirable Thinking Spreadsheet behavior. If it happens, disable it using Office Button - Excel Options - Formulas - Use table names in formulas.

Because of these convenient features, we'll always Table our data before making a Pivot Table out of it. If you're using an older version of Excel, there are no Tables, and you'll just have to Pivot Table the raw data instead.

Sorting and Filtering with Tables

Another reason people often use Tables is that they make it easier to Sort and Filter data. Each column header has a down arrow, and clicking it gives you option to show or hide specific data values, and to sort the table based on the data in that column. (Of course, you can sort tables using the normal Data ribbon Sort features as well.)

Generally you shouldn't *hide* things in your spreadsheet, and "filtering" is kind of a nice way of saying "hiding." If you'd like to look at only specific subsets of your data, a better way is to build a Pivot Table.

Creating Pivot Tables

Before creating a pivot table you'll need to get your data in the proper format. It needs to be in a table (or a Table), with descriptive labels in the top row. In this example we'll work with fictional sales data, which you can download from ThinkingSpreadsheet.com.

	A	B	C	D	E
1	Month	Region	Salesperson	Quota	Actual
2	Jan-09	Central	Ace	$50,000	$59,165
3	Jan-09	East	Deb	$75,000	$112,307
4	Jan-09	East	Keith	$40,000	$26,188
5	Jan-09	West	Kwame	$80,000	$105,702
6	Jan-09	Central	McCoy	$50,000	$41,723
7	Jan-09	East	Mel	$45,000	$56,701

Each line represents the monthly sales numbers for one of our salespeople. It contains the Month, the Salesperson's name, the Region he covers, his monthly Quota, and his Actual sales.

The first step to create a PivotTable is to click anywhere in the data, and then on the Insert ribbon click the PivotTable icon all the way on the left.

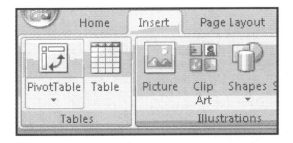

You'll get a "Create PivotTable" window, which most of the time will correctly identify the data you want. Excel's default behavior is to put the pivot table in a New Worksheet, although I prefer to put it to the right of its data, which you can do by clicking the Existing Worksheet radio button and choosing a location to the right of the data. Choose I3 and click OK.

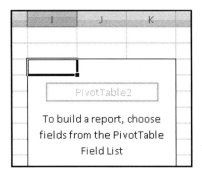

You should see a rectangle with a label (like "PivotTable1" or "PivotTable2") and the instructions "To build a report, choose fields from the PivotTable Field List." This lives over on the right:

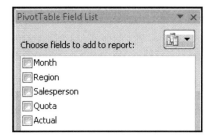

Below it are regions that correspond to the pivot table features we previously identified.

If we drag fields from the "PivotTable Field List" to those regions, they'll get incorporated into our pivot table.

The **Values** region is for fields we want to *aggregate*. If you drag an all-numeric field to Values, its *sum* will be added to the pivot table. If you drag a field that has non-numeric data in it, its *count* will be added.

The **Row Labels** and **Column Labels** regions are where we specify our *buckets*. Any field dragged to the Row Labels region will be used for bucketing along the rows of the pivot table, and any field dragged to the Column Labels region will be used for bucketing along the columns of the pivot table. You can drag multiple fields to each, in which case the buckets will be nested.

Finally, the **Report Filter** region is where you drag fields that you want to use *only* for filtering. (If you want to use a field for both filtering *and* bucketing, then just drag it to the Row Labels or Column Labels.) They'll appear above the table.

Using Pivot Tables

To start with, we'll look at our actual sales, by dragging "Actual" from the Field List into the Values section. It will show up in the PivotTable itself, but with no formatting.

Sum of Actual
4392528.325

Format it as Currency and get rid of the decimals. Now we can look at our sales by month by dragging Month from the Field List to the Row Labels section.

Row Labels ▼	Sum of Actual
Jan-09	$425,504
Feb-09	$328,644
Mar-09	$287,165
Apr-09	$455,534
May 09	$403 790

It's a little bit irritating that our row labels are called Row Labels rather than something more descriptive like "Month." Click somewhere in the PivotTable, and then select the PivotTable Tools - Design ribbon that appears. Under Report Layout, switch to "Tabular Form." This will give each field you drag to Row Labels its own column, which means the PivotTable will take up more space than if you left it in Compact Form. However, each of the fields you use for bucketing will be labeled, which makes your PivotTable much easier to understand. This is a good tradeoff, and so we'll always use Tabular Form.

To break things down further by Region, drag Region to the Column Labels section.

Sum of Actual	Region ▼			
Month ▼	Central	East	West	Grand Total
Jan-09	$100,888	$195,196	$129,420	$425,504
Feb-09	$70,429	$204,325	$53,890	$328,644
Mar-09	$102,683	$116,354	$68,128	$287,165
Apr-09	$120,273	$187,334	$147,927	$455,534

Each cell represents the sum of the Actual amounts that fall into its bucket. So the Actual sales in January in the East region were $195,196. You could have computed that from the original data with SUMIFS() or array formulas, but a PivotTable is much faster and more dynamic.

If you only want to look at the data for East Region, there are two ways to filter the Pivot Table down. The less-preferable way is to click on the down arrow next to Region, which will allow you to unselect regions. If you uncheck West and Central, the Pivot Table will behave (and calculate) as if those rows didn't exist.

Sum of Actual	Region	
Month	East	Grand Total
Jan-09	$ 195,196	$ 195,196
Feb-09	$ 204,325	$ 204,325
Mar-09	$ 116,354	$ 116,354

The down arrow next to Region has turned into a filter icon to show that some of the Regions have been filtered out.

A better method is to (after rechecking West and Central) drag Region from Column Labels to Report Filter, at which point it becomes a dropdown box above the PivotTable that you can click and filter.

Region	East
Month	Sum of Actual
Jan-09	$195,196
Feb-09	$204,325
Mar-09	$116,354

Now we can answer questions about just the East region sales data. Which was the best sales month? With only 12 months of data we can eyeball it, but if there were more we could sort. Click on any of the Actual amounts, and then either right-click and choose Sort - Largest to Smallest or on the Data ribbon click the Sort Z-A button.

Region	East	
Month ▼	**Sum of Actual**	
Dec-09	$215,806	
Feb-09	$204,325	
Jan-09	$195,196	
Sep-09	$191,936	

In the East region, December was the best sales month, followed by February. If you want to see the results for the West region instead, just change the filter to West region.

Region	West	
Month ▼	**Sum of Actual**	
Apr-09	$147,927	
Jan-09	$129,420	
Sep-09	$128,238	
May-09	$126,673	

The PivotTable is again sorted by Actual sales amounts, even though that's a different order for the months.

Subtotals and Grand Totals

Still with Actuals in the Values section, drag Month and then Region to Row Labels.

Month		Region		Sum of Actual
⊟ **Dec-09**		Central		$159,485
		East		$215,806
		West		$110,029
Dec-09 Total				**$485,320**
⊟ **Apr-09**		Central		$120,273
		East		$187,334

By default Excel shows subtotals for every Row Label (and every Column Label) but the last. On the PivotTable Tools - Design ribbon, there's a Subtotals feature where you can enable or disable subtotals altogether. You can also enable or disable them for specific fields. If you right-click anywhere in the Month column of the PivotTable, you'll get a menu with the option to disable subtotals just for Month.

You can of course re-enable them the same way.

Alternatively, you can enable or disable subtotals in the Field Settings popup, which you can get to either by clicking Field Settings on the PivotTable Tools - Options ribbon, or by clicking the down arrow next to Month under Row Labels.

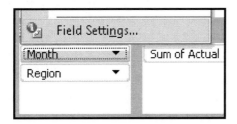

Whenever your PivotTable has more than one row, Excel will automatically add a Grand Total row at the bottom. And whenever it has more than one column, Excel will automatically add a Grand Total column at the right.

You can enable and disable these Grand Totals using the Grand Totals pull-down menu on the PivotTable Tools - Design ribbon. You can also enable or disable them on the Totals & Filters tab of the PivotTable Options popup, which you can get to either by clicking on PivotTable options in the PivotTable Tools - Options ribbon, or by right-clicking on the PivotTable and choosing PivotTable Options.

Value Field Settings

When you drag a field into the Values section, Excel will by default aggregate numeric fields with Sum and other fields with Count. To change this, right-click on one of the Values in the Pivot Table and change the Summarize Data By option to Max or Min or whatever you like.

You can also change the aggregation method by clicking the down arrow next to the field under Values and choosing Value Field Settings.

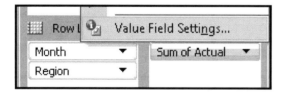

Alternatively, you can click in the value field in the PivotTable and then choose Field Settings on the PivotTable Tools - Options ribbon.

For the most part, each option behaves like its corresponding function. Sum finds the SUM() of the values in each bucket, ignoring values that aren't numbers. Max finds the MAX() of the values in each bucket, and so on. The only one that's non-intuitive is Count, which is *the number of rows that have non-blank values* in each bucket. (Typically your data won't have blank values, and so Count will simply count the number of rows in each bucket.) There's a Count Numbers option that behaves like COUNT().

The Value Field Settings menu has another tab that allows you to change how the aggregates are displayed. You should avoid most of these options, as they make your PivotTable supremely breakable. For instance, you could display the Actual amounts as "% of the amount in the Central Region," which works when your Row Labels consist just of Region but which produces lots of #N/A errors once you change them.

Accordingly, we'll focus on the difficult-to-break ones, which are the most useful anyway. The most common (and default) is Normal, which simply shows the data as is. The other ones we'll use are "% of Row," "% of Column," and "% of Total."

Still with Actual in the Values section, put Month as the Row Label and Region as the Column Label. The Pivot Table is probably still sorted largest to smallest, so either click the down arrow next to Month and choose "Sort Oldest to Newest" or click on one of the months and then click the "Sort A to Z" button on the Home ribbon.

Sum of Actual	Region			
Month	Central	East	West	Grand Total
Jan-09	$ 100,888	$ 195,196	$ 129,420	$ 425,504
Feb-09	$ 70,429	$ 204,325	$ 53,890	$ 328,644
Mar-09	$ 102,683	$ 116,354	$ 68,128	$ 287,165
Apr-09	$ 120,272	$ 187,224	$ 147,027	$ 455,524

Now go into the Value Field Setting for Actual and on the Show Values As tab change it from Normal to % of Row.

Sum of Actual	Region			
Month	Central	East	West	Grand Total
Jan-09	23.71%	45.87%	30.42%	100.00%
Feb-09	21.43%	62.17%	16.40%	100.00%
Mar-09	35.76%	40.52%	23.72%	100.00%
Apr-09	26.40%	41.12%	32.47%	100.00%

The underlying data hasn't changed, but Excel no longer displays the Actual amounts. Instead, it shows what percentage each bucket contains of the total in its row. By design, the numbers in each row sum to 100%, as you can see.

You can similarly show the values as % of Column, which behaves analogously. With that setting, the numbers in each *column* will sum to 100%.

Finally, you can show the values as % of Total, in which case all the numbers in the Pivot Table will sum to 100%.

Sum of Actual	Region			
Month	Central	East	West	Grand Total
Jan-09	2.30%	4.44%	2.95%	9.69%
Feb-09	1.60%	4.65%	1.23%	7.48%
Mar-09	2.34%	2.65%	1.55%	6.54%

The total for each row is the percentage of the overall Actual values contained in that row's buckets, and similarly for columns.

Most of the time, though, you'll just Show Values in the Normal way.

Tweaking Buckets

We've seen that you can change the order of the Row Labels or Column Labels by sorting. You can also change them by clicking and dragging.

Change the Show Values As back to Normal, if you haven't already, and put Salesperson as the Row Label (and nothing as Column Label).

Salesperson ▾	Sum of Actual
Ace	$ 558,637
Deb	$ 1,182,161
Keith	$ 331,773
Kwame	$ 989,891

Let's say you want to see Kwame at the top of the list. Select the cell containing his name and mouse over the top dark border until the four-way arrow appears.

Keith	$ 331,773
Kwame	$ 989,891
McCoy	$ 573,136

Click and drag it to the top, where you want it to go. A fuzzy bar will appear to indicate its destination.

Salesperson ▾	Sum of Actual
Ace	$ 558,637
Deb I3:J3	$ 1,182,161
Keith	$ 331,773
Kwame	$ 989,891
McCoy	$ 573,136

Release the mouse button, and you'll see your new order.

Salesperson ▾	Sum of Actual
Kwame	$ 989,891
Ace	$ 558,637
Deb	$ 1,182,161
Keith	$ 331,773

You can move more than one name at a time, too, just by selecting multiple names before dragging.

Manual Groups

Imagine your salespeople work in teams, and that you'd like to look at Keith and Deb's combined numbers. Keith and Deb are already next to each other, but if they weren't you'd have to re-order the Row Labels so they were.

Select both their names, right-click, and choose Group.

Salesperson2 ▼	Salesperson ▼	Sum of Actual
⊟ Kwame	Kwame	$ 989,891
⊟ Ace	Ace	$ 558,637
⊟ Group1	Deb	$ 1,182,161
	Keith	$ 331,773
⊟ McCov	McCov	$ 573 13c

Excel has created a new virtual Field called Salesperson2, which is the same as Salesperson except that for every row where Salesperson was Keith or Deb, Salesperson2 is the unhelpful Group1. Click on Group1 and type Keith/Deb to rename it. Salesperson2 is also not a helpful name, so go into its Field Settings and change it to SalesPair.

Finally, remove Salesperson from from Row Labels, and you'll see the new data by SalesPair.

SalesPair ▼	Sum of Actual
Kwame	$ 989,891
Ace	$ 558,637
Keith/Deb	$ 1,513,934
McCov	$ 573 13c

At this point you can group together other Salespeople (like McCoy and Mel). To undo a grouping simply right-click on a group and choose Ungroup. If you eliminate all the groups, so that in every case SalesPair and Salesperson have the same values, the SalesPair field will vanish altogether, since it no longer does anything.

If you wanted to add Ace into the Keith/Deb group, you probably shouldn't simply group those SalesPairs together. When you Group together cells that already contain a grouping (like Keith/Deb), Excel will create a *new* field (Salesperson3) so that it can preserve the Keith/Deb grouping at the SalesPair level. If your goal is really to replace Keith/Deb with Keith/Deb/Ace, you should first Ungroup Keith/Deb and only then Group the three Salesperson rows back together.

Automatic Groups

When you have Date or Time data in one of your Fields, Excel will do some sorts of groupings automatically. Get rid of all the Row Labels and replace them with Month.

Right-click on any date in the Row Labels and choose Group. You'll get a popup window with the option of automatically grouping by Month, Year, or several other choices. If you have several years of data (which we don't), you might find this useful.

Changing the Data

There's two problems with Group By. First, if you have a lot of fields in your Row Labels, it's a pain to group them together. More importantly, if you ever add new values to the field, they won't be grouped.

For instance, imagine we need to group our Salespeople by the first letters of their names. It's easy enough to group Keith and Kwame together and to group McCoy and Mel together. But once we hire a Kyle, he won't be included in the "K" grouping until we manually Ungroup it, drag him to the right place, and then reGroup it. This is far from Thinking Spreadsheet.

A better solution is to build this grouped field into the data itself. It's easy enough to add a Letter column that calculates the first letter of the Salesperson column. And if your data is in a Table, Letter will automatically populate when you add more rows.

Then when you build a Pivot Table out of your data, you'll already have the desired Letter field without having to do any grouping at all. This is often the best solution!

Technique: Calculated Fields and Items

So far we've only looked at each Salesperson's Actual sales, but probably you also want to see how they're doing against their Quotas. Let's start with Salesperson as the Row Labels (sorted alphabetically if they're not already), and both Actual and Quota as Values (both formatted as Currency with no decimal places).

Salesperson ▾	Values	
	Sum of Actual	Sum of Quota
Ace	$ 558,637	$ 605,000
Deb	$ 1,182,161	$ 925,000
Keith	$ 331,773	$ 500,000
Kwame	$ 989,891	$ 960,000

We'd like to see each Salesperson's variance from Quota, both in absolute ($ difference) terms and relative (% difference) terms.

The simplest thing to do is to calculate it outside the Pivot Table in column L. For instance, in L5, you could compute Ace's variance as

=K5-J5

and fill down.

Salesperson ▼	Values		
	Sum of Actual	Sum of Quota	
Ace	$ 558,637	$ 605,000	$ 46,363
Deb	$ 1,182,161	$ 925,000	$(257,161)
Keith	$ 331,773	$ 500,000	$ 168,227
Kwame	$ 989,891	$ 960,000	$ (29,891)

This works if you type the formula out, but if you try to choose K5 by clicking on it, you're likely to end up with a monstrosity like

=GETPIVOTDATA("Sum of Quota",$I$3,"Salesperson","Ace")

which is a "feature" that someone on the Excel team added several years ago to make your life difficult. On the PivotTable - Options ribbon, click the down arrow next to Options and uncheck the Generate GetPivotData feature, and hopefully you'll never see it again.

This makes it easier to create formulas based on the Pivot Table data, but it's still not the best idea. Once your formulas start living outside the Pivot Table, they lose all the Pivot Table functionality.

For instance, if you add Month as a Row Label above Salesperson, your formulas will all be overwritten. (And if they weren't, for example, if you had them in column M, then they'd refer to the wrong data.)

Calculated Fields

When you need to do calculations on the data in the Pivot Table, it's easier to use a Calculated Field. Clear the formulas in column L. Then, on the PivotTable Tools - Options ribbon, under the Formulas dropdown, choose

Calculated Field.

In the window that pops up, call the Field "Variance" and specify its formula as

=Actual - Quota

(You can choose field names by double clicking on the list it gives you.)

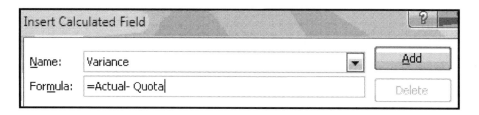

Click "OK" and you'll get a "Sum of Variance" field added to the Values section.

	Values		
Salesperson ▼	**Sum of Actual**	**Sum of Quota**	**Sum of Variance**
Ace	$ 558,637	$ 605,000	$ (46,363)
Deb	$ 1,182,161	$ 925,000	$ 257,161
Keith	$ 331,773	$ 500,000	$ (168,227)

Similarly, you can add a "PctVariance" field with the formula

=Variance/Quota

It's important to understand that when calculating items, Excel aggregates first, and calculates second. We defined Variance as Actual - Quota. This means that for each bucket Excel takes the sum of the Actual amounts and subtracts from them the sum of the Quota amounts. (Of course, if it computed Actual - Quota for each line and then summed them up, it would get the same result.)

This is more important for understanding PctVariance, which is

(Sum of Variance for this bucket) / (Sum of Quota for this bucket)

not

Sum of (Variance / Quota) for every row of data in this bucket

To see why this is important, think about a salesperson who in January has Quota 10 and Actual 20, and in February Quota 20 and Actual 10. His PctVariance just for January is +100%, and his PctVariance just for February is -50%. But you can't simply combine these to get his overall PctVariance, which is 0%, since his total Quota and total Actual are both 30.

If you use Calculated Fields a lot, you'll likely get this wrong at some point and find it very frustrating, so remember aggregate then calculate.

Calculated Fields as Row Labels?

Unfortunately, you can't use Calculated Fields as Row Labels or Column Labels. As we discussed earlier, you'd sometimes like to bucket by the first letter of the Salesperson's name, which (in theory) you could do with a Calculated Field using the formula

=LEFT(Salesperson,1)

If you try this, you'll discover that Calculated Fields can only be placed in the Values area. This also means that the calculations should be formulas that produce *numbers*, since Pivot Table aggregations will (except for Count) ignore non-numeric data.

Calculated Items

Besides calculating new fields, you can also calculate items within fields. For instance, you could add an item called "AceDeb" to the Salesperson field with the formula

> =Ace+Deb

The AceDeb row would show the results of adding together everything from the Ace row and everything from the Deb row. Unlike if we Grouped them, their individual rows will stick around, which means that all of our totals become very misleading.

If you use a Calculated Item, you should disable Totals for Rows and Columns as appropriate. Mostly, though, you should avoid Calculated Items, as they're more confusing than helpful.

Refreshing Data

One reason that pivot tables aren't orthodox Thinking Spreadsheet is that they don't immediately reflect changes in their underlying data. Pivot tables work with an *in memory* copy of the data, and when the original data changes you have to explicitly tell the pivot table to update its copy with the latest.

To get new data, right-click anywhere within the table and choose the Refresh option. This Refresh option can also be found on the PivotTable Tools-Options ribbon.

Also, because of this behavior, if you create a pivot table based on a lot of data, when you save the workbook Excel will store both the original data and the pivot table's copy of it, which makes your file twice as large (and twice as slow to open and save and close) as it might otherwise be. You can disable this behavior by opening up the PivotTable Options menu (either by right-clicking or by finding it on the PivotTable Options ribbon) and on the Data tab unchecking Save source data with file. If you make this change, when you close and re-open the spreadsheet you won't be able to make any changes to the table until you explicitly Refresh it. Alternatively, you can check the "Refresh data when opening the file" box, which you might also want checked if your data contains RAND() or TODAY() or other functions that might have new values since the last time you saved the workbook.

Example: Baby Names, Revisited

Go back to

http://www.ssa.gov/OACT/babynames/

and download the top 1000 baby names from 2009, this time checking the radio button to include Number of Births. Copy the results and Paste-Special-Text into a new spreadsheet. You may have to clean up the headers a bit.

	A	B	C	D	E
1	Rank	Male	Male#	Female	Female#
2	1	Jacob	20,858	Isabella	22,067
3	2	Ethan	19,664	Emma	17,716
4	3	Michael	18,677	Olivia	17,246
5	4	Alexander	18,025	Sophia	16,742

These data, it turns out, are not in a good form for Pivoting. Certain Fields (Name and Number) are repeated twice in each row, once corresponding to Male and once corresponding to Female. This severely limits the data's "pivotability."

A more "pivotal" way to structure the data would be

GenderRank, Name, Babies, Gender

which converts the distinction between Male and Female Names into a distinction between Male and Female *rows*.

To make your Pivot Tables as useful as possible, never repeat the same type of value within a row. Instead give each instance its own row with a field capturing the distinction, so that you can pivot and filter on it.

We'll need to transform the data into a more Pivot-friendly format. First, rename column A to GenderRank. Why GenderRank? Because some names appear in both lists. For example, your final data will have the rows

    12,Addison,10567,Female
    866,Addison,240,Male

The description GenderRank makes clear that the 12 in the Female Addison row is its popularity as a Female name, while the 866 in the Male row is its popularity as a Male name.

Rename column B to Name and column C to Babies. Next, we need to Cut the Female names and Paste them beneath the Male names. However, as you've learned to check by now, the Female names all have extra spaces at the end, which means we need to clean them up. The quickest way to do this is by entering the formula

    =TRIM(D2)

in F2, filling down to F1001, Copying F2:F1001, Paste-Special-Valuing it over D2:D1001, and Clearing out column F. Now Cut the Female names and numbers from D2:E1001 and Paste them into B1002:C2001.

Copy the GenderRanks 1 to 1000 from A2:A1001 and Paste them again in A1002:A2001 next to the Female names. Finally, label the names as Male in D2:D1001 and Female in D1002:D2001. After all that, your data should look like this:

	A	B	C	D
1	GenderRank	Name	Babies	Gender
2	1	Jacob	20,858	Male
3	2	Ethan	19,664	Male
4	3	Michael	18,677	Male
5	4	Alexander	18,025	Male

Now convert the data into a Table. Once we have our Pivot Table, we're going to want to bucket by the first letters of the names. It would be severely unpleasant to have to create these groupings manually. Instead, we'll add a new column to our data that contains the first letter of each name.

Type Letter in E1, and the Table will automatically expand. Then if you just put the formula

=LEFT(B2,1)

in E2, the Table will fill it down automatically.

	A	B	C	D	E
1	GenderRank ▼	Name ▼	Babies ▼	Gender ▼	Letter ▼
2	1	Jacob	20,858	Male	J
3	2	Ethan	19,664	Male	E
4	3	Michael	18,677	Male	M
5	4	Alexander	18,025	Male	A

Now make a Pivot Table from this data and put it in H3. Drag Letter to the Row Labels, Gender to the Column Labels, and Babies to the Values section. Finally, set Babies to display as % of Column, and you've quickly recreated our earlier analysis.

Sum of Babies	Gender		
Letter	Female	Male	Grand Total
A	18.21%	10.93%	14.18%
B	3.47%	5.64%	4.67%
C	5.60%	9.59%	7.81%
D	2.28%	6.40%	4.56%

Actually, our earlier analysis counted how many names started with each letter, while this version counts how many babies were given such names. To completely recreate the previous, you could change the Sum aggregation to Count, which would count each name only once.

Androgynous Names

Since our data is in a Pivot Table, we can quickly do further analysis. For instance, let's say we want to see which names are popular for both Males and Females. Put Name as the Row Label, Gender as the Values, and no Column Labels. Since Gender contains text, Excel aggregates it by counting rows. The names with a count of 2 necessarily appeared in both the Male and Female lists, while the names with a count of 1 appeared only in one or the other.

If you sort by "Count of Gender" from Largest to Smallest, you'll get all the androgynous names at the top.

Name	Count of Gender
Sage	2
Morgan	2
Kasey	2
Addison	2
Reese	2

(Yes, apparently there are baby boys out there named Sage. Good luck in middle school, guys.)

Select all the androgynous names and Group them together. Excel will create a Name2 field, with our androgynous names listed as Group1, which you should probably relabel as Androgynous. Drag it to the top, Group the remaining names, and change their label to Gendered.

Finally, rename the Name2 field to NameType, and get rid of the Name Row Label.

NameType ▼	Count of Gender
Androgynous	138
Gendered	1862
Grand Total	**2000**

Now we can ask "What are the most popular androgynous names?"

First, though, we have to decide what we mean by most popular. We could look at Sum of Babies, which would highly rank names with lots of babies, although this would include names very popular with one Gender but barely popular with the other. We could look at Min of Babies, which would rank them solely based on the less popular gender. Let's look at both.

Drag NameType up to the Report Filter section and filter down to Androgynous so that we only see rows with those names. Remove Count of Gender from the Values section and replace it with Babies (which will default to Sum). Drag a second instance of Babies to the Values section (it will get called Babies2) and change its Value Field Setting to Min. Finally, drag Name to the Row Labels.

NameType	Androgynous ▼	
	Values	
Name ▼	**Sum of Babies**	**Min of Babies2**
Addison	10807	240
Alexis	11845	2006
Ali	1092	282
Amari	1702	627

Now sort the Pivot Table by Sum of Babies from Largest to Smallest.

	Values	
Name ▼	**Sum of Babies**	**Min of Babies2**
Jayden	18820	1738
Logan	15013	682
Ryan	13502	516
Alexis	11845	2006
Dylan	11785	543

Androgynous names given to the most babies are Jayden, Logan, Ryan, and Alexis. In every case the Min is much smaller than the Sum, which means that each of those names skewed heavily toward one Gender or the other.

If you sort by the Min instead, you'll see names with slightly more balance, like Riley, Peyton, Hayden, and Jordan. If you wanted more balance still, you could look at the Standard Deviation, which should be small precisely when the two data points going into it (Male and Female) are pretty close to each other. However, the standard deviation would also be low if the name was the 1000th most popular for each gender, so you'd have to play around a bit until you found what you wanted.

A Frivolous Bug

Clear all the fields out of the pivot table and just put Name as a Row Label. Excel sorts the names in a curious order:

April, June, August, Aaden, Aaliyah, Aarav, Aaron, . . .

It's easy to see that the Names that are also months are being somehow treated as months, which are numbers, which get sorted before text. This is not what you want to happen, but I don't know of a way to fix it.

I discovered this bug in a previous career, where I routinely built pivot tables on data involving IATA codes for major airports. I noticed that SAT (San Antonio) always got sorted first, before ABQ (Albuquerque), ALB (Albany), ATL (Atlanta), and so on. This puzzled me for the longest time until one day my data included SUN (Sun Valley, Idaho) and JAN (Jackson, Mississippi), which also were sorted at the beginning, which allowed me to figure out that Excel was treating text that might mean a date as meaning a date.

As far as I can tell, this odd sorting behavior is limited to Pivot Tables.

Technique: Pivot Charts

If you click anywhere on your Pivot Table and insert a chart, Excel will create a Pivot Chart, which (as you might guess) is a chart that you can interact with like a Pivot Table. Excel won't let you make a Pivot Scatter Chart, which means that you should only make Pivot Column (or Bar) Charts and Pivot Line Charts.

Fields that are Row Labels become Categories on the x-axis, and fields that are Column Labels become different Series in the chart. Our histogram of Baby Names by First Letter, with Babies in the Values section (displayed as % of Column), Letter as the Row Labels, and Gender as the Column Labels, becomes the the Column chart

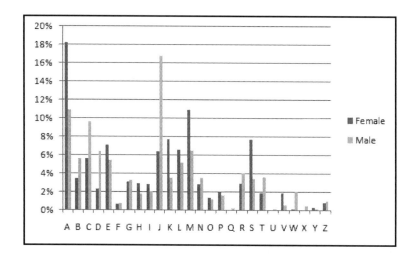

with Letter as the Axis Fields (or Category) and Gender as the Legend Fields (or Series). Now we could switch to the overall histogram (ignoring gender) either by removing Gender from the Columns of the Pivot Table or by removing it from the Legend Fields of the Pivot Chart.

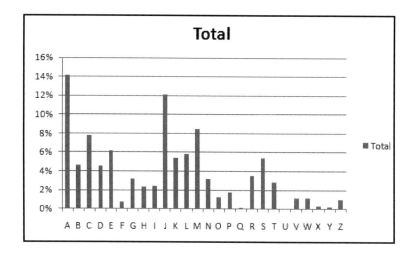

As you'll quickly see if you start making Pivot Charts, changes you make to the Pivot Table like adding Fields or filtering or sorting data are automatically reflected in the Pivot Chart, and vice versa. Sometimes this seems like a feature and other times it seems like a bug.

CHAPTER 23

GOAL SEEK AND SOLVER

Throughout this book we've mostly been solving problems by starting with known parameters, constructing appropriate formulas, and looking at the outputs. Sometimes, though, you'd like to do the opposite – start with a desired output, create formulas, and then try to *find* parameters that produce the output you want.

For example, in our "Closing the Honors Gap" example, we constructed formulas that took as input the threshhold for receiving graduation honors (and also information about the distributions of scores) and then used trial-and-error to choose a threshhold that resulted in equal honors for both schools.

Trial-and-error is rarely an efficient way to solve problems, though, which is why Excel provides Goal Seek and Solver.

Goal Seek

Goal Seek is by far the simpler of the two. It will try to make a specific cell equal a specific value by changing only one other cell.

For example, let's say you want to find a number that when multiplied by itself equals 2. In a new worksheet in cell A2 enter the formula

=A1*A1

Then we just need to find a value for A1 that makes A2 equal to 2.

On the Data ribbon, in the Data Tools section, under What-If Analysis, choose Goal Seek and input those parameters into the menu that pops up.

Click OK, and Excel will try to find a solution to your problem.

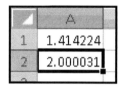

It doesn't get you exactly to the goal, but it's pretty close.

Goal Seek doesn't always do what you want, though. If you recall our "closing the honors gap" example, we needed a cutoff level such that NORMDIST(cutoff,85,3,TRUE) and NORMDIST(cutoff,84,5,TRUE) were equal. Using trial-and-error, we found that a cutoff of 86.5 worked.

We can try the same in Goal Seek. In cell A1, put the original cutoff of 90, and in A2 put the difference between the honors percentages:

   =NORMDIST(A1,85,3,TRUE)-NORMDIST(A1,84,5,TRUE)

Goal Seek only lets you choose actual values as goals. So when your goal is to set two quantities equal to each other, you have to tell Goal Seek to set their difference to 0.

But when you try to Goal Seek A2 to 0 by changing A1, Excel finds a cutoff of 99.93 (at least on my computer), which turns out to be the solution "don't honor anyone." This (as well as the other trivial solution "honor everyone") both satisfy the goal of honoring both classrooms equally, but they're not the solution we're looking for.

When your Goal Seek problem has multiple solutions, Excel might not choose the one you want, and there's no simple way to force it to prefer one solution over another. For that, you need Solver.

Solver

Solver does everything Goal Seek does, and many things Goal Seek doesn't. As a result, there's not really any reason ever to use Goal Seek. In fact, I'm not sure why I included the previous section.

Installing Solver

For some reason that possibly makes sense to someone, Solver isn't installed by default. If it's installed, you'll find it on the Data ribbon in the Analysis section. If it's not, then possibly there won't even be an Analysis section.

If you can't find Solver, install it using the following steps:

1. Click on the Office logo in the top left corner
2. Click the Excel Options button at the bottom of the next window
3. Choose the "Add-Ins" option on the left of the next window
4. Next to where it says Manage, make sure "Excel Add-Ins" is selected and click the Go button
5. Check the box by Solver Add-In and click OK

And now you're ready to start solving things!

Using Solver

A Solver problem has three main components.

The first is the **Goal**. As in Goal Seek, the goal consists of a Target Cell. However, whereas in Goal Seek you needed to specify a target *value* that you were trying to get that cell to equal, Solver also lets you specify a goal of Max (make the value in the target cell as large as possible) or Min (make the value in the target cell as small as possible). Most of the interesting uses of Solver involve Max or Min.

The second component is the **Changing Cells**, which are the one or more cells you want Solver to adjust in pursuit of the Goal. While Goal Seek only allowed you to specify a single changing cell, Solver will try changing multiple cells if you ask it to.

The third component is a set of **Constraints**, which has no analogue in Goal Seek. Constraints can apply to either the cells you want Solver to change (e.g. "only try values between 0 and 1") or cells that depend on what Solver is changing.

Solver also has a variety of technical options that you can tweak; however, unless you really know what you're doing, you probably shouldn't.

Example: Optimal Alchemy

After years of research, you've perfected your lead-into-gold process. Through careful analysis, you've discovered that if you start with l pounds of lead, c cans of Crisco, and h helpers, then you can produce

$$l * (1 - EXP(-c/100)) * (1 - EXP(-h/50))$$

pounds of gold.

Your financial backers have given you $300 to produce as much gold as possible. You can get lead for $1/pound, Crisco for $10/can, and helpers for $60 each, and you want to use Solver to figure out how to optimally spend your money.

To start with, let's put all these parameters into a spreadsheet.

	A	B	C
1		Quantity	Price
2	Lead (lb)	1	$1
3	Crisco (cans)	1	$10
4	Helpers	1	$60
5	Cost:		$71
6	Budget:		$300

All the above are entered as values, except for the cost in C5, which is computed using the formula

=SUMPRODUCT(B2:B4,C2:C4)

In B8 we need to add a formula to calculate the amount of gold our process outputs:

=B2*(1-EXP(-B3/100))*(1-EXP(-B4/50))

And now we're ready to Solver. We'll want to set B8 to a Max by changing cells B2:B4. And our constraints? We'll need to insist that B2:B4 are all non-negative (since you can't use negative amounts of lead or Crisco or helpers), and to enforce our budget, we'll need C5<=C6.

To start with, click the Solver button, fill in the Target Cell and Changing Cells, and click the Max radio button.

Click on the <u>A</u>dd button next to the Constraints window, and input the constraint that B2:B4 must be non-negative.

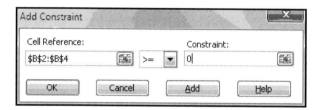

Click the <u>A</u>dd button on this menu, input the second constraint C5<=C6, and click OK.

The Solver box will now include your constraints, and you're ready to click Solve.

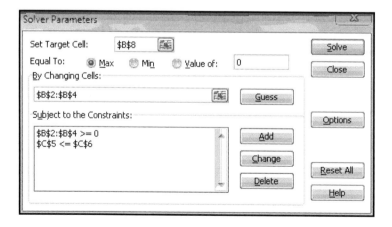

While it's running, Solver will show progress in the bottom left corner of the Excel window, indicating what step it's on and the value it's solved to.

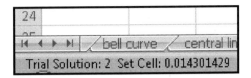

After several steps it will inform you that it's stopped, and once you click OK you can see Solver's optimal solution.

	Quantity	Price
1		
Lead (lb)	102.1965	$1
Crisco (cans)	9.73061	$10
Helpers	1.674956	$60
Cost:		$300
Budget:		$300
Output:	0.312174	

With our budget (and current prices), we can produce 0.31 pounds of gold.

Integral Constraints

Your investors point out that current labor law forbids you from hiring 1.674 helpers, and that Helpers really needs to be a whole number. Solver has an "int" constraint that will force this.

Click Solver again. Unlike Goal Seek, it remembers the parameters we last used, so we just need to add one more constraint. Click the Add button, choose B4 as the Cell Reference, and as the middle option choose "int." Click OK, and Solve again.

	Quantity	Price
1		
Lead (lb)	91.99431	$1
Crisco (cans)	8.800569	$10
Helpers	2	$60
Cost:		$300
Budget:		$300
Output:	0.303882	

Solver satisfied the new "int" constraint by increasing the helpers to 2, paid for by using less lead and Crisco. This change lost us about 0.1 pound of gold.

There's also a "bin" constraint that allows a cell only to take on the values 0 and 1.

Optimization problems with "int" and "bin" constraints are very difficult, and Solver doesn't always do a good job with them. Use these constraints sparingly.

Some General Solver Tips

Be Constrained

For example, "make A2 as large as possible by changing A1" is a pretty open-ended problem. If you have a constraint like "A1 must be between 0 and 1" then the range of values Excel has to look at is much smaller, and it's much more likely you'll get a good result.

Be Smooth

The smoother the function you're trying to optimize, the better results you'll get. Solver works best when your function has the following two features:

1. If some set of inputs produces a certain value, then "nearby" inputs should produce a similar value.
2. If tiny increases in one of the inputs result in a larger (smaller) value, then moderately larger increases in the same input should result in a larger (smaller) value still

The first is easier to check, and it's important because it means that inputs near the optimal inputs produce values near the optimal value. This allows Solver to gradually work its way toward an optimum by finding better and better values.

As an extreme (bad) example, imagine trying to maximize the function

=IF(A1=1,1,0)

which equals 0 unless A1 equals 1. This means that when Solver is looking at 0.9 or 0.99 or 0.999, the function value is still 0 and so it has no idea that it's close to the optimal input. Solver is pretty much useless for problems like this.

On the other hand, if you're trying to minimize the formula

=ABS(A1-1)

which measures how close A1 is to 1, then inputs near 0.5 produce outputs near 0.5, and inputs near 0.9 produce outputs near 0.1, which allows Solver to focus its search nearer the latter and away from the former.

The second condition rules out "jerky" functions that "change direction" frequently.

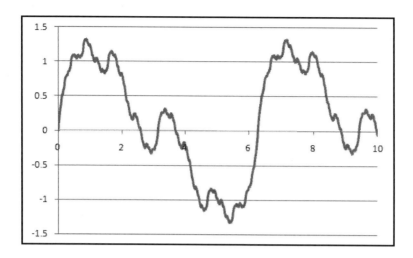

This called a Weierstrass function, and I approximated it in Excel as

=   SIN(A1*POWER(2,0))/POWER(2,0)
    +SIN(A1*POWER(2,1))/POWER(2,1)
    + ...
    +SIN(A1*POWER(2,23))/POWER(2,23)

(Mathematically the sum should go on forever, but Excel chokes once the powers of 2 get too large, so I had to cut it off at 23.)

When Solver is trying to find a Max, it tries to figure out what "direction" to move in in order to increase its output value. When the function is "jerky," the right direction for a small move is often the wrong direction for a larger move, and Solver won't do a good job.

But Don't Be Too Smooth

If your function is completely flat in places, Excel will often call that plateau a max or a min, even if it isn't. Solver uses small changes to figure out how to adjust the parameters; if small changes don't change the function value at all, Solver might decide it's done.

Be Unique

A value can be a *local* maximum (larger than everything near it) without being a *global* maximum (larger than everything else). In the jerky function illustrated in the last section, there is a local maximum near the input value 3, but it's plainly not the global maximum.

If the function you're trying to optimize has multiple local maxima, it's likely that Solver will find a local maximum that isn't the global maximum.

Be Diverse

When you have multiple local maxima, the value Solver finds depends on its starting point. You should always try running Solver with several different starting values to find the most optimal optima.

For instance, returning to the jerky function example, if you run Solver with the initial value set to 4, it ends up finding the local maximum near 3.4. But with the initial value set to 0, it finds the global maximum near 0.84.

Be Clever

This is good advice in general, not just when you're using Solver.

CHAPTER *24*

MACROS, CUSTOM FUNCTIONS, AND PHILOSOPHY

Many advanced Excel users are experts at the un-Thinking-Spreadsheet techniques of Macros and Custom Functions. After a philosophy lesson, we'll talk about why you should try to avoid these techniques.

Philosophy

Throughout this book we've tried to emphasize the Thinking Spreadsheet philosophy, which roughly corresponds to the following paradigm:

> A spreadsheet is a grid of cells filled with data and formulas. The formulas make it so that the values in some cells depend in a straightforward way on the values in other cells and change in a predictable way as soon as the values they depend on change.

A spreadsheet that relies on its data being sorted breaks this paradigm, as it's possible to make changes to your data that aren't correctly reflected downstream in formulas. Similarly, static menu-driven tools like Regression and Histogram produce outputs that never change even as the underlying data changes, and are accordingly not Thinking Spreadsheet.

Many Excel "power users" are experts at VBA, which is the programming language built into Excel. In a previous life even *I* was an expert in VBA.

Then one day I was meditating and achieved a form of enlightenment that I eventually codified into Thinking Spreadsheet. I realized that the essence of Excel was in analyzing relationships involving structured data, not in writing computer programs. I haven't written a line of VBA code since.

Now, there's nothing *wrong* with computer programming. I enjoy programming computers as much as you do. But as we've seen throughout this book, the strengths of spreadsheets are based on using formulas to represent relationships. For most spreadsheet-sized data analysis problems, the cleanest, the most effective, the quickest, and the easiest-to-understand solutions are the ones that involve creating formulas. If you're going to use spreadsheets, you should use spreadsheets' strengths.

Of course, when you need to analyze millions of rows of data, coding is probably essential, but with millions of rows of data you wouldn't be using Excel anyway. Part of the Thinking Spreadsheet philosophy is that Excel is an improper outlet for your code-writing urges. Channel them elsewhere.

Macros

Macros are automated sequences of commands. In their simplest form they don't require any programming, as you can simply "record" and "replay" them. For instance, you could record the sequence

1. Insert a new column between columns F and G
2. Copy the data from column A
3. Paste-Value it into the new column G

and assign it to a certain key combination, so that (for example) whenever you entered Ctrl-Alt-I, Excel repeated the above sequence of steps. If you want to get more elaborate, you can write computer code to specify the steps the macro should take.

As should be clear by now, actions like this break the spreadsheet paradigm. Furthermore, they make your spreadsheets terrifically opaque. There's no obvious indication that Ctrl-Alt-I does something special, and you're likely to forget about it if you don't open the spreadsheet for a long time.

It's possibly even worse if you remember it, as there's no simple way to *understand* what the macro actually does. You'd have to go into the Visual Basic window (Alt-F11), find the appropriate code, and then try to figure out what happens when you run it. In short, by using macros you forfeit many of the features that make spreadsheets useful, and you make your spreadsheets harder to understand and easier to break. Please avoid them.

Custom Functions

The other reason some people write code in Excel is to create custom functions. When SUM() and EXP() and VLOOKUP() don't meet their needs, they write their own functions, often with clever names like VLOOKUP2() and VLOOKUP3() and VLOOKUPJOEL(). This is a guaranteed way to make your spreadsheets difficult to understand, since most people looking at your work won't know what VLOOKUPJOEL() does.

I'm willing to be slightly accommodating here. If you work in some sort of organization that routinely requires additional functions, then I have no objection to your adopting a standard set of *shared* custom functions. For instance, serious financial modelers often use third-party add-ins that provide a huge range of custom functions that do things like option pricing and curve bootstrapping. To the extent these functions are truly shared, they become part of your local version of Thinking Spreadsheet, and (insofar as everyone with whom you share your spreadsheets uses them) they don't make your spreadsheets any more difficult to understand.

However, this does not give you license to write your *own* personal custom functions, a practice that violates the principles of Thinking Spreadsheet just as do macros. Get it done with standard formulas or don't do it in Excel.

Chapter 25

Final Projects

Here are some data analysis problems for you to apply what you've learned. Because data I find on the web today might not be there for you tomorrow, I've made the relevant datasets available at ThinkingSpreadsheet.com. I'll also keep posting new projects on the website as I come up with them.

Counting Letters

The file **WordList.txt** shows approximately 100,000 "crossword words." Create a histogram showing how many times each letter appears in the list. Make sure to count every letter of every word, not just the first letters.

Where's Starbucks?

The file **Starbucks.csv** contains the Address, Latitude, Longitude, and City of every known Starbucks as of sometime in 2006. The City field contains data like "New York New York 10119" and "Toronto Ontario M5C 2W5" and "Vienna Vienna 1210."

Find a way to classify every Starbucks as "US," "Canada," or "Other." A quick, simple method that is occasionally wrong is preferable to a perfect method that takes all day.

411

After this, extract the State and build a histogram to find which states had the most Starbucks.

Using the longitude and latitude data, find the Starbucks location with the greatest number of other Starbucks nearby. You'll have to decide how to define and measure "nearby."

Soccer Standings

The file **MLS.txt** contains the results of what should be every Major League Soccer game from 2009. It's not in a very pleasant format, though. It has lots of unnecessary asterisks, and the data are all crammed together in one column. The fields are as follows:

- Date of Game
- Home Team
- Home Team Goals
- Away Team Goals
- Away Team

First, clean and transform the data so that each row corresponds to a single game.

After that compute each team's record of wins, losses, and ties. Find the records just for home games, just for away games, and overall. Similarly, compute each team's goals scored and goals allowed.

Soccer teams are ranked by "points," where each win counts as 3 points and each tie counts as 1 point. Investigate whether goals scored and goals allowed can be used (either separately or together) to predict wins, losses, ties, or points.

JOLTS

The file **JOLTS.xlsx** contains data from the government's Job Openings and Labor Turnover Survey. The "Data" tab contains the actual survey results. Each data series has an ID like JTS00000000HIL. The "Series" tab contains descriptive details *about* each series, with one row per Series ID. Looking there, you'd find that the previously mentioned series has a dataelement_code of "HI." This is actually a lookup key; if you find "HI" in the DataElement tab, you'll see that it represents Hires.

Use these data to figure out which industries are growing. In particular, look at industry-by-industry growth in Job openings from the 2006-2007 time period to the 2008-2009 time period.

As a first step, Table the data in the Data tab. Add a column to show what Data Element each row represents. You'll need to first use series_id to figure out each row's dataelement_code, then dataelement_code to figure out the corresponding dataelement_text. Go through a similar two-step process to bring in Industry, at which point you can create a Pivot Table of the data.

Put Industry and series_id as Column Labels and use Report Filter to show only the "Job openings" series. You'll find that there are still four series left for most of the industries (but only two for some of them). Add whatever additional fields you need to filter down to just the one relevant series per Industry.

With the appropriate filters in place, create 2006-2007 and 2008-2009 buckets and compare them by Industry. Where are the jobs?

If you want to explore these data further, the Description tab contains all the details you should need.

Economic Assistance

The file **EconomicAssistance.csv** contains foreign aid data since 1946, broken down by recipient country and program. Each year's data is in its own column, which isn't a good format to use in a pivot table.

Transform the dataset into a pivot-able format. You should end up with four columns of data: Country, Program, Year, and Amount. Delete any rows with zero Amounts and build a pivot table. Find the biggest aid recipients and best-funded programs at five-year intervals from 1950 up to 2005. Are they what you expected?

Proposition 8

The file **Prop8.csv** lists the contributions both for and against California's Proposition 8, which outlawed same-sex marriage.

Similar Zip Codes tend to be near each other, which means that you can use "First three digits of Zip Code" as a decent proxy for Location. Add this field to the data, and then investigate which parts of California strongly supported the proposition, which parts strongly opposed it, and which parts were more ambivalent. Does it make more sense to look at total contributions or number of contributions?

Outside of California, which states were most supportive and most opposed? Which locations outside of California were most interested in the outcome?

The 4-Minute Mile

The file **Mile.xlsx** contains all the official IAAF-era world records for running the mile, both for men and women.

I copied them from Wikipedia, which has an unfortunate tendency of putting junk in its tables. Here, some of the Times have asterisks, and all of the Dates have footnotes, so you'll need to clean both those columns.

For each Date in the data, find the Male record and Female record as of that date. (There's a way involving running totals that requires the data to be sorted, and a way involving array formulas that doesn't.)

Examine how the difference between the Male record and the Female record is changing over time. What's the longest time that the Male record has gone without improving? The Female record? At present, how long has it been since either has changed?

Population Growth

The file **Population.csv** contains the world population for every year from 1950 to 2010. The growth doesn't seem to be linear, since population doesn't increase by the same amount each year.

Compute the year-over-year log changes. Since they're not constant, the growth isn't exponential either. Extrapolate the recent trend in the log changes to predict future population growth. What does your model predict the population will be in 2050? Does the population in your model ever reach 10 billion? When does it peak, if ever?

Tweet of the Union

The file **Tweets.txt** contains a filtered subset of the output of Twitter's sample feed during the 2010 State of the Union Address. To get it down to a manageable size, it only includes lines that contain one of the terms "president," "state," "union," "speech," "obama," or "sotu."

Get the tweets into Excel. Examine the data and find a way to extract just the text of each tweet, the username of its tweeter, and its language. Who were the most prolific tweeters?

Tweeters often decorate their tweets with #hashtags, which always start with a # and end at a space or punctuation or the end of the tweet. Create a histogram showing the most popular hashtags in these tweets. Some tweets contain multiple hashtags and some tweets contain none, so make sure to deal with both situations.

What Color is Baby Poop?

The folks at CrowdFlower showed 10,000 color samples to people and asked them to name the colors.

http://blog.crowdflower.com/?p=11

You can find their results in the file **ColorNames.csv**. Colors on computers are typically specified in terms of how much red, green, and blue they contain. These are captured here in the columns **r**, **g**, and **b**, whose values are between 0 and 1.

Workers 7, 8, and 20 each labeled a different color as "baby poop." Use the dataset to figure out less ambiguous names for each of these colors.

ABOUT THE AUTHOR

Joel Grus lives in Seattle, where he builds spreadsheets and writes books.

If you have any questions or comments or feedback about *Thinking Spreadsheet*, he would love to hear from you.

You can email him at joelgrus@gmail.com or visit the book's website at ThinkingSpreadsheet.com.

Printed in Great Britain
by Amazon